LIMITS OF CITIZENSHIP

LIMITS OF CITIZENSHIP

MIGRANTS AND POSTNATIONAL MEMBERSHIP IN EUROPE

Yasemin Nuhoğlu Soysal

THE UNIVERSITY OF CHICAGO

CHICAGO AND LONDON

Yasemin Nuhoğlu Soysal is assistant professor of sociology at Harvard University and an affiliate of Harvard's Center for European Studies.

The University of Chicago Press, Chicago 60637
The University of Chicago Press, Ltd., London

Printed in the United States of America
03 02 01 00 99 98 97 96 95 94 5 4 3 2 1

ISBN (cloth): 0-226-76841-4
ISBN (paper): 0-226-76842-2

Library of Congress Cataloging-in-Publication Data

Soysal, Yasemin Nuhoğlu.
Limits of citizenship : migrants and postnational membership in Europe / Yasemin Nuhoğlu Soysal.
p. cm.
Includes bibliographical references and index.
ISBN 0-226-76841-4 (cloth). — ISBN 0-226-76842-2 (paper)
1. Citizenship—Europe. 2. Aliens—Civil rights—Europe. 3. Alien labor—Civil rights—Europe. 4. Immigrants—Civil rights—Europe. 5. Europe—Emigration and immigration—Government policy. I. Title.
JN94.A92S69 1994
325.4'09'045—dc20 94-16331
CIP

♾ The paper used in this publication meets the minimum requirements of the American National Standard for Information Sciences—Permanence of Paper for Printed Library Materials, ANSI Z39.48-1984.

CONTENTS

ILLUSTRATIONS

Figure

Tables

ACKNOWLEDGMENTS

My primary thanks go to John Meyer and Ann Swidler, both of whom have profoundly influenced my thinking: John Meyer by teaching me the importance of questioning the questions of sociology and of envisioning the "larger picture," and Ann Swidler by inspiring me with her enthusiasm to search for crucial paradoxes in sociological inquiry. From the beginning of this project, they have been endless sources of support. I feel privileged to have the opportunity of working with and knowing them.

Peter Katzenstein read this work on more than one occasion and at various stages, and at each stage his probing insights, astute criticisms, and support have been invaluable. My deep gratitude also goes to John Boli, Gary Freeman, Ron Jepperson, and Mark Miller for their detailed readings and extremely effective comments. Orlando Patterson, Bill Alonso, and Alan Wolfe provided me with perceptive queries that contributed to the improvement of this book. I thank Seymour Martin Lipset for his continual support and encouragement over the years.

Throughout the project, I have benefited enormously from and enjoyed my conversations with Francisco Ramirez, John Boli, Frank Dobbin, Ron Jepperson, Miriam Feldblum, David Strang, Connie McNeely, and Marc Ventresca. They provided the best friendship and intellectual sustenance. For pertinent discussions and helpful comments at various stages of this project, I thank Carol Conell, Len Hochberg, Steve Krasner, Philippe Schmitter, and Aage Sørensen. I am also grateful to the members of the Comparative Institutions Group and the Stanford Women's Cultural Project at Stanford University for many hours of fun and spirited discussions. I presented parts of this work to various audiences and received valuable comments and criticisms that forced me to clarify and strengthen my arguments. I would particularly like to mention the Student/Faculty Workshop at the Department of Sociology, Harvard University; Social Policy and Citizenship, and State and Capitalism groups at Harvard University's Center for European Studies; and the Immigration Workshop at the Center for European Studies, New York University. My thanks to Ari Zolberg and Martin Schain, the organizers of the NYU Immigration Workshop, for lively discussions and sojourns in my favorite city.

Data collection for this project required extensive logistic planning and thus the assistance of many individuals. My warmest appreciation goes to Gero Lenhardt, Marlis Buchmann, Barbara Schmitter Heisler, Jan Rath, and Catherine de Wenden, all of whom have been generous of time, support, and friendship. I am also indebted to all of the friends who helped me find the crucial resources and contacts in the migration capitals of Europe. In particular, Mesut Akın and Murat Metin (London), Adil Alkan and Ali Rıza Özkan (Berlin), Tülin and Mete Uygur (Stockholm), Mehmet Emin Yıldırım (Amsterdam), Necmi and İlkay Demir, and Sabri Ateş (Brussels), and Ümit Metin (Paris), not only facilitated my connection to migrant worlds, but also extended their generous hospitality and provided crucial help with translations.

The indispensable financial support for this research came from grants by the Center for European Studies and the Institute of International Studies, both at Stanford University; the MacArthur Foundation; and the Social Science Research Council Berlin Program for Advanced German and European Studies, for which I am most grateful. I would like to thank the Berlin Program, particularly Professor Martin Kohli, for facilitating many aspects of my research and stay, and to Professor Karl Ulrich Mayer for generously offering me a friendly refuge at the Berlin Max Planck Institute.

At the University of Chicago Press, Doug Mitchell proved true to his splendid reputation. His wit and enthusiasm made the whole process exceptionally enjoyable. Claudia Rex, of the University of Chicago Press, and Lauren Rusk provided editorial assistance.

A very personal appreciation goes to my parents, Melek and İlyas Nuhoğlu, whose affection has always been boundless and their support unconditional. Babür, Hale, Ömer, Suat, and Mine have been absolutely great in every way. To Levent, I owe it all, "with love and squalor."

CHAPTER ONE

Introduction

This book is about the changing institution and meaning of citizenship in contemporary nation-states. A new and more universal concept of citizenship has unfolded in the postwar era, one whose organizing and legitimating principles are based on universal personhood rather than national belonging. To an increasing extent, rights and privileges once reserved for citizens of a nation are codified and expanded as personal rights, undermining the national order of citizenship. The case of guestworkers, whose membership in European host polities contradicts predominant conceptions of citizenship and the nation-state, manifests these changes.

In the postwar era, all of the major industrialized countries of Europe recruited foreign workers to meet their immediate demands for labor. Assuming a sovereign nation-state with a unified citizenry, European governments saw the employment of guestworkers as a temporary expedient, and expected those individuals to remain outside the cohesive bounds of the national polity. The official position was that foreign workers could be sent home at will, upon the decline of their productivity or when unemployment rose. However, the guestworker experience has defied these original expectations and plans. Despite increasing unemployment and formal policies of repatriation, the host states have not succeeded in sending their guestworkers away. Guestworkers are now permanent, and form large, "foreign" communities within the host societies. More strikingly, guestworkers without formal citizenship status have been incorporated into various aspects of the social and institutional order of their host countries. They participate in the educational system, welfare schemes, and labor markets. They join trade unions, take part in politics through collective bargaining and associational activity, and sometimes vote in local elections. They exercise rights and duties with respect to the host polity and the state. Guestworkers are thus empirical anomalies with regard to predominant narratives of citizenship.

The participation of guestworkers in the host polity as social, political, and economic actors with a wide range of rights and privileges contests the foundational logic of national citizenship. Citizenship defines bounded populations, with a specific set of rights and duties, excluding "others" on the grounds of nationality. Yet guestworkers, who are formally and empirically constituted as aliens within the national collectivity, are nonetheless granted rights and protection by, and thus membership in, a state that is not "their own."[1]

How can we account for the apparent anomaly of guestworker membership? Why have European states extended the rights and privileges of their citizens to migrant workers? What legitimizes the host states' responsibility for foreigners living within their borders? What does the guestworker experience mean for accounts of citizenship facilitated by a nation-state model?

My inquiry into these questions challenges the predominant assumption, both scholarly and popular, that national citizenship is imperative to membership in a polity. As I show in the case of postwar migrants in Europe, incorporation into a system of membership rights does not inevitably require incorporation into the national collectivity. The guestworker experience attests to a shift in global discourse and models of citizenship across two phases of immigration in the twentieth century. The model of national citizenship, anchored in territorialized notions of cultural belonging, was dominant during the period of massive migration at the turn of the century, when immigrants were expected to be molded into national citizens. The recent guestworker experience reflects a time when national citizenship is losing ground to a more universal model of membership, anchored in deterritorialized notions of persons' rights.

This new model, which I call *postnational,* reflects a different logic and praxis: what were previously defined as national rights become entitlements legitimized on the basis of personhood. The normative framework for, and legitimacy of, this model derive from transnational discourse and structures celebrating human rights as a world-level organizing principle. Postnational citizenship confers upon every person the right and duty of participation in the authority structures and public life of a polity, regardless of their historical or cultural ties to that community. A Turkish guestworker need not have a "primordial" attachment to Berlin (or to Germany, for that matter) to participate in Berlin's public institutions and make claims on its authority structures. It is such postnational dictums that undermine the categorical restraints of national citizenship and warrant the incorporation of postwar migrants into host polities.

In this book, by means of a comparative study of the incorporation and membership of guestworkers, I pursue a dual analytical agenda. First, I examine in detail the incorporation regimes—that is, patterns of discourse and policy—of major western European countries, and provide a conceptual framework to explain the differences in incorporation. I show how European host countries, each with an elaborate state system designed to manage the membership of its domestic population, have expanded these systems to incorporate foreign residents. Second, I relate the contemporary reconfiguration of membership in European nation-states to changes in world-level models and discourses that contest and complicate the national order of citizenship. For this agenda, guestworkers reflect the existing logic of membership in particular polities and the wider changes in the institution of national citizenship.

Variation in Incorporation Regimes

While global discourses and models increasingly penetrate national frameworks, spurring the incorporation of guestworkers, polity-specific modes of membership still shape the patterns that incorporation takes in specific European countries. Host polities, drawing upon their institutionalized resources and understandings of membership, develop distinct strategies, policy instruments, and organizational arrangements to incorporate migrants. Take, for instance, the contrast between Sweden and Britain.

In Sweden, where individuals characteristically participate in various aspects of public life through legally recognized corporate groups, the incorporation of migrants involves collective interchange and centralized organizational activity. State policies produce "official ethnicities" and arrange for their highly formalized, structured participation in the Swedish polity. Like the members of other corporate groups, migrants are represented by their own associations, in this case defined by national origin or culture, through appropriate administrative and consultative structures. Furthermore, in Sweden, incorporation emphasizes policy instruments that target the welfare and social rights of specific migrant groups. Thus, it is only through their official corporate identity and standing that migrants gain access to rights and public services.

In Britain, on the other hand, membership in the polity is organized around the individual. In this context, the civil rights and labor-market participation of individual migrants become the most visible instruments of incorporation. Antidiscriminatory legislation concerning housing and jobs constitutes the cornerstone of state policy, which aims to enhance the opportunity patterns of migrants. Incorporation assumes much more society-level participation and differentiated organizational activity. Whereas in Sweden professionally and nationally organized elites act as intermediaries between the state and migrant groups, in Britain, the initiatives that address migrant issues are local and voluntary.

Thus, variations in modes of incorporation among states do affect migrants' strategies and participation in host societies. In Sweden, religious demands of migrant groups are accommodated through formalized consulting between the central state and migrant associations. To secure provision for religious education classes, religiously appropriate school meals, or celebration of religious festivals, Muslim organizations appeal to the Swedish Association of Free Churches, which represents them to the state bureaucracy. In Britain, for such causes, migrant associations actively engage in local politics. They canvas city councils, school boards, and local deputies to make their demands known and generate change.

When systematically scrutinized, cross-national differences reveal how host states and their foreigners encounter each other. In accounting for variations in incorporation, I make a comparative argument about the effects of polity-specific membership models in the field of immigrant policy. In other words, I assert that patterns of incorporation can be associated empirically with the institutionalized modes and the organizing logic of membership in particular polities.

In doing so, I intend to reverse one of the driving presuppositions of immigration literature: the notion that guestworkers' situations and cultures predict how they participate in and interact with host societies. Most of the literature attributes a weighted causality to migrants' own conditions—customs, traditions, ethnoreligious background, and so on. In contrast, I privilege the institutional repertoire of host political systems, which afford the model and rationale for both state and migrant action.

In the chapters that follow, I examine the incorporation of migrants in European host polities through a study of political models and discourses of membership at both the nation-state and world level. As these models and discourses become increasingly intertwined, the global modalities of rights reverberate through nation-state-level arrangements and premises of citizenship. Together, they constitute the topography of membership in contemporary polities.

Global Paradoxes of Membership

In the postwar era, if one facet of the discourse and praxis of immigration is the closure of national polity, the other is the expansion of the same polity beyond national closure. While the first involves boundary construction through restrictive policy measures and national(ist) narratives, the other is about "border crossings" (Rosaldo 1989)—a constant flux of people, the extension of rights of membership to foreigners, and narratives of multiplicity. This apparent paradox is only intelligible if world-level institutional frameworks and processes are taken into consideration. By omitting the global element and focusing on the nation-state as the unit of analysis, much of political sociology axiomatically privileges the nationally bounded model of citizenship and bypasses the reconfiguration of contemporary membership.[2] To redress this overemphasis of the national unit, I accentuate the ways in which the global system shapes schemes of incorporation, parameters of membership, and boundaries of polity in the postwar era.

My discussion of the global system takes the symbolic and institutional order as constitutional.[3] Thus, I consider modes of discourse to be as consequential as organizational mechanisms in facilitating new understandings of citizenship. Discursive modes afford "taken-for-granted rationales" for, and "common social accounts" of patterned state action and practice—in other words, a cultural framework upon which the national actors base their meanings and actions (Meyer, Boli, and Thomas 1987; DiMaggio and Powell 1991; Jepperson 1991). Accordingly, I stress the institutionalized rules and definitions of the global system that provide models for and constraints on actions and policies of the nation-states in regard to international migration and migrants.

There is no unified, homogeneous global institutional order.

Instead, there is a multiplicity of discourses and modalities of legitimate action. Combined in complex ways, these discourses and modalities sanction different forms of activity and organizing. Hence, the global system enacts multiple institutionalized scripts, which, although equally legitimated, do not always operate in agreement and may lead to "conflicting claims and empowerments."[4] Consequently, multiply coexisting institutions and discourses may further inconsistent outcomes; but this does not mean that they necessarily create irresolvable tensions or "role conflicts" for actors. State actions, policies, and identities may reflect multiple sets of norms and institutions, equally and/or concomitantly acted upon.

Consider two institutionalized principles of the global system in regard to immigration: national sovereignty and universal human rights. Celebrated and codified in international conventions and treaties, these principles form pivotal components of postwar international migration regimes.[5] The principle of national sovereignty ordains that every "nation" has a right to its own territorially delimited state, and that only those who belong to the nation have the right to participate as citizens of the state. Over the course of the twentieth century, this articulation of national/territorial sovereignty has been consolidated as "the 'natural' political condition of humankind" (Giddens 1985:259). As a corollary to this, territorial belonging (and identity) is presumed to be determined by the parameters of national contiguity and homogeneity.

Equally emphasized in the global framework is the human rights principle, advocated and practiced by national and transnational actors. The notion of human rights, as a codification of abstract concepts of personhood, has become a pervasive element of world culture. Continual invocation of human rights establishes and advances universal contiguities and thus legitimates claims for rights and identities of "persons," from within or without national limits.

These two global precepts simultaneously constrain and enhance the nation-state's scope of action. On the one hand, nation-states are charged with expanding "responsibilities," on the basis of human rights, with respect to the foreign populations living within their borders. On the other hand, they are expected to regulate immigration and exercise border controls as a fundamental expression of their sovereignty. Indeed, it is precisely these institutionalized reifications of national sovereignty and human rights that occasion both the status of guestworker (with its implication of temporariness) and the expanded rights and duties guestworkers accrue in their host polities (their de facto membership). European states grant rights to their foreign residents, admit and provide for family members of foreign workers, extend their obligations—financial or other—to countries of origin even when asylum seekers are sent back, yet also reinforce their borders through continued attempts to restrict immigration and enact discourses of the past through nationalist narratives. In so doing, they "[act] against the background of, and thereby reproduc[e]" (Wendt 1992:413) the prevailing principles and definitions embedded in the global system.

The concurrent invocation, in nation-states' rhetoric and praxis, of national sovereignty and universal human rights engenders paradoxical correlations. This means, for one thing, an incongruity between the normative and organizational bases of rights. While the source and legitimacy of rights is increasingly located in the transnational order, individual rights continue to be organized differentially, country by country, and bear the imprint of polity-specific forms of membership and incorporation. A similar disparity appears between two constitutive aspects of citizenship—identity and rights. Whereas rights, and claims to rights, become universalized and abstract, identity is still conceived of as particular and bounded by national, ethnic, regional, or other characteristics.

These apparent contradictions precipitate around the constructs of the bounded, territorialized nation-state and universal, deterritorialized rights, creating a dialectical tension. Nation-states and their boundaries persist as reasserted by regulative immigration practices and expressive national identities, while, at the same time, the universalistic rights of personhood transcend these boundaries, giving rise to new models and understandings of membership. Consequently, a more universalistic model of membership and rights comes to contest the exclusive model of citizenship anchored in national sovereignty.

Research Strategy and Organization

This book is based on a detailed, comparative study of state incorporation patterns and changes in the membership of guestworkers over time. The study encompasses the major European countries with prominent populations of migrants, both economic and political, concentrating particularly on the postwar period. Western Europe, which has moved furthest in blurring the national boundaries around economic, cultural, and political units, provides a distinctively prolific site for investigating the changes in the institution of citizenship.

Postwar international migration is characterized by a multiplicity of forms: labor migration, political migration, postcolonial migration, and migration within common markets. These migratory flows, in turn, have produced a host of immigrant strata: legal temporary or permanent migrants, political refugees, illegal migrants, ex-colonial citizens, and common-market citizens. While the rules governing their entry, residence, and employment differ, the common characteristic of these populations is their noncitizen status. Though, strictly speaking, the term *guestworker* does not represent all of these forms and strata, I employ it as a general category in reference to noncitizen migrant populations.

The first component of my analytical agenda concerns cross-national patterns of incorporation. For comparison, I confine my case countries to the Federal Republic of Germany (Germany, hereafter),[6] France, the Netherlands, Sweden, Switzerland, and the United Kingdom. Affected and motivated by similar labor-market conditions and long- and short-run economic trends, all of these advanced industrialized countries imported foreign labor after World War II, either through explicit state programs or through migration of a more spontaneous nature. They also have accepted a large number of political refugees. Except for France and, to a certain extent, the United Kingdom, none of these countries have been immigration countries in the traditional sense: that is, migrants were not considered as permanent inhabitants and prospective citizens upon their arrival.[7] Despite their shared experience, these European host states have generated different policies and organizational structures in incorporating migrants. Having controlled for socioeconomic factors by the choice of case countries enables me to draw cross-national comparisons that focus explicitly on the effects of polity-specific institutional resources and forms of membership.

My analysis systematically identifies and orders varying dimensions of incorporation with respect to distinct membership models. I examine how polity-specific forms of membership shape and maintain state discourses, policies, programs, and budgets that concern migrant populations, as well as the organizational activity and participation of the migrants themselves. I also investigate the extent of the rights and privileges granted to foreigners in host polities. For this purpose, in order to achieve a broader analytical base, I add Austria, Belgium, Canada, Denmark, and the United States to the original six countries.

Then, I extrapolate from the emerging forms of incorporation and membership of migrants to draw inferences about how global factors transform the national order of citizenship. I elaborate on the extent to which the concepts of universalistic rights and personhood are ingrained in the global institutional order and its discourse, and provide substantiating instances of their influence on state action and policy, and on migrants' claims to rights.

My concern in this study is the organization and articulation of incorporation policy and membership rights, not their implementation and practice. The realization of policies and rights invariably involves a discrepancy in implementation, which, in the case of guestworkers, correlates with persisting social and economic inequalities. Clearly, the degree to which policies are implemented and rights are exercised has relevance to how migrants experience their membership in host polities. However, since my main interest in this project is to capture the wider changes in the institution of citizenship itself, my analysis is not designed to address the consequences of implementation.

Data for this project were collected mainly through on-site interviews and archival and documentary research in the countries involved. From spring of 1988 through fall of 1991, I made prolonged visits to these countries, including a stay of over a year in Berlin. I conducted extensive interviews with officials from relevant ministries, municipalities, and other administrative agencies; with representatives of pertinent welfare organizations, trade unions, and the specialized agencies that cater to migrants; and also with the leaders of migrant associations. As for migrant associations, I concentrated on those of migrants from Turkey, who constitute the largest foreign population in Europe. Aside from interviews, I participated in migrants' associational and cultural activities. These engagements afforded me valuable insight into migrants' interactions with host polity institutions.

I also interviewed qualified informants on international migration, such as scholars from various European research institutions, members of national research councils and governmental advisory boards, and officials of international organizations. The relatively small size and interconnectedness of the countries of Europe, and the tight networks among scholars, researchers, and officials facilitated my access to crucial resources and contacts. (See appendix A for a list of the offices, agencies, and organizations at which the interviews were conducted.) The interviews provided a comprehensive body of information on the formal structures and arrangements of particular countries, as well as an understanding of the prevalent discourses. I conducted the interviews open-endedly but used a structured questionnaire to ensure their comprehensiveness.

Further systematic data on state policies, regulations, and budgets were compiled from relevant governmental documents and other written sources: statistical reports, research and policy papers, and annual reports. I also made extensive use of the documents, reports, and brochures put out by migrant organizations. Additional data were obtained from the publications of the International Labor Organization (ILO), the European Community (EC), and the Organization of Economic Cooperation and Development (OECD).

The next chapter is a brief account of the history of international migration and its interaction with the construction of the nation-state system and national citizenry in Europe. I discuss the characteristics of contemporary migration systems, emphasizing discrepancies between the assumed models and the demographics of postwar migrant populations.

Chapter 3 lays out the main premises and guiding ideas of this inquiry. I argue that the incorporation of postwar migrants is shaped by two factors: the institutionalized modes and organization of membership in particular polities, and larger changes in the institutional and discursive order of rights at the global level. I introduce a typology of membership models—corporatist, liberal, and statist—as a framework for understanding and analyzing incorporation. Chapters 4 and 5 use these models to identify and explain the different incorporation patterns that have emerged in European host countries.

Chapter 6 discusses the implications of different patterns of incorporation for the collective organization and participation of migrants, focusing on the ways they respond to the new institutional environments encountered in the host societies. I argue that the models of membership and organization available in each polity, rather than the cultural particularities of migrant groups, predict the collective forms and patterns of migrant organization.

Chapters 7 and 8 address the question of the changing institution and meaning of citizenship in the contemporary nation-state system. Chapter 7 reviews the membership status of guestworkers, concluding that they are incorporated into many of the rights and privileges that constitute the basis of citizenship. Chapter 8 argues that national citizenship is no longer the main determinant of individual rights and privileges, and that these rights are now codified in a different scheme, one that emphasizes universal personhood rather than nationality. I then delineate the emerging model of membership that I call postnational. Finally, I consider the implications of the postnational model for the duality of the persistence of the nation-states and the advent of a new citizenship.

CHAPTER TWO

International Migration and the Nation-State System

Large migratory flows and the use of foreign labor are not new. There have always been population movements (voluntary, planned, or forced) across territorial boundaries. Prior to guestworker programs, other forms of foreign or recruited labor were common; the slavery and indenture systems in the Americas, for example, are well-known passages in the history of world labor movements (Sassen-Koob 1980). In Europe, neither the presence of large numbers of aliens nor widespread foreign labor, often portrayed as unique to the postwar period, is a novel development. Early European literature on immigration shows that by the end of the nineteenth century there were already significant numbers of Irish workers in

Britain, Spaniards in France, Italians in Switzerland, and Poles in Germany, popular images of whom were not greatly different from those of postwar guestworkers (Rhoades 1978).[1] What distinguishes postwar migration from previous waves is not its magnitude, although even a glance at the numbers shows that the proportion of foreigners living in countries other than their own has increased significantly throughout the world, but, rather, the definition of the relationship between the "other," or "alien," and the host polity. This relationship has changed over time as the nation-state has emerged and crystallized, and as it has been transformed and restructured.

International Migrations and the Advent of the Nation-State

A chief characteristic of the contemporary world system is that economic production and trade increasingly take place on a transnational level, while populations are still bound within nation-states by the instruments of citizenship and sovereignty (Wallerstein 1974; Zolberg 1981). This discrepancy has created inconsistencies between capital investment and labor force allocation that have resulted in the movement of both these resources (Sassen 1988). Within the modern nation-state system, it has been relatively easy to move capital around, whereas the free movement of populations has been problematic. Nation-states with well-defined boundaries and sovereignty rules present obstacles to labor migration.

A historical reading of international labor migration reveals that it has been closely tied to the unfolding of the European nation-state system and the development of the institution of citizenship. The concept and category of international migrant is a product of the nation-state system and its ideologies of national membership. The creation of a specialized terminology—with, for instance, a distinction between emigrants (people who go beyond national frontiers) and immigrants (people who cross frontiers from the exterior)—manifests the strict definition of national boundaries and sovereignties (Rocha-Trindade 1988). It is no coincidence that the first statistics on international migration were collected after the Napoleonic wars (Taft and Robbins 1955), a period characterized by the intense efforts of the French state to construct a national polity.[2]

The following is a schematic history of the emergence of nationally codified polities and thus of international migration.[3]

Before settling down in agricultural societies, human beings were generally "on the move"; all continents experienced a succession of migratory waves (McNeill 1987; Taft and Robbins 1955). Labor control first became an instrument of societal organization in agrarian systems. Slavery in ancient city-states and then feudalism, in various forms and on various continents, introduced societal and legal arrangements that hindered the free movement of labor.[4] Feudal societies were characterized by individuals who were "fixed" to their localities through primordial or quasi-legal ties—local and communal attachments, personal allegiances to manor and estates, and serfdom.

Although immobility, or perceived immobility, was a reality for the bulk of the population, feudal societies experienced mobility of other kinds. First of all, invasions and conquests, which resulted either in compulsory movements of local populations or resettlements, were still very much a part of European history until the fourteenth century (Davis 1974; Smith 1986). Second, certain categories of people, especially the higher strata, were not bound to the land by the rules of serfdom but were free to move. Artists, artisans, and scholars, regardless of their regional origins, were invited by kings and courts to exercise their skills. Ecclesiastics also enjoyed a great deal of mobility: clergy and members of religious orders could move from kingdom to kingdom, monastery to monastery, to spread their teachings. Christianity and Islam were, after all, translocal institutions, embracing many cultures and peoples. Mercenary armies, composed largely of foreigners, were an important part of European militaries into the nineteenth century, until the ascendance of national mass conscription and prohibitions on foreign enlistment (Thomson 1990; Tilly 1990). Many people moved to other states to sell their military and paramilitary services. Finally, trade and transactions among geopolitically distant lands contributed much to the mobility of a merchant class dating back as early as the 1200s (Abu-Lughod 1989a).

This picture began to change in the fifteenth century with the breakdown of the feudal organization of society. Existing sources of authority were supplanted by the state as the sole sovereign power. As a result of this shift in authority, individuals were freed from their primordial ties and a direct link between the state and the individual was established, undermining the importance of other bonds in the society. With the rise of absolute monarchies in the seventeenth and eighteenth centuries, the king became "less an overlord of a feudal nobility and more the supreme ruler of the nation" (Bendix 1977:56; see also Anderson 1979). A related development, from the late eighteenth century on, was the redefinition of the populace, from subjects of monarchs to citizens of states, and an emerging overlap between the state and the nation as the principal definer of citizenship. This involved a concerted effort on the part of the state to mold individuals into citizens and to match state boundaries with nationalities, and resulted in fierce wars among and within states.

All these developments had a twofold impact on international migration. On the one hand, the abolition of serfdom and the disintegration of earlier forms of societal organization created an immense mobility, particularly among the lower strata, which had previously been tied to the land. Individuals dislodged from their customary settings adopted new identities and moved to new locales, from rural areas to urban sites. An ease of transportation, the result of new technological developments, also contributed to the increasing mobility of individuals. The "European discoveries" of other lands spurred overseas migration, disturbing the existing migratory patterns within Europe (McNeill 1979). Migration transcended the limits of Europe, reaching across the Atlantic, where the state as an organizing rule had not yet developed. The surge of Europeans brought many settlers to the Americas—missionaries, soldiers, mercenaries, and religious dissenters, along with economic refugees—at the violent expense of natives. This pattern of migration was accompanied by the first colonial ideologies of the European states, which lead to the reinvention of forced labor, through the systems of indenture and slavery.

On the other hand, as nation-states solidified and the international state system crystallized, new restrictions on the mobility of populations were introduced. European states, while freeing individuals from the traditional sources of authority and according them rights and privileges, at the same time created boundaries around their populations. With the French Revolution, the nation-state emerged as *the* form of political organization and nationality as the condition of membership in a polity. The Revolution codified individual rights and freedoms as attributes of national citizenship, thus linking the individual and the nation-state.[5] Citizenship acquired exclusionary properties through compulsory education, conscription, and national welfare, all of which defined culturally unified and sacred entities by creating boundaries around them (Anderson 1983; Hobsbawm and Ranger 1983; Weber 1976). These institutions erected a variety of barriers—physical borders, ideological boundaries, national languages, and moral obligations to the state—all of which impeded migration. The labor of individuals was reconstructed as a national resource, and individual capacities were defined as central to national economic and social progress. As it became increasingly important who was in and who was out, the states attempted to control any movement of population across their borders by means of elaborate immigration laws. In the early twentieth century, passports and national identity cards were introduced, formalizing the status of the national citizen and, by contrast, the alien.

Nevertheless, individual rights and liberties, which were embedded in the concept of citizenship, opened the way for many forms of immigration. Pursuit of economic well-being stimulated major population movements to new geographies of employment in the nineteenth and early twentieth centuries. During this period, around 52 million Europeans left their countries and about 72 percent of them settled in North America (Moch 1992:147), where national definition was not yet as exclusive as it was in Europe.

Contemporary International Migrations: Guestworker Systems

With the consolidation of the nation-state and nationalism in the twentieth century, international migration took a different course. Western industrialized countries became large-scale importers of workers, while government control, protective legislation, and compulsion came to dominate population movements. Accordingly, the pre–World War II period exhibited the following characteristics.

- A decrease in European emigration, with greater numbers moving in than out. German emigration, for example, dropped from over 1 million to less than 300,000 between 1890 and 1900 (Böhning 1978:15).
- An increase in the number of migrants returning to their home countries. In the 1910s, the rates of return from the United States were 63 percent for northern Italians, 56 percent for southern Italians, 51 percent for Spaniards, 41 percent for Russians, 31 percent for Poles, and 21 percent for Germans (Piore 1979:151).
- Early forms of temporary migration designed to keep citizenship intact: the indentured labor system of the British and Dutch colonies, and increased use of seasonal workers. In the Caribbean, the need for additional labor for sugar production was met by the importation of a half-million workers from India, "who typically came on five-year contracts with free transportation both ways" (Sassen-Koob 1980:6). Seasonal migrant workers recruited from distant tribes were frequently used in African plantations and mines (Amin 1974).
- An increase in immigration by foreigners who were easily assimilable, like those from colonies or previous colonies to core countries (Böhning 1979a).
- The establishment of systematic immigration rules and alien controls in many European countries by the end of the World War I (Hammar 1985e).
- A tightening of control even in the United States. The Congressional laws of 1921 and 1924 introduced a quota system to "maintain the cultural and racial homogeneity of the United States by the admission of immigrants in proportions corresponding to the composition of the white population" (Böhning 1979a:189).
- Political relocations of populations to homogenize language and culture within national boundaries. In

the course of nation-state formation and redefinition, many states have coercively relocated or expelled their ethnic minorities. Large numbers of people were exchanged between various European countries from 1918 to 1939. The most notable were 1.1 million Poles from Russia to Poland; 700,000 Germans from western Poland to Germany (Tilly 1978:61); and, by the Treaty of Lausanne, 190,000 Greeks to Greece from Turkey and 388,000 Muslims to Turkey from Greece (Davis 1974:101).

- In some states, as part of an attempt to make citizenship and nationality correspond, the ex post facto definition as alien of certain groups, which previously had been part of the polity (Jews in Europe, Armenians in Turkey, and Chinese in Malaysia).

As the shortage of workers in the industrialized Western countries became more acute, especially after World War II, restrictions on the inflow of populations were relaxed—though in a "mercantilistic fashion," which is to say, that "laborers were welcome, even actively recruited, but not supposed to stay or to bring their families" (Böhning 1978:16). Between 1950 and the early 1970s, Austria, Belgium, Germany, France, Luxembourg, the Netherlands, Sweden, and Switzerland all admitted large numbers of foreign nationals as guestworkers into their countries. France and Germany, for instance, each received more than two million foreign workers. And in the same period the number of foreigners in the Swiss labor force multiplied seven times, from 90,000 to 700,000 (Castles and Kosack 1973:32–40).

Most of the foreign labor came from the Mediterranean countries of Italy, Spain, Portugal, Greece, Yugoslavia, Turkey, and Morocco. However, not all migrant workers were part of official guestworker systems. Britain, France, and the Netherlands received large numbers of migrants from their colonies or former colonies (India and Pakistan, the Caribbean, Algeria, Surinam and Indonesia). Although colonial workers had a legal right to permanent residency and a more privileged status in general, they, too, were treated as temporary. As colonies acquired independence, European states redefined their relationships with ex-colonial populations. Algerians in France, Surinamese in the Netherlands, and Pakistanis in Great Britain are now defined as aliens and subject to general immigration policies.

In the early 1980s former labor-exporting countries of Europe, such as Italy, Spain, Portugal, and Greece, also began to receive large numbers of migrants, most from the southern Mediterranean—Morocco and Tunisia—but also from Senegal, Gambia, Ethiopia, the Philippines, Sri Lanka, and, more recently, from the Balkans. By 1990 foreign residents numbered 70,000 in Greece, 108,000 in Portugal, 415,000 in Spain, and 781,000 in Italy (SOPEMI 1992). In all these cases, migrant workers comprise both skilled and unskilled labor, both men and, increasingly, women. The majority are employed either as industrial workers or in the service sector, while a notable category of the self-employed is emerging among the more established migrant groups.

Guestworker systems are widespread in other regions of the world as well. In South Africa, such systems are set up for workers from "homelands" and from other African countries. The United States had its formal experience with guestworkers during the Bracero program, and still carries out such arrangements officially and unofficially with Mexico.[6] Japan has a foreign minority of about 800,000 Chinese and Koreans, whose forebears were brought over as forced labor in the 1920s and '30s (Holloway 1989). In addition, Japan employs about 50,000 South Americans of Japanese descent, and an estimated 300,000 foreigners, mostly from Iran, Pakistan, and Bangladesh, work and reside there illegally (Holloway 1989; Salt 1992:1102). In Africa, Libya, the Ivory Coast, Gabon, Zaire, Zimbabwe, Ghana, and Nigeria have been the main destinations for foreign labor from other parts of the continent. In Latin America, Venezuela employs Colombians in oil production, and Argentina receives workers from Chile, Bolivia, and Paraguay. The eastern European countries, especially the former Soviet Union, Czechoslovakia, and the Democratic Republic of Germany, used large numbers of Vietnamese, Mozambican, Angolan, and Ethiopian workers.[7] In the oil-producing Gulf emirates, where the percentage of foreign labor significantly exceeds that of national workers (ILO 1984), temporary migration is used to protect the "identity" of local people (Böhning 1978). Most foreign laborers in the Gulf are from other Middle Eastern countries, notably Egypt, North Yemen, Palestine, and Jordan, but they also come from Asian countries, such as Pakistan, the Philippines, Korea, Sri Lanka, and Thailand. Since 1967, Palestinians in the occupied territories have been recruited as unskilled workers into Israel's labor markets (Semyonov and Lewin-Epstein 1987). In addition, there is a sizeable work force of Palestinians, Egyptians, and Turks in Libya, Iraq, and Saudi Arabia. The list and combinations of sending and receiving countries have grown impressively with time, undermining political and geographical distance and rationalities.

Temporariness is the formal characteristic that all contemporary labor migration systems share. The principle of temporariness has been institutionalized in guestworker systems. As the name implies, guestworker programs are designed to satisfy immediate labor force demands by importing temporary workers (Rist 1978). The governing assumption is that foreign workers can be sent back at times of unemployment. The migratory flow is expected to behave in accord with labor market requirements; and economic cycles are considered the main determinant of immigration regimes.

The normative model of migration developed within this framework is essentially an "exclusionary" one, supported by ideologies of nationhood and citizenship. In contrast to the "inclusionary" model of the nineteenth-century immigrations, which depicts a system that favors the penetration and integration of new migrants, the "exclusionary" model sanctions cohesive cultural and population boundaries (Baker et al. 1985). As reflected in official statements and ideologies, guestworkers are not expected to partake in the national culture or polity.

The guestworker experience, however, challenges this normative model. Foreign worker populations have become permanent, contrary to official government policies and rhetoric. Foreign labor recruitment had formally ceased throughout western Europe by 1974. Yet, the former labor-importing countries face growing numbers of foreign residents, because of low return rates, ongoing family reunification, and natural population growth. In addition, political refugees have become a substantial component of international migration flows. Between 1986 and 1990, the average yearly growth of foreign populations was 9.2 percent in Austria, 1.3 percent in Belgium, 3.7 percent in Germany, 4.6 percent in the Netherlands, 4.5 percent in Sweden, and 3.2 percent in Switzerland (SOPEMI 1992:17). Increasing unemployment and repatriation programs have not expedited mass-scale return of former guestworkers.[8] And despite further restrictive efforts, European states have not been fully successful in preventing new flows of migrants from abroad.

Demographics of Migrant Populations in Europe

Currently, about 15 million migrants in Europe are foreigners in their countries of residence, which is to say that they do not have a formal citizenship status. Of these, only 5 million are European Community nationals. Well over half of the foreigners have the status of permanent resident alien, which can be established by living in host countries for a period of from two to ten years. There are also an estimated 3 million undocumented foreigners residing in western European countries.

Tables 2.1 and 2.2 summarize trends in the proportion of foreigners in selected European countries with respect to total population and total labor force in the postwar period. The major growth in foreign populations took place before the mid-1970s, rising from an approximate 5 million in 1960 to some 12 million in 1976 (table 2.1). Since then, foreign populations have grown steadily but more slowly, except in France and Switzerland, where they have stabilized. The proportion of foreigners in the work force decreased in all countries between 1975 and 1987, except in Belgium, where a notable increase occurred (table 2.2). However, at the end of the decade, the foreign labor population in most European countries rose again.

By 1990, foreigners in the western Europe made up between 3 and 16 percent of their host country's total population, with less than 4 percent only in Denmark and Britain, whereas in 1960 foreigners amounted to more than 4 percent of total population in only three countries: France, Germany, and Switzerland. Large foreign populations now inhabit France, Germany, Belgium, and especially Switzerland, where foreigners number

Table 2.1. Foreign Population in Selected European Countries (absolute, in thousands, and as percentage of the total population)

	1960		1976		1990	
	Absolute	%	Absolute	%	Absolute	%
Denmark	17	0.4	91	1.8	161	3.1
Britain	—	—	1,542	2.9	1,875	3.3
Netherlands	118	1.0	351	2.6	692	4.6
Austria	102	1.4	271	3.6	413	5.3
Sweden	191	—	418	5.1	484	5.6
France	—	4.7	3,442	6.6	3,608	6.4
Germany	686	1.2	3,948	6.4	5,242	8.2
Belgium	453	4.9	835	8.5	905	9.1
Switzerland	495	9.2	1,039	16.4	1,100[a]	16.3[a]

Sources: Penninx (1986) for 1960 and 1976 figures for countries except Denmark; Danmarks Statistik (1989) for Denmark; SOPEMI (1992) for 1990 figures.

[a] Excludes seasonal and frontier workers.

Table 2.2. Foreign Labor in Selected European Countries (absolute, in thousands, and as a percentage of the total work force)

	1975		1985–87		1990[a]
	Absolute	%	Absolute	%	Absolute
Denmark	—	—	50[b]	1.8[b]	—
Netherlands	216	4.4	169	3.0	200
Britain	1,696	6.5	1,123[c]	4.5[c]	933
Sweden	251	6.0	215	4.9	258
Austria	185	6.1	146	5.1	236
France	1,900	8.5	1,658	6.9	1,554
Germany	2,120	8.0	1,834	7.9	2,025
Belgium	278	6.9	403	10.0	—
Switzerland	711	24.0	567	18.2	670

Sources: Sassen-Koob (1980:10) for 1975 figures; Perotti, Costes, and Llaumett (1989:39) for 1985–87 figures; SOPEMI (1992) for 1990 figures.

Note: Data reported are not always comparable; in certain cases foreign labor refers only to foreign wage and salary earners, excluding the self-employed and unemployed. Also, frontier and seasonal workers are generally not included.

[a] Includes the unemployed, except in Britain and the Netherlands.

[b] 1982 figures.

[c] 1986–1988 average (SOPEMI 1989:55).

one-sixth of the total population, and almost one-fifth of the work force.

Foreign workers in various countries represented from 2 to 18 percent of the total labor force by 1990, the lowest in Denmark and the highest in Switzerland. These numbers are striking, especially if we consider that labor migration to Europe formally ended in 1974, and that unemployment throughout western Europe has risen.[9] Overall, foreign populations show a demographic increase, in spite of decreasing opportunities for work.

This increase has been reinforced in the 1990s by an upsurge of refugees. In western Europe, the number of asylum seekers increased from 65,400 in 1983 to 544,400 in 1991 (Rogers 1992: 1121). Despite restrictive regulations,[10] asylum remains a privileged form of migration. Attempts to stop or repatriate asylum seekers receive international attention, and are heavily debated within and outside Europe. According to one estimate, on average, 30 percent of applicants are granted asylum in Europe. Among those rejected, 75 to 85 percent stay in the country of asylum, nonetheless (Rogers 1992:1122).

Table 2.3 shows the proportion of naturalizations in relation to foreign population in various European countries. Even after a considerable length of residence in host countries, migrant populations remain foreign. The average length of residence for migrant workers in Europe is more than 15 years, whereas the annual rate of naturalization is relatively low, only 1.9 percent, on the average (1990 figure). In addition, naturalization rates have not changed significantly over time; where they have, they have decreased rather than increased. Only in France and Germany has there been a rise in the last decade, albeit minimal. Belgium, Switzerland, and Germany have especially low percentage rates. Sweden's uncharacteristically high percentages may be accounted for by its large proportion of political refugees, who in general naturalize at higher rates. Table 2.4 further illustrates the relatively low incidence of naturalization in various host countries.

In the decade of the mid-1970s to the mid-1980s, the number of foreigners naturalized in Germany did not exceed 6 percent. Sweden, Switzerland, and France naturalized from 10 to 13 percent of their foreign populations. The rather high figure for the Netherlands reflects a significant proportion of ex-

Table 2.3. Annual Naturalizations as a Proportion of the Foreign Population

	1976	1980	1990
Belgium	0.8	1.0	0.2
Switzerland	1.5	1.8	0.8
Germany	0.4	0.4	1.0
France	1.1	1.2	1.5
Denmark	2.6	3.8	1.9
Netherlands	1.1	4.1	2.0[a]
Britain	4.2[b]	3.0[c]	2.9
Austria	2.6	2.9	2.9
Sweden	4.8	4.9	3.7

Sources: Penninx (1986) for 1976 and 1980 figures for countries except Denmark; Danmarks Statistik (1989) for Denmark; SOPEMI (1992) for 1990 figures.

Note: The numbers reported may not be comparable across cases; changes in nationality because of marriage or birth are not always reported.

[a]The drastic drop was mainly caused by a change in the Dutch Naturalization Act in 1988.

[b]1975 figure.

[c]1981 figure.

Table 2.4. Naturalizations, 1975–84

	As Percentage of Total Foreigners	As Percentage of Total Population
Germany	6.0	0.5
Sweden	10.4	2.4
Switzerland	10.4	1.5
France	12.7	0.9
Netherlands	18.6	0.7

Source: Perotti, Costes, and Llaumett (1989:36).

colonial residents, mostly Surinamese, who were granted citizenship. In any case, at current rates of naturalization, it may well take at least one hundred years before the foreigners all become citizens of their host countries—assuming a constant stock of foreigners, of course (see de Rham 1990:179).

Note that, unlike countries such as the United States, Canada, and Australia, with historically high immigration rates,

European states do not grant citizenship on the basis of *jus soli*, birth in the territory. France and Britain apply the principle of jus soli conditionally, with certain requirements of residence and registration. In Europe, assumption of nationality is not automatic; immigrants, and their children born in the host country, have to contend with relatively restrictive naturalization procedures. Normally, there is a waiting period for application for citizenship in the host country: five years in Belgium, France, the Netherlands, Sweden, and Britain; seven years in Denmark; ten years in Austria and Germany; and twelve years in Switzerland. In some cases, immigrants must also fulfill further conditions, such as good conduct (no criminal record), sufficient knowledge of the language and means of subsistence, or assimilation (see Brubaker 1989b, Niessen 1989, and de Rham 1990).

In the 1990s, countries with more restrictive, lineage-based rules (Belgium, Germany, Switzerland, and the Netherlands) have widened access to citizenship (SOPEMI 1992). Switzerland (since 1990) and the Netherlands (since 1991) have allowed for dual citizenship. A 1991 act in Belgium grants citizenship to third-generation immigrants automatically, and second-generation immigrants under the age of 12 can become citizens at the request of their parents. In Germany, the 1990 Foreigners Law, and a 1993 government decree, made virtually automatic the naturalization of immigrant children between the ages of 16 and 23 who were born or had lived in Germany more than eight years. During the same period, the French government tightened its nationality code, which had guaranteed automatic citizenship at age 18 to immigrant children born in France. Under the new legislation, to become citizens, immigrant children need to apply formally between the ages of 16 and 21.

Yet, difficult procedures and requirements only partially explain the low naturalization rates. Recent surveys show that many eligible migrants do not plan to give up their original nationality. According to a nationwide survey of foreigners conducted by the Ministry of Labor and Social Affairs of Germany in 1986, half of those surveyed planned to remain permanently or at least for "many years to come," but only 6 percent expressed interest in taking on German citizenship (*Der*

Tagesspiegel, 8 August 1986). The few surveys taken in other European countries support the assertion that immigrants, even in the second generation, tend to be reluctant to become nationals of their host countries (de Rham 1990). When the inclination exists, it is often accompanied by demands for dual citizenship. In a 1993 survey commissioned by the Social Services Ministry of North Rhine-Westphalia, more than half of the foreigners polled indicated interest in becoming German citizens if the laws allowed dual citizenship (Reuter news agency, 27 September 1993). In fact, even in traditional immigration countries, the propensity for becoming citizens of the host country is lower than before. In Canada, for example, of the 4 million immigrants entering the country between 1945 and 1975, only 1.5 million became citizens (Ferguson 1974:38). In the United States, according to the Immigration and Naturalization Service statistics, currently about 37 percent of legal immigrants apply for citizenship, in comparison to 67 percent in 1946 (*New York Times,* 25 July 1993).

All of these statistics reveal the foreign yet permanent character of postwar migrants in Western countries. Despite their permanence in European polities, migrant populations have not been incorporated as part of a formal citizenship scheme. This circumstance contradicts the traditional model of immigration, predominant in American literature, in which foreigners are expected to be absorbed, in time, as naturalized citizens. In earlier immigration systems, incorporation assumed that foreigners would be transformed into formal citizens and assimilated into the cultural patterns of the national polity, mainly through socialization in schools.[11] Immigrants were either treated as prospective members and eventually naturalized, or else not considered part of the polity and categorically excluded, as were turn-of-the-century indentured Chinese laborers in the United States. The condition of postwar migrants defies such binary precepts embodied by classical models of immigration. As I show later, even though postwar migrants are largely foreign, they are incorporated into various institutions and structures of host societies. They are formally included in state policies, share in governmental budgets, welfare schemes, educational systems, and trade unions, and are accorded many rights and privileges of citizenship.

Consider, however, the classical depiction of guestworkers in the literature:

> It is crucial that the workers who are admitted should be "guests," not immigrants seeking a new home and a new citizenship. . . . They are brought in for a fixed time period, on contract to a particular employer; if they lose their jobs, they have to leave; they have to leave in any case when their visas expire. They are either prevented or discouraged from bringing dependents along with them. . . . Mostly they are young men or women in their twenties or thirties; finished with education, not yet infirm, they are a minor drain on local welfare services (unemployment insurance is not available to them since they are not permitted to be unemployed in the countries to which they have come). Neither citizens nor potential citizens, they have no political rights. The civil liberties of speech, assembly, association—otherwise strongly defended—are commonly denied to them, sometimes explicitly by state officials, sometimes implicitly by threat of dismissal and deportation. (Walzer 1983:56–57)

How do we explain, then, the growing foreign populations in western European countries, even in times of economic stagnation and restrictive policies? How can we interpret the discrepancies between assumed models, on the one hand, and demographics and institutional incorporation of guestworkers, on the other? What accounts for the increasing rights and privileges of aliens who continue to reside in host societies without formal citizenship status? And why is it not possible to sustain exclusionary guestworker systems that are immanently entrenched in national models of citizenship? The chapters that follow examine patterns of incorporation of contemporary guestworkers, testifying to changes in the membership status of postwar migrants and the relationship between the alien and the host polity.

CHAPTER THREE

Explaining Incorporation Regimes

The incorporation of postwar migrants is shaped both by the historically encoded membership systems of European host polities and by global changes in the concept and organization of individual rights. In the postwar era, world-level pressures toward more expanded individual rights have lead to the increasing incorporation of foreigners into existing membership schemes. However, by extending membership beyond national citizenry, these pressures also work to transform the existing models, making national citizenship peculiarly less important.

Analyzing the incorporation of guestworkers into European polities, my study takes a different course than works that concern how well migrants adjust to host society culture and institutions. Whether they call this process "assimilation," "integration," or "adaptation," such studies share a common approach. They assume an individual-level process, and they emphasize the demographic, social, or cultural characteristics of migrants as the major explanatory variables.[1]

Commonly cited indicators of integration are migrants' degree of satisfaction with life in the host country, their adherence to the values of society, occupational achievements and income mobility, the educational attainment level of their children, rates of intermarriage, and the relative absence of discrimination. Such research attributes variations in the nature and degree of integration mainly to factors specific to migrant groups: their demographic characteristics, labor market and social status, and cultural and religious elements brought from their home countries. For instance, to explain the integration process of Turks in German society, "Islam" and the "Turkish village culture" are invoked, necessarily with a monolithic characterization. The basic premise of such studies is the simple dichotomy of the "traditional" versus the "modern": the presumed clash between the cultural values of migrants, and the norms and structures of European systems. This integrationist perspective posits and necessitates a process in which migrants are to adopt modern norms and partake of the values of the host society, thus becoming better adjusted and more satisfied individuals.[2]

My own perspective differs from that of such studies on two grounds. First, I am concerned with the macro-level process whereby a guestworker population becomes part of the polity of the host country. I call this process *incorporation*. Whether or not migrants are "well-adjusted," adapting to the life patterns of the host society, they do become incorporated into its legal and organizational structures and participate in various activities of the polity. Guestworkers gain access to many rights and privileges initially accorded only to citizens. They become part of welfare schemes; they participate in housing and labor markets, and get involved in business; they take part in politics through conventional and unconventional structures, including local elections, consultative institutions, work councils, and collective bargaining. Incorporation is a wider process that takes place independently of the integration of individuals or perceptions of such integration. Second, to explain incorporation, I look at the institutions of a host society, rather than at the cultural background or individual characteristics of migrants. The ways in which migrants interact with host polities and organize their experience are significantly affected by the models and resources available in those polities. Hence I propose that the institutionalized modes and organization of membership in host countries should be studied as the principal determinants of the incorporation of migrants.

Incorporation Regimes as Policy Discourse and Organizational Structures

Located within a competitive international system, the nation-state embodies the project of "warmaking" (Tilly 1990) and "national progress" (Meyer 1980). To this end, modern states take charge of ensuring and distributing collective goods (e.g., welfare, education, employment), and enhancing individuals as productive entities. This task entails the expansion of public space and regulation, and necessitates the incorporation as members of everyone living within the borders of the polity. Individuals in turn (as members) participate in various polity-level activity routines and central structures, thus, in the national project.

Historically, as the state has expanded and permeated new domains of social action, its responsibility has extended to different strata of society—workers, women, and children. The state has incorporated a larger and larger proportion of the population into its jurisdiction and into the public realm (Thomas and Meyer 1984; see also Foucault 1979, 1980). In this process, incorporation has affected the national citizenry through the establishment of citizenship rights and national institutions. However, in the postwar era, even foreign populations are incorporated into the institutions of the polity. In accordance with expanding notions of universalistic personhood, noncitizens, as much as citizens, are entitled (and authorized) as productive individuals wherever they reside.

Modern polities follow distinct patterns in incorporating their foreigners. One of primary analytical aims of this book is to account for the different incorporation regimes that have emerged in European host polities. In using the term *incorporation regime,* I refer to the patterns of policy discourse and organization around which a system of incorporation is constructed.[3] All states develop a set of legal rules, discursive practices, and organizational structures that define the status of foreigners vis-à-vis the host state, and the forms and boundaries of their participation in host polity institutions. The chapters that follow elaborate on the policy discourses of various European incorporation regimes, on the one hand, and the organizational arrangements that accompany particular regimes, on the other. I examine the officially stated policy goals and language; the specific policy instruments and budgets; the administrative and organizational structures for the formulation and implementation of policy; the legal framework defining the status and the social, economic, political, and cultural rights of migrants; and the migrants' associational and participatory schemes.

Explaining Immigration and Incorporation Policy

The extant literature on state policy and action pertaining to immigration and guestworkers in Europe customarily focuses on country-level political and economic variables, failing to note the larger institutional processes that frame and configure national contexts. Traditional theorizing essentially takes the form of functional explanations. Such analyses view foreign worker policies as reflections of the economic needs and interests of both nation-states and the capitalist classes. They argue that foreign labor enables the separation of production and reproduction and also functions as a "shock absorber" to cushion fluctuations in demand, providing flexibility to restructure labor markets. Through the creation of secondary markets and control of the labor supply, nation-states are thus expected to deflect market inefficiencies and periodic economic crises.[4]

The "interest" arguments assume the temporariness of foreign labor and assign nation-states an absolute position from which to regulate immigration in the national interest. Yet, postwar migrants are permanent, and nation-states do not seem to dispense with their foreign populations even when they are no longer "functional."

The permanence of foreign workers defies arguments for the projected economic functionality of guestworker schemes. In view of family unification policies and the extension to guestworker populations of health, education, and other welfare benefits (unemployment, sickness, and old age pensions), the presumed function of foreign workers as shock absorbers or labor substitutes becomes questionable. Indeed, the literature on the economic consequences of postwar European immigration is, at the very least, controversial (Freeman 1986). Hollifield (1992:141–66), for instance, shows that from the mid-1960s through the 1980s, in various sectors of the French economy, the use of foreign labor did not differ significantly from the use of citizen labor. During periods of economic decline, foreign workers were laid off in somewhat greater numbers than native workers, but, rather than return to their own countries, they remained as part of the French labor market, joining the unemployment line.

Postwar migration has coincided with expanding individual and membership rights that undermine the logic of guestworker systems and make it hard for host states to sustain exclusionary schemes. As nation-states accord guestworkers the rights and privileges of citizens, categorical differentiation between foreign and native workers becomes untenable. Functionalist explanations fail to acknowledge these changes in the parameters of membership. They also fail to recognize that the self-definitions and interests of nation-states are conditioned by the institutional rules of the global system. Host states articulate their interests and mobilize new policies and strategies according to what is "acceptable" and "available" within the broader institutional environment. Acting within a framework that emphasizes expanded notions of rights and membership, many European host states have redefined their interests. Rather than insist on repatriation policies, they have found interest in strategies that promote labor-market training for second-generation guestworkers. The theme of "the need to incorporate" guestworkers has supplanted that of their "temporariness" as the dominant discourse.

It should be apparent that I do not propose to bracket out

economic factors. Clearly, labor market conditions, along with wars and demographics, affect immigration—and always have (Tilly 1978). After all, a primary reason for the massive flows of labor in the postwar era is afforded by the transnational character of the world capitalistic system (Sassen 1988) and the openness of international markets (Hollifield 1992). However, it is less clear why these economic conditions should lead to the incorporation of foreign workers and their families into various institutions of the polity and citizenship rights, since this was not necessarily the case with the previous forms of imported labor, such as indentured workers.

Conventional political factors, such as party systems, electoral politics, and ideologies of different groups within a given national polity, have also been considered as explanatory variables in relation to guestworker and immigration politics (Freeman 1979; Layton-Henry 1992; Messina 1989; Saggar 1992; Schain 1988). In this vein, prevailing political party positions and programs (for example, conservative versus social-democratic) can be advanced as a determinant of the varying policies and degrees of responsibility assumed by different governments.

Studies reveal that, until the mid-1980s, immigration was one of the least politicized policy areas on the political agendas of most European countries.[5] Only since then have immigration issues become politicized. Debates on immigration have gained momentum especially with the new migratory flows connected to the reorganization of political geography in the former Soviet Union and in Eastern Europe. On the one hand, Western governments have deployed immigration and asylum as a symbolic decorum to reinforce their legitimacy by claiming mastery over their borders. On the other hand, with the rise of right-wing parties, immigration has become a contested issue in electoral and party politics (Feldblum 1990; Schain 1988). The far right, which uses anti-immigration rhetoric to mobilize and create a constituency, forces the "problem of asylum-seekers" into a prominent position on the public agenda.[6] Such rhetoric finds resonance among the mainstream parties, particularly in electoral politics. By including regressive measures and language regarding "asylum abuse" in their election platforms, mainstream parties lend further legitimacy to the problematizing of immigration (Husbands 1992). This exclusive stance, however, does not preclude host governments or major political parties from adopting more inclusionary policy positions toward migrants already in the country.[7]

What is striking about immigration politics is that, in most countries, there has been general agreement across the political spectrum on basic immigration policy. In both Sweden and the Netherlands, major decisions concerning immigration have been supported by political parties whether they are in power or in opposition (Hammar 1985d; Entzinger 1985). In Britain, France, and Switzerland, immigration has been a much more politicized issue, but even in those countries party politics have not differed significantly, regardless of who was in power while the immigration policies were shaped (Hammar 1985e). British legislation on immigrants has generally been supported by both the Conservative and Labour parties (Layton-Henry 1992; Saggar 1992). Similarly, in Germany, in 1993, changes made to the Basic Law regarding the right to asylum enjoyed bi-partisan support from conservatives and social democrats. These patterns of convergence indicate that variations in the ideological orientation of parties are not likely to explain variations in policy. Major political parties more often than not exhibit a propensity for alignment rather than dissention in their immigration politics and platforms.

Arguments of functionalist interest and party politics remain at best partial explanations of the postwar migration experience. The institutionalized schemes of membership in European polities and the larger changes in the parameters of citizenship, both of which affect and delimit the interaction of guestworkers with their host polities, do not figure into these analyses. In contrast, this book assigns primacy to wider institutional variables as an explanatory framework with which to differentiate and account for the European incorporation regimes.

My central argument has two components. The first emphasizes institutionalized state systems—the conceptual and organizational configuration of the political order within which states frame their action. Differences in incorporation regimes reflect the different collective modes of understanding and organizing membership in host polities. Encountered with new contexts and populations, nation-states invoke existing codes and schemes of membership. Thus, the prevailing principles, discourses, practices, and organizational structures that address membership are the source of variations in incorporation regimes across polities. In other words, incorporation styles bear the imprint of collective paradigms of membership that persist over time.[8]

The second component of my argument emphasizes world-level factors, transnational discourse and structures that provide the normative framework for incorporation regimes, both enabling and constraining them. Organizational and ideological changes in the nation-state system—the expansion of transnational economic and political structures and a growing focus on personhood and the rights of individuals—influence the configurations of incorporation regimes and tend to standardize the status of postwar migrants. Although the preeminent models of membership persist over time and reconstitute themselves in incorporation regimes, new models do emerge and innovations occur as nation-states extend their structural capacities to new segments and populations and as new global discourses permeate their boundaries.

Membership Models and Incorporation Patterns

One of the basic premises of this book is that the way new migrant populations are incorporated depends on the type of polity they encounter, with respect to its institutional resources and legitimate models of membership. By membership models, I mean the institutionalized scripts and understandings of the relationship between individuals, the state, and the polity, as well as the organizational structures and practices that maintain this relationship. These models constitute a repertoire for states, as well as societal actors, to draw upon, in constructing new strategies of action and policy.[9] They provide the language, concepts, resources, and mechanisms for the formal understanding and organization of incorporation. Consequently, policies and organizational arrangements concerning the incorporation of new migrant groups are isomorphic with the preeminent models of membership in host polities.

The discussion that follows introduces a typology of membership models and outlines the implications of these models for the incorporation of migrants. Figure 3.1 is intended to facilitate a discussion of two dimensions that define the membership models. The legitimized locus of action and authority in a polity specifies to whom the action is oriented and from whom the action is expected in a given social situation. Some polities locate more authority in the state; others, within society, as epitomized by the individual or corporate groups. The organizational configuration—whether the public space and authority are centralized or decentralized—specifies the locus of organizational resources and the extent of organizational capacities. This configuration determines to what extent state, public, or voluntary local structures initiate and control social functions and organizing. The typology defined by the intersection of these two dimensions identifies four membership models: corporatist, liberal, statist, and fragmental.[10]

In the corporatist model, membership is organized around corporate groups and their functions. Corporate groups—defined by occupational, ethnic, religious, or gender identity—are emphasized as the source of action and authority. These groups assume certain "natural" rights vis-à-vis the state. Individuals gain legitimacy and access to rights by subscribing to the wider collective groups through which they participate in different arenas of the social order. The corporatist model is centrally organized and collectively oriented, and corporate groups are tied closely to the administrative structures that

Locus of Action and Authority	Organizational Configuration: Centralized	Organizational Configuration: Decentralized
Society	I. Corporatist Sweden, Netherlands	II. Liberal Switzerland, Britain
	— Germany —	
State	III. Statist France	IV. Fragmental Gulf oil countries

Figure 3.1. Typology of Membership Models

support their existence. This model emphasizes public interest and the welfare of social groups. Elaborate state structures or state-sponsored institutions develop to provide social services.

Since the state is responsible for the collective good, governments in corporatist polities generate clear top-down policies for the incorporation of migrants, with an emphasis on standardized protection and services. Corporatist polities have formal avenues by which new populations can gain access to decision-making mechanisms and pursue their interests. In these polities, the pattern of incorporation is vertical: migrants are incorporated collectively, through their participation in the intermediary structures sponsored by the state. The pattern is one of official incorporation with an emphasis on social and welfare rights. Sweden and the Netherlands exemplify the corporatist pattern.[11]

The liberal model, in contrast, legitimizes the individual as the source of action and authority. Individuals and their interests supersede other institutions in society. Most political action and organization is effected by individuals and private associations, not formal centralized structures. Weak central authority and a loosely organized state apparatus characterize the liberal polity. The decision-making process is decentralized, and local authorities play an active role in developing and implementing policy concerning the citizens' social welfare. Voluntarism at the local level compensates for public functions not performed by the centralized authority and structures.

In the liberal model, with the absence of an administrative organ to act as the agent of the collective interest, the labor market is the main instrument of incorporation. Since liberal polities do not provide state-sponsored formal structures through which new populations and their interests can be incorporated, private and voluntary associations proliferate. Thus, these polities generate a horizontal incorporation pattern at the societal level through local voluntary associations, in which migrants are incorporated as individuals. Britain and Switzerland, each in its own way, are examples of the liberal pattern.

The statist model takes the form opposite that of the liberal one. The state as a bureaucratic administrative unit constitutes the locus of sovereignty and, to a great extent, organizes the polity. Individuals and their activities are defined as elements of, and subordinate to, the state. As the main provider and initiator of most public services, the central state intervenes actively in societal functions. The political process and decision making are also centralized, and, in the main, collective action and organization take place with respect to the centralized state apparatus and categories.

Statist polities are like liberal ones in terms of interacting with the citizens as individuals, but their mode of operation is top-down. Again, like liberal polities, they lack intermediary structures that can link migrant groups and their collective interests to the state and its administrative organs. Migrants are incorporated as individuals, but with much more state involvement. Statist polities also anticipate associational incorporation, but at a more national level. The centralized nature of politics drives the action and organizing of migrants to national and state levels. Migrant groups target and organize in opposition to the state, creating "social movements" in the traditional sense. The statist pattern is most clearly apparent in France.

Germany's membership model combines the corporatist and statist patterns. Its organizational structure displays many characteristics of the corporatist model, but, as is the case in France, the state has a strong presence in the political order as the locus of sovereignty. And despite its federative political system, which necessarily decentralizes administrative structures, the public sphere is centralized and bureaucratic. Highly centralized semi-public bureaucracies, trade unions, churches, welfare institutions, business organizations, and professional chambers actively take part in formulating public policy, and have strong links to the state.[12] Thus, Germany exemplifies a statist corporatist pattern.

In the last model, the fragmental, although the state holds sovereign rule, it is organizationally weak and circumscribed in its interaction with society. Instead, "primordial" groups such as the family, clan, and church, dominate social and public life. In this case, the incorporation of migrants is partial. Migrant populations participate in labor markets, but not necessarily in other societal or institutional structures. This model summarily characterizes such labor-importing countries as the oil-exporting Gulf states. Fragmental polities afford a good case to probe the emerging global models of membership that this book studies in the case of Europe. Further research on non-Western immigration and incorporation regimes is needed for a more complete understanding of the changing nature of citizenship.

These distinct models of membership provide the schemes within which new entrants to the polity are incorporated. Corporatist polities incorporate guestworkers as collective groups through vertically structured, formal organizations, while liberal and statist polities incorporate them into an associational structure, as individuals. In the corporatist model, the pattern is official and formal; incorporation takes place through state-sponsored intermediary organizations. In the liberal model, incorporation occurs at the societal level through local associations, with more active participation by migrants. In the statist model, the pattern is also associational but occurs at a centralized level.

The typology that I propose here emphasizes systems of rules that are directly pertinent to the construction of membership in a polity—the ways individuals are authorized to participate in authority structures and take part in public life, and the ways their rights and duties are organized. The membership models are intended not as categorical totalities but as frameworks within which to situate the particularities of state incorporation regimes and policies. As such, the typology may not apply to other domains of public order. Any given polity hosts multiple systems of rules, each regulating different policy or issue areas. So, for example, in Switzerland, whereas incorporation policy manifests a liberal pattern, industrial policy may be formulated in a more "corporatist" setting of conflict negotiation and social partnership (Katzenstein 1985). Similarly, despite the preeminence of the state's executive authority in the system as a whole, the French polity may display "corporatist" tendencies in the organization of certain aspects of its social security sector (Esping-Andersen 1990; Freeman 1989).

The chapters that follow present a detailed account of the attributes of various incorporation regimes. A close examination of the ways in which migrant populations are incorporated provides further insights regarding the institutionalized models and characteristics of membership in particular polities.

Global Discourses of Personhood and Membership

The incorporation of guestworkers and the extension of membership to "foreign" elements are only intelligible when we take the dynamics of and changes in the global institutional order into account. New institutionalist approaches in macrosociology contend that world-level rules and definitions are integral to the constitution of national institutions and social entities, such as state policies and bureaucracies, national economies, education, welfare, gender, and the individual (see esp. Thomas et al. 1987). Accordingly, global discourse and systems of rules provide and legitimize models of membership and the array of institutions that organize membership and the rights it entails. In the postwar era, a number of global processes have contributed to the expansion of membership and rights in national polities: the institutionalization of ideas of self-determination and equality through decolonization, the affirmation of "human rights" as a world-level organizing principle in legal, scientific, and popular conventions, and the extension of a state's responsibilities beyond the national framework (e.g., development-aid schemes, refugee programs, hunger relief efforts, and "democratization" projects).

These trends point to an intensifying discourse about the individual and human rights that is transmitted as global norms and models by a number of inter- and transnational agencies. In this vein, many world-level organizations take an active interest in international migrants and situate them within the bounds of human rights discourse. Through norm diffusion and direct policy influence, these organizations contribute to the redefinition of migrant status and rights, opening the way to an extended construction of membership.

The twentieth century has seen an impressive elaboration of the political, economic, and social rights of the individual citizen.[13] New forms of rights are introduced, as conceptions of personhood and its attributes are amplified. In addition, the scope of legal rights has expanded to cover new groups who were previously outside the national polity. Even nature—animals and plants—has acquired protection under law (Turner 1986b).

In the postwar era, massive decolonization not only led to the active involvement and mobilization of newly independent countries as equal partners at the international level, but also ushered in an awareness and assertion of their rights within universalistic parameters. This, in turn, contributed to the broadening and recasting of global discourse on rights. Parallel to the celebration and codification of "different but equal" cultures and "otherhood" through transnational agencies such as the UN and UNESCO,[14] postwar Europe has moved toward a more universalistic approach to membership and participation in the polity. New social movements have coalesced around individual and collective rights, contesting the accepted notions of citizenship in European polities. Consequently, a variety of cultures and subcultures have been incorporated into the social domain and institutions of citizenship: women, gays and lesbians, environmentalists, regional identities and interests, and youth subcultures, as well as immigrants.

Postwar discourse on rights crystallizes around the idea of personhood. It involves a conception of human persons in abstract, universal terms, supported by scientific theories and ideologies.[15] As a social code, personhood is not an idealistic, Hegelian notion but one rooted in highly structured discourses, economies, and politics. This scientifically encoded human personness constitutes the normative basis of an expanding citizenship. In the postwar era, the rationalized category of personhood (and its canonized international language, Human Rights) has become an imperative in justifying rights and demands for rights, including those of nonnationals in national polities.

Although ideas of human rights are not new to the West, these principles have systematically become legitimate international concerns and an integral component of international relations only in the twentieth century (Sikkink 1991).[16] Human rights are now a pervasive feature of global public culture. They are object of much public debate and social action and organization, enveloping and engendering a wide range of issues—from the protection of ethnic minorities and their cultural heritage to the right to development and employment; from political participation and sexual politics to the right to enjoy peace and access to the amenities of a "better" life and a "healthy" environment. The media images of the United Nations' "peace" missions, the Human Rights Awards distributed by the Reebok Corporation, and Amnesty International's mega rock concerts on behalf of humanitarianism further cultivate the legitimizing moral message of human rights discourse in everyday social spaces and routines.

As such, human rights principles amount to more than formal arrangements and laws. They constitute a binding discourse, according frameworks that render certain actions conceivable and meaningful. Like development (Ferguson 1990), progress (Meyer 1980), and freedom (Patterson 1991), human rights is a world-level organizing concept. Embedded in collective narratives, it presents itself as "ontological" and "self-evidently necessary"—that is, it is inconceivable to "dismiss" the idea of human rights, "just as it must have been virtually impossible to reject the concept 'civilization' in the nineteenth century, or the concept 'God' in the twelfth" (Ferguson 1990: xiii).

The concept of human rights, along with those of development, progress, and freedom, provides ways of understanding and interpreting the world order. As institutionalized prescriptions, they provide the criteria differentiating the first world from the third, west from east, and north from south. National governments are evaluated (and disciplined) by the "international community" on the basis of their realization of progress, development, and human rights. Transnational agencies produce ranking statistics and records through well-established evaluation schemes (e.g., productivity counts, measures of educational output, healthcare inventories, accounts of cultural multiplicity, and registries of political dissent). New nation-states promptly incorporate these "high" principles into their constitutions as state goals and individual entitlements. Even when there is disagreement as to their definition and extent, these principles are taken for granted and acted upon as "facts" (Meyer and Rowan 1977).[17]

This is not to assert that the discourses of universalistic

rights and personhood are automatically adopted by or authoritatively imposed on national/local actors; there are no centralized global-level structures to impose these norms and principles. Global discourse affects national outcomes in two significant ways. First, as I have mentioned, such discourse results in collective cognitive maps that allow social entities—individuals, groups, nation-states—to justify resource allocation, articulate legitimate dispositions, and perform effects. Second, global discourse creates new actors and collective interests which, in turn, exert pressure on existing systems. Once codified and materialized through conventions, legal instruments, and recursive deployment, this discourse becomes a focal point for interest-group activities and public attention. It enables mobilization, opens up an array of legitimate claims, and amplifies action. Hence, migrant self-organizations, advocacy groups, and international agencies, as well as sending governments, appeal to dominant human rights principles and develop discursive and organizational strategies around them.[18]

It is against this background of intensified discourse on rights and personhood that the incorporation of guestworkers into European host polities should be read. The trends toward elaboration and standardization of the legal status and rights of migrants, and expansion of national and transnational institutional arrangements for incorporating them signify a reconfiguration in the predominant European schemes of citizenship. The change is from a model of national citizenship to one of postnational membership, predicated on notions of personhood.

The next three chapters seek to discern and expound incorporation regimes and patterns in European polities, by employing the foregoing explanatory framework. I analyze both the common and varying dimensions of incorporation regimes and systematically sort their dimensions of variation across membership types. In particular, I examine to what extent the institutionalized membership models and organizational principles of polities are reflected in state incorporation regimes and the resulting collective organizational patterns of migrants. In so doing, I provide a more refined typology and discussion of the properties of incorporation regimes.

CHAPTER FOUR

Discourses and Instruments of Incorporation

The rationalization and institutionalization of the category "international migrant" is a new phenomenon in Europe. Although many European countries had previous experience with foreign labor and migration, the formulation of a comprehensive policy regarding incorporation of migrants did not occur until the middle or late 1970s. And only in the past two decades have European states produced explicit administrative structures, measures, and programs that affect the lives of migrants in host societies (Hammar 1985e).[1] Given the relatively short history of guestworkers in Europe, it is striking how elaborate and extensive a sphere of action states and other organizations, profit and nonprofit, have built up around them. International migrants have been increasingly addressed by a wide array of organizational and administrative structures, local and central procedures, policy instruments and budgets. States, as part of their expanding responsibilities, either extend existing policy schemes and organizations or develop new, though not necessarily coherent, ones to manage the incorporation of new populations.

The policies and the accompanying organizational structures that have emerged reflect the predominant models of membership in specific polities. Whether membership in a polity is primarily based on collectivities or on the individual affects how the state incorporates new migrants. Polities organized around the membership of corporate groups actively incorporate migrants as collectivities, through group-oriented instruments, budgets, and organizational structures. In polities where membership is organized around the individual, the labor market becomes the main conduit of incorporation. Migrants are expected to participate in the existing institutions of the host society as individuals, and state policies aim to enhance "opportunity structures."

Sweden and the Netherlands: Migrants as Corporate Groups

In Sweden and the Netherlands, migrant populations are defined by their collective identities. As collective groups, their position vis-à-vis the state is clear, and is a statutory position similar to that of other corporate groups in society. These states generate elaborate and highly organized policy regarding the incorporation of migrant groups.

Both countries refer overtly to "ethnic minorities" in their policy discourse. The Swedish case is especially interesting, because Sweden lacked extensive encounters with ethnic minorities other than Lapps and Finns before the postwar labor migration started. Sweden used to be one of the most "ethnically homogenous" societies in Europe (Hammar 1985d), unlike the Netherlands, which historically has been composed of religious minorities. Nevertheless, Sweden defines new migrant groups by their collective ethnic identity, which is considered a "natural" social grouping, and treats them like other corporate groups, in accord with the underlying corporatist mode of its membership.[2]

The immigration policy Sweden adopted in 1975 is based on three objectives: equality between immigrants and Swedes, freedom of cultural choice for immigrants, and cooperation and solidarity between the native Swedish majority and various ethnic minorities (Ministry of Labor 1984:11–12). Despite explicit reference to ethnic groups, the government's position is that Swedish policy does not foresee migrant communities persisting as cohesive ethnic entities over time (Lithman 1987). The officials I interviewed at various government offices including the National Immigration Board (SIV), the central agency responsible for migrants, repeatedly emphasized this point. They asserted, rather, that migrants are expected to integrate as individuals into Swedish society. However, the framework and instruments the Swedish state uses to promote this integration are themselves collectivist and reinforce ethnicity.

The corporatist pattern is readily revealed in the instruments of policy that Sweden has developed.[3] First of all, religious and ethnic minorities are given the constitutional right to "express and develop their cultural heritage." This right, recognized as one of the main principles of Swedish policy—freedom of cultural choice—in practice means mother-tongue education for children of "linguistic minorities," as well as ethnic radio and television broadcasting. The Swedish Broadcasting Corporation, which is by statute required to "give special consideration to ethnic minorities," produces radio and television programs in migrant languages (Lithman 1987). Moreover, various forms of literature in migrant languages, including newspapers and periodicals, receive state subsidies. In 1988, the Swedish government subsidized around seventy publications, in more than twenty different languages, catering to foreign communities (SIV 1987c).

Second, migrant organizations are regarded as natural channels for the incorporation of their constituencies. As formal bodies, they are expected to maintain the link between migrants and institutions of Swedish society. Thus, Swedish policy provides for the creation and nationwide organization of migrants' associations. The central government maintains an elaborate system of financial support for these organizations. Migrant groups are defined as ethnic groups when they reach 1,000 members. They are then incorporated into a central plan that closely resembles the state funding scheme for all other Swedish organizations (interview: SIV, Popular Movements Section).

The general Swedish model, in which societal organizations are recognized as representatives of different segments of the population and are therefore given a significant role as "formal partners" of the state (Boli 1991), constitutes the background for the Swedish policy emphasis on migrant organizations. In this context, migrant organizations are seen to represent the interests of their respective communities. The state provides avenues for the participation of migrant organizations at the national level through consultative bodies and advisory councils. Each "nationality" is represented by its federations at councils attached to ministries and other administrative agencies. In terms of participatory and funding arrangements, migrant organizations have the same statutory position as other Swedish umbrella organizations.

Dutch policy resembles Sweden's, both in content and form. The main goals of the Dutch "ethnic minorities policy," as the official papers term it, were formulated in 1981 as follows: "to create the conditions necessary to enable minority groups to attain equal rights and participate in society, to reduce the social and economic disadvantages suffered by minority groups, [and] to prevent discrimination and to improve the legal position of minorities where necessary" (Ministry of Home Affairs 1983:3).

Dutch incorporation policy, like that of Sweden, is based on collective categories. Official policy specifies the following minority categories: Moluccans, residents of Surinamese and Antillean origin, migrant workers and members of their families from recruitment countries, Gypsies, and refugees. Interestingly, not all of these categories are ethnic; nevertheless they are defined and organized as ethnicized collective identities vis-à-vis the state. Collectivity in this sense is not cultural, but functional. Chinese and Pakistanis, for example, are not specified as ethnic minorities, since "they are assumed to have no problems with their participation in Dutch Society" (Rath 1988:628).[4]

Similarly, Dutch policy ethnicizes religion and defines it as an affair of minority policy to be incorporated within the "ethnic minority" schemes. The Dutch state supports financially the Islamic associations of Turkish migrants on grounds that religious organizations are "a very *natural* form of 'self-organization' for people coming from cultures with a strong religious base" (emphasis added).[5] This reasoning ignores the fact that such religious organizing is not part of "Turkish tradition" and is unconstitutional in Turkey.[6] On the other hand, Dutch policy does not support the Islamic organizations of Pakistanis or Palestinians because those groups are not officially defined as ethnic minorities (Rath, Groenendijk, and Penninx 1991).

For both Dutch and Swedish policy, then, classification itself is an essential policy instrument and activity; and the arbitrariness involved reflects the exogenous and functional standing of the officially constructed categories.

Dutch policy stresses as one of its goals giving members of ethnic minorities the opportunity to "become emancipated within their own communities" and "gain an independent place" in society (interview: Ministry of Home Affairs, Directorate for the Coordination of Minorities Policy [DCM]). Emancipation assumes a process through which the new migrant groups are elevated to equal status with the dominant groups in Dutch society. The term *emancipation* has its origin in the historical process of religious liberation that, in the early twentieth century, resulted in a Dutch polity segmented along religious lines (Hoppe and Arends 1986). Emancipation has meant the organization of social, cultural, and political functions along denominational "pillars"—Catholic, Protestant, and Secular—each with a separate system of schools, welfare and health organizations, and unions.[7] Although the pillarization of Dutch society gradually disintegrated in the postwar period, current policies toward migrants still reflect this legacy (Entzinger 1985).

The two areas of policy in which the legacy of pillarism is most apparent are education and broadcasting. Within the existing legal system, migrant groups can secure charters for their schools and run their own radio and television broadcasts, all publicly funded.[8] More directly, Dutch policy has provisions that give priority to the support of minority cultures and their organizations. The provisions include a Government Grant Scheme for the Welfare of Minorities that directly finances migrant organizations. The rationale for this support is grounded in the discourse of emancipation. As one of the directors of minorities policy at the Ministry of Home Affairs explained in an interview, "Dutch society has historically been a society of minorities, a society of emancipated minorities; the Catholics, Protestant groups, laborers, women. And, now the emancipation of immigrant minorities. That is the background of our policy for strengthening the self-organizations of immigrant groups. These organizations can serve to make the Dutch society acquainted with the interests of immigrants and their eventual emancipation."

Hence, in addition to providing financial support to migrant organizations, Dutch policy encourages the participation and consultation of minority groups at both national and local levels. Consultative councils for each ethnic minority group facilitate their participation at the national level. Political parties, trade unions, and welfare agencies make similar arrangements. All of these measures are designed to provide a bridge between migrant groups and Dutch institutions, which are presumed to be in natural disparity.

In the late 1980s, Dutch policy shifted in emphasis from "emancipation" to "reduction of disadvantage and discrimination," another principle expressed in the 1981 policy document (Entzinger 1987; interview: Netherlands Scientific Council for Government Policy). The government's 1991 *Action Program on Minorities Policy* has no special section on the goal of emancipation; most of the program was devoted to eliminating social and economic disadvantage and discrimination experienced by members of migrant groups (SOPEMI-Netherlands 1991). As unemployment has grown, the government has increasingly focused on discrimination in the labor market and education. Consequently, there has been much less emphasis on promoting separate institutions for migrant groups. For instance, the government has been considering whether to combine the national organizations that provide services along ethnic lines by 1994. Despite this change in priorities, the term emancipation is still a part of the official language, although it has taken a new meaning. In its 1993 Action Program on minorities, the government retitled the emancipation project "Women, Emancipation, Minorities," merging migrant groups with broader categories of the disadvantaged in Dutch society (SOPEMI-Netherlands 1992:53).

The instruments and budgets that have evolved within the framework of Swedish and Dutch migrant policy target certain ethnic groups and the institutions that cater to them as collectivities. The major fields of government policy and spending are reception services for newcomers; specific employment projects and vocational training courses for certain categories of migrants; host-country language training for adults; mother-tongue classes in the school system for migrant children;[9] information and social services; and support for migrant organizations and cultural activities.

In Sweden, the total budget for migrant policy for the 1983/84 fiscal year was estimated at 2,000 million crowns (SKr) ($300 million; Hammar 1985d:38).[10] Table 4.1 summarizes state funding of major programs in the fiscal year 1987/88.

In the Netherlands, the "minorities budget" consists of funds allocated to finance measures directed toward minority groups. In 1981, the total amount in the minorities budget was 720 million florins (Fl) ($374 million; Entzinger 1985:78); in 1988 it rose to 797 million Fl ($414 million). Table 4.2 shows roughly how the money was distributed in 1988. The budget further itemizes the funds on the basis of minority categories. For example, the allocation for social welfare, health, and

Table 4.1. Swedish State Spending on Immigrant Programs, 1987/88 (Swedish crowns and U.S. dollars, in millions)

Grants to municipalities for Swedish language instruction	244.0 SKr	$ 39.5
Study allowance to participants in language instruction	108.0	17.5
Language support in schools for children of immigrant and other linguistic minorities	835.0	135.3
Grants to national immigrant organizations (including religious groups)	18.5	3.0

Source: Lithman 1987:24, supplemented by an interview at the SIV, Information Section.

Table 4.2. Distribution of the Netherlands' 1988 Minorities Budget (Dutch florins and U.S. dollars, in millions)

General policy instruments[a]	28 Fl	$ 14.6
Employment	161	83.7
Education	312	162.2
Housing	68	35.4
Social welfare, health, and culture	194	100.9
Other	34	17.8
Total	797 Fl	$414.5

Source: Ministry of Home Affairs 1987/88.
[a] Figure includes 2 million Fl ($1.04 million) reserved for research on minorities.

culture includes money for group-specific social service organizations, both local and national. It also includes funds reserved for migrant associations.

The existence and extent of such specialized budgets in Sweden and the Netherlands demonstrate that migrants constitute separate, formalized categories in central state programs, and that they are incorporated into legal and formal organizational structures as collectivities.

Switzerland and Britain: Migrants as Individuals

The migrant policies of Switzerland and Britain are more individual-oriented and decentralized than those of Sweden and the Netherlands. An emphasis on the individual migrant is reflected in both the context and organization of Swiss and British policy. Migrants are not defined by their corporate standing; they are regarded as individuals whose position in the host society is determined largely by their participation in the labor market. Unlike the corporatist polity, where the state actively incorporates new groups through centralized policy instruments, the liberal polity rejects formal, codified policy focused on collective groups. Rather, it emphasizes the individual migrant and labor market processes as the loci of incorporation.

Swiss policy, as stated by the officials of the Swiss federal government, is upheld by three principles: stabilization/equilibration [numerical regulation] of the foreign population, improvement of the labor market structure, and integration (interview: Federal Commission for Aliens [EKA], and the Federal Aliens Office).

Although controlling the inflow of migrants has now become a concern for all host countries, in Switzerland, numerical regulation is a well-established policy instrument. It serves the major aim of federal migration policy, which is to control the size of the foreign population in accord with labor market demands. The regulation is accomplished by setting yearly quotas for the numbers of foreigners to be admitted, which the federal government determines in consultation with labor authorities as well as business associations and trade unions.[11] In fact, the single most important policy decision about migrants made at the federal level is the determination of quotas of foreign workers that each canton can import. Apart from regulating the flow of migration, the Swiss federal state has little legal or organizational involvement in migrant affairs.[12]

The key term of the Swiss policy on migrants is "integration," rather than "emancipation" or "mutual coexistence," terms which came up persistently in interviews with Dutch and Swedish officials and migrant leaders. According to Swiss federal authorities, integration denotes an individual-level process and means that "the foreigner must find himself in a situation in which he can realize and succeed in his professional and personal life in Switzerland" (interview: EKA). Although integration is cited as one of the pillars of federal policy, this principle is not manifest in a centrally organized set of measures directed to specific migrant groups. The federal state does not assume an active role in the incorporation process. It expects migrants to become integrated through existing occupational and market structures. While the Dutch and Swedish authorities I interviewed constantly stressed the importance of migrants' self-organizing, Swiss officials pointed to market mechanisms as the principal framework for integration.

Historically, Swiss society is organized at the level of the canton and commune, which are highly autonomous and correspond practically to linguistic communities. The state recognizes territorial divisions along linguistic lines, but does not grant legal ethnic status to these collectivities. This means that individual identity is regionally rather than ethnically defined (Schmid 1981a; Hoffmann-Nowotny 1986), and that the concept of membership mainly refers to locality, or *gemeinde*, rather than to a centralized corporate identity and community.[13]

Within this framework, integration of migrants does not assume a corporate, or collective orientation, either. There is no special state support for migrant identities or migrant organizations, which is notably different from the strategies employed by the Dutch and Swedish states. Migrants are expected to integrate as individuals into the communities where they live. Asked why Switzerland has no federally organized policy of incorporation, an official at the Federal Aliens Office said confidently, "[foreigners] are not integrated at the federal level; they integrate where they live, where they work, through their interaction with Swiss people, with their partners at work. . . . Part of our job is to take care that people who are being admitted do integrate themselves as quickly as possible with the Swiss population."

Although British policy differs in emphasis and origins, its general principles resemble those of the Swiss. British policy also addresses the individual migrant rather than migrants as a collective category; and, in its strategies, it too is decentralized. In Britain, "racial equality" is the dominant theme of migrant policy. This focus stems from Britain's history with ex-colonial and Commonwealth immigration (Freeman 1979). Early immigrants were considered British citizens with full legal rights; thus, no special measures were thought necessary, other than a series of legislative acts to accord them equal footing with the rest of society (Layton-Henry 1985). But even with an influx of new immigrants who lack legal status as Commonwealth citizens, British policy has not changed much. The officially stated goal of British policy is to facilitate integration by enhancing "equality of opportunity" and promoting "good race relations" (CRE 1988). To this end, the government has issued a number of acts prohibiting discrimination against racial and ethnic minorities in education, housing, and employment. The 1976 Race Relations Act is the most comprehensive one and the basis for many antidiscriminatory codes.

Yet, although policy discourse in Britain stresses race relations (and even the existence of a "multi-ethnic" society), there are no indications that migrants are viewed or treated as collective groups. In this context, "favorable race relations" means employing legal actions against discrimination in individual cases rather than acting on behalf of any particular group or creating special mechanisms to deal with migrant groups as separate entities. The main policy focus is to provide opportunities in labor and housing markets for migrants who are otherwise discriminated against and cannot realize their individual capacities. The 1988 report of the Commission for Racial Equality, the main government agency responsible for the integration of migrants, clearly expresses this orientation: "[The Commission is] concerned for social justice and ensuring that the law is respected, but also works to build up the capacity of people who may have been denied access to opportunity" (CRE 1988:7). Such a goal accords with that of Swiss policy, which also stresses individual opportunity; but, unlike Switzerland, Britain has instituted extensive legal mechanisms and strategies toward this end.

Thus, in liberal cases, the main policy aim becomes that of providing opportunities for and removing obstacles to individual migrants' integration into existing institutions of society, so that they can gain those benefits already offered by the system. In Britain, policy instruments formulated within this framework include legal strategy and action designed to protect individual migrants' interests and to abolish restrictions that affect foreigners as individuals (CRE 1988). In Switzerland, the major policy instruments are measures to improve the structure of the labor market, which is seen as the main avenue of integration; in an interview, an official of the Federal Office of Industry, Small Business, and Labor (BIGA) remarked: "the better position you have on the job market, the better you are integrated." Accordingly, such provisions as vocational training, language support in schools, and adult education are introduced to strengthen migrants' standing vis-à-vis the labor market.

Since there are no federal instruments designed to serve migrant groups, it is hard to talk about Switzerland in terms of an incorporation budget, as I did with the cases of Sweden and the Netherlands. The budget and the content of policy instruments change significantly from canton to canton. In general, expenses include establishing contacts between the Swiss and foreigners; training social workers, teachers, and volunteers who work with migrants; and providing information, Swiss language courses, and vocational training. The financial sources for these activities can be both public and private: cantonal and communal governments, church groups, foreign consulates, corporations, and trade unions. The dispersed nature of these resources creates further difficulty in generalizing about the Swiss budget of incorporation.

In broad terms, the 1982 budget can be summarized as follows (EKA 1982): about 2.5 million Swiss francs (SFr) ($1.7 million) was allocated for the activities of federal and local public organizations whose main purpose is to facilitate integration. This amount includes personnel costs. Church communities spent over 10 million SFr ($6.9 million) for social help to foreigners. For vocational training, the federal government and the cantons provided about 2 million SFr ($1.4 million), that is, 2 SFr ($1.40) per migrant. When compared to state spending in the Netherlands for the same budget item, 80.5 Fl ($42) per migrant (Ministry of Home Affairs 1987/88), the lack of direct state involvement in the Swiss case stands out. On the other hand, the Swiss business community spends a large amount on vocational and language training, although the figures are not available.

In Britain, the main instruments of integration and budget item is a set of measures the state has developed against discrimination. One of the CRE's specific purposes is to realize and enforce these measures by means of codes of practice in different areas (e.g., employment and housing). In 1991, the Commission spent around £632,000 ($1,097,200) for information, publication, and research activities (CRE 1991). In addition, it supports local voluntary organizations, including ethnic ones, that offer services to migrants such as youth training and counseling, employment campaigns and projects, advice services and community centers, language training, and aid for elderly members of ethnic minorities. In 1991, the Commission distributed about £5.3 million ($9.2 million) to groups and projects committed to the cause of antidiscrimination and to social services for migrants.

Apart from the general activities of the CRE in the field of discrimination, Britain has no centrally defined policy instrument; migrants are largely taken care of in their localities. Local educational authorities allocate funds for teaching English to migrant children in schools; a total of £35 million ($60.7 million) was spent in 1976 for this purpose, £15 million ($26 million) of which was contributed by the central government (Layton-Henry 1985). Local administration also provides some funding to voluntary service associations to help with their expenses, such as half-time staff and rent.

These measures do not add up to a national incorporation policy that fosters corporate groups and identities, comparable to the policies of Sweden and the Netherlands. For instance, the British government has rejected suggestions that schools offer an Asian language as the compulsory modern language in areas with a substantial migrant population (CRE 1988). Arrangements for mother-tongue teaching are in large part private and voluntary, outside regular school hours. Similarly, even though the British educational system allows schools owned by religious organizations to receive substantial financial aid from local education authorities, no non-Christian schools (except for a few Jewish ones) have had such status accorded them.[14]

Policy instruments that serve the general population are expected to benefit migrants as well. Various programs designed to improve living conditions in inner city areas, collectively termed "Urban Aid," have been in effect since 1977. The priorities of the Urban Aid program have changed over time, from more social and welfare provisions to more economic projects whose aims are the "creation of wealth and environmental regeneration, thus, improvement of living and working conditions of immigrants" (interview: Home Office, Research and Planning Unit). Some city councils devote part of their urban aid budget to the voluntary associations sector, in order to support initiatives aimed at satisfying the needs of immigrants. Migrant organizations can also use these grants.

A more direct source of financing from the central government for local services is provided by Section 11 of the 1966 Local Government Act, designed to meet what are loosely called the "special needs" of immigrants. The funding under this act is almost exclusively used for educational projects

(FitzGerald 1986). Local authorities in areas with ethnic minorities can claim reimbursement up to 75 percent, mostly for the salary costs of teaching English to migrant children. In accord with general British policy, the emphasis is again on projects and programs that "integrate immigrants better, to use mainstream services better, or to play their part along with the majority white population in public life" (interview: Home Office, Research and Planning Unit), instead of the sorts of initiatives that would encourage migrants to develop a separate collective identity and organization.

France: Individual Migrants, Centralized State

The French state also defines migrants as individuals, but takes a much more centralized approach to their incorporation. In contrast to Britain and Switzerland, in France the central state is more actively involved with, and bears more responsibility toward migrants in terms of their general welfare, since most social functions are already centralized and organized by the state.

The centralized formation of the French polity and its political system intensifies discourse and action regarding migrants at the national level. One manifestation of this, for example, is the preoccupation with issues of citizenship and nationality in the context of immigration (Hollifield 1989). Moreover, within this framework, the concept of incorporation acquires a very state-centric meaning; it assumes uniformly equal individuals vis-à-vis the state. This assumption disallows specialized action or intermediary structures on behalf of migrant groups. As one French official insisted, special treatment or institutions for migrants would be considered a breach of "the relationship between state and the citizen" (interview: Ministry of Social Affairs and Employment, Directorate of Migrant Populations). The French concept of integration favors, instead, the access of individual migrants to "normal" (non-group-specific) services and institutions (interview: Social Action Fund [FAS]). It is generally believed that "a formal guarantee of access to legal rights and social participation is sufficient to create equality" (Verbunt 1985: 145).

In the French polity, ethnic or religious minorities are not officially or legally recognized categories (Lochak 1989). When comparing French migrant policy to that of other European countries, one of the FAS directors I interviewed commented that "the French state has a definitive purpose of integration . . . but integration more as individuals than as communities. In fact, the concept of community has no relevance in the French system." This statement epitomizes the secular and "republican" understanding of French membership that detaches the rights and capabilities of the individual from corporate entities. This model clearly contrasts with the corporatist one, in which the state constructs "ethnic minorities" through legal and organizational mechanisms, as a means for incorporation. In France, migrant policy is unconcerned with collective categories. Instead, market and educational processes emerge as the main instruments for incorporating individual migrants, but with direct state intervention.

The centralized, individualistic character of the French model colors various policies. The school system attempts to foster equality by deemphasizing regional, ethnic, or religious orientations, and stressing uniformity (Boyzon-Fradet 1992; Verbunt 1985). Since 1976, following a European Community directive, primary school curricula have included mother-tongue classes for migrant children. However, these courses are usually sponsored by the governments of the sending countries, and are taught by foreigners certified by the appropriate French state agency. The concept of "migrant organization" is also problematic in the French case, since the system prefers open organizations that admit both migrants and French (interview: FAS). Until 1981, restrictive regulations on the associational activity of foreigners discouraged the foundation of migrant organizations. Since then, a growing number of migrant associations have sprung up, and are increasingly acknowledged by state authorities as proper representatives of migrant interests.

The more direct policy instruments of the state aim to equip migrants with the skills to gain access to the institutions of French society. To this end, the Social Action Fund for Immigrant Workers and their Families (FAS) was founded in 1958 to assist "the social and professional insertion of foreign workers and their families through the implementation of social

Table 4.3. FAS Budget, 1989 (French francs and U.S. dollars, in millions)

Housing (42.3%)		520 F	$ 89.4
administration	66.6%		
temporary housing	27.8		
new housing	4.8		
equipment of foyers	0.8		
Education (27.6%)		340	58.5
vocational training	58.4%		
language	33.7		
integration of youth	4.4		
mother-tongue	2.5		
Social and cultural (26.8%)		330	56.8
general social services	43.1%		
cultural activities and information	32.0		
pre-school activities	9.3		
neighborhood life	8.2		
youth associations	7.4		
Other[a] (3.3%)		40	6.9
Total		1,230 F	$211.6

Source: FAS (1988a).

[a]Includes 2 million F ($344,000) for research.

programs." The FAS has an elaborate budget, which covers the main aspects of migrants' lives: housing, education, and training, as well as social and cultural activities. The FAS finances various organizations, firms, and institutions for their services in these areas. Education is especially emphasized to facilitate the integration of migrants and to develop their qualifications for the labor market (FAS 1989b). In 1988, the FAS financed 2,800 projects, mostly small-scale ones receiving between 50,000 francs and 100,000 francs (F) ($8,600 and $17,200), but also some major operations adding up to millions of francs (FAS 1989a). The number of projects funded had been only 180 in 1972 and 536 in 1980. Between 1970 and 1989, the budget of the FAS increased ten times from 140 million F ($24.1 million) to 1,230 million F ($211.6 million). In 1989, the budget was distributed among "sectors of intervention" as shown in table 4.3.

In 1990, the Ministry for Urban Affairs instituted a new policy and budget to improve the "integration of the most disadvantaged populations into their urban environment," targeting areas with a high concentration of migrants. This scheme provided 100 million F ($17 million) for 60 pilot sites in 1991 (SOPEMI 1992:61).

Though specialized, such instruments do not aim to promote the collective incorporation of specific migrant groups. Instead, they are temporary measures designed to "expose [migrants] to the French way of life" and to "help their transition to French institutions" (interview: FAS). The FAS itself was projected to be a temporary structure to facilitate the integration of migrants into the "common" institutions of the French polity. However, it now is almost 35 years old and has evolved into a more active and specialized body, with programs that cater to migrants, as it is evident from the growth in its budget and functions. Furthermore, the FAS increasingly supports the initiatives of migrants themselves, "considering that they are the best agents of their own insertion." According to one of its directors, the FAS considers it crucial "to keep a balance between integration and preservation of cultures of origin." This goal, though contradictory to the principles of the French integration model, points to a new emphasis in policy in the last decade, best exemplified by the government's *Vivre Ensemble* campaign of the mid-1980s that celebrated the diversity of cultures in France (Ministry of Social Affairs and National Solidarity 1986). The state has also started to provide financial support for ethnic festivals and other cultural activities of migrant groups. This trend mirrors a more general shift toward recognizing and teaching regional languages in French schools (*New York Times*, 3 May 1993). Nevertheless, these "multiculturalist" tendencies in policy remain within the bounds of "republican citizenship," deemphasizing collective incorporation and reifying individual membership.[15]

Germany: A Mixed Case

Germany exhibits aspects of both corporate and statist membership and incorporation. Unlike policy in Sweden and the Netherlands, German federal policy does not explicitly refer to "ethnic minorities," and makes no special provisions for the participation of migrants as collectivities. However, in organizational terms, a centralized and corporate pattern of incorporation has developed, in accord with other German institutional structures. This pattern is most visible in the organization of social services to migrants. The welfare of foreigners is mainly the responsibility of trade unions and the major social service organizations, which are highly centralized and closely connected to the state both financially and organizationally. Migrants are assigned to these agencies according to their religious and national orientations.

Because of the German federal political and administrative structure, migrant policy and its implementation differ considerably among local states *(Länder)*, as well as between the states and the federal government. There is no nationally formulated policy, except for some principles that serve as guidelines for the local states. The principle of integration, as stated in the official texts, is general and does not target collective groups:

> Integration implies offering fair and equal opportunities in education, on the labor market, and in society at large. . . . Integration also calls for considerable effort from the foreigners themselves to adjust to the living conditions prevailing here. . . . Finally, integration also calls for a gradual reduction of the social and cultural gap separating nationals and non-nationals, together with an increase in mutual tolerance and acceptance. (Commissioner for Foreigners' Affairs of the Senate of Berlin 1985:9)

Different cultural existences are acknowledged, but they are not given an institutional status through which foreigners are expected to organize as corporate entities. In the words of the federal government's commissioner in charge of foreigners' affairs, integration requires "making the foreigners part of society and the working life, while respecting their national, cultural, and religious characteristics without discriminating against them" (quoted in Şen 1987:17).

Although German integration policy is not centrally defined or coordinated, its instruments are centrally organized. There is a federal budget allocated specifically for foreign populations, the main items of which are language and vocational education, social services, and publicity and information. A

Table 4.4. Budget of the Federal Ministry of Labor and Social Affairs for the Integration of Foreigners (German marks and U.S. dollars, in thousands)

		1968	1973	1978	1983	1985
Publicity and information	DM	350	950	1,398	1,673	1,840
	$	203	551	811	970	1,067
Social services	DM	2,500	11,536	22,666	33,357	36,600
	$	1,450	6,691	13,146	14,347	21,228
Language and vocational education	DM	321	2,577	6,606	49,537	50,000
	$	186	1,495	3,832	28,732	29,000
Total	DM	3,171	15,063	30,670	84,567	88,440
	$	1,839	8,737	17,789	49,049	51,295

Source: Federal Ministry of Labor and Social Affairs 1985.

large portion of this funding goes to centralized, semi-public institutions that organize and manage social and educational services for migrant groups.

The most important instrument of German integration policy is vocational training, which aims to fit migrants into occupational categories and strengthen their position in the labor market. Especially for the second generation, vocational integration is promoted as the main gateway for entering German society (interview: Federal Ministry of Labor and Social Affairs). Furthermore, the government supports the education of migrant children by funding classes that address their special needs. The federal budget also funds programs to help adult migrants find better jobs and take advantage of social programs available to them. Table 4.4 demonstrates a considerable increase in the amount of money that the federal state spent on vocational education, as well as other instruments of policy, over time. Altogether, the budget jumped from a mere 3.2 million German marks (DM) ($1.8 million) in 1968 to 88.4 million DM ($51.3 million) in 1985. In 1990, around 90 million DM ($52.6 million) was allocated to this budget.

Although there are generally agreed-on principles and rules at the federal level, the states have autonomy, especially with regard to educational and cultural matters. Consequently, local policies of integration vary in emphasis and content. Berlin, for example, has developed more specific, and group-oriented measures. The importance given to migrant identities is apparent in the following statement of the Berlin Commissioner for Foreigners' Affairs (1985:9):

> The underlying concept from which the Senat proceeds . . . is that, for many non-nationals, adherence to tradition represents a necessary component of the integration process. For, only if one is secure in the knowledge that one's cultural identity is unchallenged can one have the inner self-assurance to open oneself up to an alien environment.

The Berlin Senate also emphasizes measures to promote the integration and equality of foreigners in legal, administrative, and social areas, to ensure "the peaceful living together of people of different origin, nationality, and religion" (Commissioner for Foreigners' Affairs of the Senate of Berlin 1992:3). Accordingly, in 1984, the Berlin Senate allocated more than 100 million DM ($58 million) for integration purposes (Commissioner for Foreigners' Affairs of the Senate of Berlin 1985). A large percentage of this money was used for school programs, including classes catering to the "specific needs" of migrant children. Moreover, in some districts, courses on migrant language and culture have been incorporated into general school curricula. Again in 1984, Berlin's government spent approximately 800,000 DM ($464,000) on "fostering the cultural traditions of Berlin's non-national population groups." A wide range of activities organized by migrant associations and groups are funded by the Berlin government, through a yearly budget of 1 million DM ($580,000; interview with the Commissioner). Since 1980, similar policies and measures have been developed in other parts of Germany, notably Hamburg, Hessen, and Bremen.

CHAPTER FIVE

The Organization of Incorporation

In the postwar era, European welfare apparatuses have become more apparent both in the expanse of their activity spheres and their organizational structures. Elaborate public and private schemes have developed to administer and provide for the welfare of various segments of national citizenry. European host countries, encountering guestworkers, have drawn upon the same schemes to manage the incorporation of their new residents.

The ways European host polities organize the incorporation of their guestworkers vary widely, however, depending on their understanding of incorporation and their predominant models of membership. While, in corporatist and statist polities, the state and its bureaucracy has a strong presence in the organization of incorporation, liberal polities, in contrast, generate decentralized incorporation through local and voluntary associations. Corporatist polities, furthermore, produce a set of formal organizational structures and intermediary institutions that offer centralized channels for the collective participation of migrants. Similar intermediary structures are either missing or are much less formalized in statist and liberal polities. What is common across European countries is that incorporation has become a field increasingly subject to state action and policy; the host polities assume increasing responsibilities, regardless of whether incorporation takes a centralized or decentralized form.

Centralized Incorporation, Corporate Participation

What immediately strikes a researcher in Sweden and the Netherlands is how highly organized and centrally formulated the field of immigration is. The bureaucratic, corporate pattern of policy and politics in these countries yields two organizational outcomes: elaborate, fairly centralized administrative agencies and a network of umbrella organizations and consultative commissions that act as intermediaries between the state and the migrant groups.

Incorporation in Sweden is the responsibility of public authorities, at both local and state levels (see appendix B, table 1).[1] The immediate social services, housing, education, and health care, are provided by municipal authorities, many of which have established separate immigration boards and service bureaus. At the national level, a group of central administrative departments are charged with handling various aspects of incorporation. The Swedish Labor Market Board (AMS), for example, implements an extensive labor market policy that includes training and employment projects directed toward specific migrant groups. However, the primary authority for the organization and coordination of migrant affairs is the National Immigration Board (SIV), under the Ministry of Labor. The responsibilities of SIV range from issuing visas and work permits and granting citizenship to conducting research on "ethnic relations" and funding migrant organizations. Besides implementing and supervising policy, the SIV also assumes the tasks of "[supplying] information to and about immigrants, and [acting] as an intermediary between Swedish society and organizations of immigrants and minorities" (SIV 1987a). Over time, the SIV has grown both organizationally and in its responsibilities. Currently it has six divisions and thirty-eight sections, and between 1981 and 1988 the number of its employees increased from 300 to 1,800 (interview: SIV, Information Section).

Though local authorities have a substantial degree of autonomy in their dealings with migrants, incorporation in Sweden is remarkably centralized. Local authorities coordinate their own efforts closely with those of the SIV and replicate the national discourse and organization. The centralized character of Swedish policy is sustained by the constant communication and consultation that takes place between central and local levels, instead of being dictated by a top-down bureaucracy as is the case in France. Rather than issue directives to the local authorities, the SIV provides advice, guidelines, and support, and oversees local practice on migrant affairs (SIV 1987a; Hammar 1985d). National and local administrative officials regularly meet to discuss policy and issues.

In addition to centralized administrative agencies, the Swedish organizational structure includes a large number of national-level commissions and advisory councils, formed to address issues of immigration. This is symptomatic of general Swedish policy making, which involves continual exchange and "structured consultation" between the administration and interest groups (Heclo and Madsen 1987). Some commissions have a permanent status and play a significant role in initiating, formulating, and evaluating policy. The Swedish Commission for Immigrant Research (DEIFO) is one such commission, which evaluates policies that affect migrants and advises the government on the programming of those policies. Migrant policy is, in fact, formulated on the basis of reports generated by such commissions and advisory councils (see Hammar 1985d).

Both Sweden and the Netherlands are known as highly organized polities. Every societal group has a "well-organized national body" that speaks for its interests; these organizations are regarded as a necessary and permanent fixture of the policy-making process (Heclo and Madsen 1987). Thus, it is not surprising that, in Sweden, a consultative council, with representatives from different interest groups, is attached to every ministry and state agency. What is interesting is that the same consultative and participatory channels are extended to migrant groups, thereby incorporating even foreigners into the formal structures of the polity. Migrants are regularly represented as corporate entities, in various consultative councils. For example, the Immigrants' Advisory Council of the Ministry of Labor includes representatives of the national federations of migrant groups. The SIV and other state agencies have similar arrangements. Lithman (1987) reports that, since the 1970s, all the major commissions that investigate migrant-related policy and issues have included representatives from migrant organizations.

The Netherlands displays a similar pattern in organizing incorporation. Policy on migrants is primarily determined at the national level, with the participation of advisory commissions like the Netherlands Scientific Council for Government Policy (WRR).[2] In contrast to Sweden, the Netherlands does not have a single centralized state agency that deals with migrant matters per se. Instead, ministerial bodies and intermediary institutions that are autonomous but fully funded by the state take charge of different aspects of incorporation (see appendix B, table 2). Nevertheless, Dutch policy is centrally organized, and coordination is an important aspect of its administration. Tellingly, the official name for the Dutch policy on migrants is the "coordinated minorities policy." The task of coordination is carried out by a group of ministerial committees, including the Directorate for the Coordination of Minorities Policy (DCM), under the Ministry of Home Affairs, and the Interministerial Coordinating Committee on Minorities Policy. The DCM further acts as a structural liaison between the national government and migrant groups. It also is in close contact with municipalities, which are responsible for administering a coordinated minorities policy of their own at the local level.

Implementation of Dutch minorities policy clearly reflects the corporatist mode of incorporation. The central state subsidizes semi-public institutions that cater to different nationalities. The Dutch Center for Foreigners (NCB) is responsible for Turkish, Moroccan, and Southern European migrants. Local foreign-workers' assistance units, originally set up by private initiatives of church groups and employers, were later united under the national umbrella of the NCB.[3] The NCB now has no organizational ties with local assistance units. It works closely with the state, participating in commissions created to deal with migrant issues, and is continually consulted about minorities policy by the government. In 1987, two similar organizations were created, one for the Surinamese (SSA) and one for Antilleans (POA).

Since the mid-1980s, in the course of restructuring its welfare system, the Dutch government has reorganized its social services for ethnic minorities (SCP 1986; de Graaf, Penninx, and Stoové 1988). As a result of the state's decision to shift funds from group-specific organizations to institutions that serve the general populace, the NCB has become more of an agent of coordination, advocacy, information, publicity, and support for migrant groups, rather than of direct social services. It functions as a center of expertise that "attempts to generate policies to achieve equality of foreigners and emancipation of ethnic groups" (interview: NCB). Local municipalities now bear the major responsibility for the welfare of migrants.

As is the case in Sweden, Dutch policy calls for various forms of consultation at different levels. A white paper on minorities policy states that, in principle, "no political decisions must be taken on proposals until minorities have had the opportunity to make their views known through participation procedures" (Ministry of Home Affairs 1983:22). During my interviews, officials repeatedly referred to this principle; at the DCM one remarked offhandedly, "I think it is a good investment for the government to listen to what the people [toward whom the policy is directed] think. . . . It can overcome a lot of polarization and can provide a better understanding of each other in the society." This principle is effected by legally required consultation and corporate representation of migrant groups. The National Advisory Council for Ethnic Minorities (LAO) was founded specifically for this purpose, to advise the government, upon request or at its own initiative, on matters relating to national policy on minorities. The LAO acts as an umbrella organization for subcouncils representing individual minority groups. The subcouncils are the federations of the eight officially recognized migrant groups: Turks, Moroccans and Tunisians, Surinamese, Dutch Antilleans, Moluccans, South Europeans, refugees, and Gypsies.[4] Similarly, at the local level, within the framework of certain grant regulations, advisory councils must include representatives from local migrant organizations. Municipalities can only receive government grants to defray the administrative costs of local minorities policy if they have undertaken procedures to consult with minority spokespersons.

Obviously these formal arrangements for consultation do not guarantee that migrant groups can affect policy decisions directly. Annual activity reports of LAO subcouncils often include discussions of the need for more emphasis on minority input (see, e.g., IOT 1986/87). My purpose here is to highlight how extensive and taken-for-granted these consultative arrangements are in the Dutch and Swedish contexts. Such arrangements indicate that immigrants, like other societal groups, are incorporated as collectivities into the state's organizational and legal framework. Furthermore, these formal consultative structures contribute to a uniform and institutionalized understanding at all levels of what policy is, by providing a common language and legitimate categories. This homogeneity of understanding and discourse was apparent in all the interviews I conducted. From ministerial staff to leaders of migrant associations, and from local officials to scholars working on immigration, interviewees consistently evoked the main principles of Swedish immigration policy—equality, freedom of choice, and cooperation. In the Netherlands, "emancipation" is invariably used as a metaphor by officials, social workers, and migrant organizers.

Decentralized, Society-Centered Incorporation

In contrast to the highly organized and centralized structure of incorporation in Sweden and the Netherlands, the liberal cases display a decentralized pattern consonant with the general organization of membership in their polities. In both Switzerland and Britain, formal structures of incorporation are less differentiated at the central level and less specific to separate migrant groups (see appendix B, tables 3 and 4).

In Switzerland, policy- and decision making at the federal

level mainly involves the determination of foreign labor quotas and their distribution among cantons. The sectoral and cantonal quotas on foreign workers are the major source of conflict between the federal state, the cantonal state, and the firms in various economic sectors (interview: Federal Office of Industry, Small Business, and Labor [BIGA]).[5] In accord with the three principles of Swiss immigration policy—stabilization, improvement of the labor market, and integration—the Foreigners Police, the Federal Department of Economic Affairs, and the Federal Commission for Aliens (EKA) form a triangle in administering and implementing the policy. The first two principles are centrally organized: the Aliens Office of the Federal Department of Justice and Police, and the Federal Office of Industry, Small Business, and Labor together control the flow of foreigners according to current quotas. In collaboration with these offices, the Central Register for Aliens has the task of keeping the accurate, continuous data on the number of foreigners in the country that the government uses to determine yearly quotas.[6] At the local level, the cantonal foreigners police administers permits together with the Cantonal Office of Industry, Small Business, and Labor (KIGA) and other labor authorities.

The third component of Swiss policy, integration, is mainly left to an advisory commission that does not have administrative capacity, the Federal Commission for Aliens (EKA). Its principal task is to "investigate the needs of foreigners, prepare recommendations, and inform the government and migrants toward integration" (interview: EKA). The federal government considers the EKA's proposals in making recommendations to the administration at the federal and cantonal levels. Since the EKA is not an administrative agency, the implementation of integration policy lies primarily with local public and private organizations.

The Commission includes members of parliament; representatives of churches, trade union federations, and social service organizations; and representatives of federal and cantonal authorities. Since 1981, the Commission has also accepted members, appointed by the federal government, from migrant groups.[7] However, migrants on the commission are not necessarily regarded as representatives of collective groups, but rather as informants who can describe the problems that migrants experience (interview: EKA). Since 1987, the Commission has also met twice yearly with the representatives of organizations of seven foreign groups (Italian, Spanish, Portuguese, Greek, Turkish, Yugoslav, and French) to discuss issues that relate to migrant communities. Since there are no set criteria for the representation of foreign organizations, personal relations influence which organizations are invited to these meetings (interview: Federation for Solidarity among Turkish Associations in Switzerland). This representative arrangement contrasts with those in Sweden and the Netherlands, where national federations of migrant groups are recognized spokespersons for their respective communities.

Other than the EKA, which is only an advisory body, there are no federal level state agencies that exclusively focus on the integration of migrants. Immigrants are expected to become integrated into general Swiss social service facilities that are mainly located at the community level. Locally, numerous public and private organizations provide information and assistance of various sorts to individuals of all nationalities. Very few of these organizations specialize in migrant-related issues.[8] Although the scope of their activities differs, they usually work on a small scale, with minimal budgets, depending on volunteers. Foreign consulates also establish and/or fund social service organizations for their own citizens, as in the case of Italian and Spanish workers (Schmitter 1980). In addition, general service organizations, such as the Swiss Red Cross, Swiss Caritas, and International Social Service in Switzerland take part in assisting migrants. The city of Bern is a typical example: in 1988, of nineteen organizations that served migrants, nine were funded by the churches, five by private initiative, four by the sending governments; only one was funded by the city and cantonal governments.

Over the years, some cantons and communes have set up offices to deal directly with the "foreigners problem" (EKA 1977). These offices are generally small-scale operations, sometimes with one or two employees, functioning without a regular budget. They differ in organization and operation, but usually work to facilitate integration by organizing activities, generating information, and initiating contact between Swiss and foreign communities (interview: City Coordination Office for Foreigners' Affairs, KSA, Zurich). In addition, some cantons and communes have established consultative commissions that include representatives of social institutions and, in some cases, foreigners, appointed by the cantonal or communal governments. In the early 1990s there were about twenty such consultative councils at the communal level, and eighteen at the cantonal level.

In Britain, a policy emphasis on "race relations" is evident in the way incorporation is organized. The major agency dealing with migrants is the Commission for Racial Equality (CRE). Founded in 1976 under the Race Relations Act, the CRE directly reports to the Home Office. There is also a minister of state responsible for matters of race and immigration, but the minister does not supervise or coordinate activities.

As a central agency, the CRE is charged "to work towards the elimination of discrimination; to promote equality of opportunity and good relations between persons of different racial groups; and to keep under review the Race Relations Act and to draw up and submit to the Secretary of State proposals for amending it" (CRE 1988:14). The Commission also provides legal services and represents individuals in cases of discrimination, and conducts investigations into various sectors to uncover discriminatory practices.[9]

The CRE is the main channel through which government is informed of issues that affect minorities, but it has never been considered as a representative body for ethnic minorities. The CRE's twelve commissioners include people from varied ethnic groups, but they are appointed, by the Home Office, as "individuals who have something to contribute on minority related issues" rather than as representatives of their communities (interview: CRE). In this sense, the CRE resembles the EKA in Switzerland. Furthermore, there is no institutionalized interaction between the CRE and the government. Unlike, for example, the Dutch Center for Foreigners (NCB), the CRE is not regularly consulted by the government, even though it is the main agency overseeing minority issues and proposing solutions.

The Race Equality Councils (RECs) are autonomous, voluntary organizations that work closely with the CRE to achieve similar aims at a local level. The RECs (known before 1990 as

Community Relations Councils) were created to facilitate the "transition" of New Commonwealth migrants into British society, by "transmitting the norms and values" of British society to its new members (Rath and Saggar 1987). They started as voluntary organs, from local initiatives. In time, they acquired a more formal role and status, but they are still locally based, voluntary associations rather than statutory bodies.[10] The RECs' size and strength, and their relationship with local authorities, as well as with migrant groups, differ widely from one municipality to another (Gay and Young 1988). In general, their function is stated as promoting equal opportunity and fighting discrimination at local levels. RECs are expected to represent ethnic minorities and their interests in dealing with the local authorities. However, they do not have formalized structures for the representation of ethnic groups as separate constituencies. Indeed, their representativeness is highly questioned by the migrant communities themselves.[11]

In addition to the RECs, some local authorities have established their own "race equality units" to promote equal opportunity in services and employment, in accord with the 1976 Race Relations Act. The nature and functions of these units vary. Some involve consultative mechanisms through which members of ethnic minorities participate. In general, though, there is no formal agreement on the status of these bodies. In fact, by the late 1980s, a number of local authorities had abolished them or were considering uniting them under "broader-based equal opportunities units" (Runnymede Trust 1989b:10).

As in Switzerland, local authorities provide a portion of the social services, many of which are not specific to migrants. The voluntary sector and "self-help" organizations play a vital role in meeting the social needs of migrants (Johnson 1987). Funding sources for the voluntary sector include the CRE, local authorities, and the various "urban aid" projects, as well as any private funds the voluntary sector can mobilize.

Since the late 1980s, both Switzerland and Britain have moved toward a more organized and coordinated implementation of policy. Each government has made efforts to establish regular contacts between the various levels of administration. One of the recently formulated aims of the EKA is to work with cantonal, regional, and communal service agencies, as well as with foreigners' organizations, to further the integration of migrants (EKA 1987). Thus the EKA meets with local organizations and authorities twice a year in order to develop guidelines for harmonizing their policies. A similar trend is apparent in Britain, where the CRE has been trying to assume a coordinating role and organize local RECs into a formal network. This process includes a forum in which the Commission and the RECs together set priorities and plan national and regional strategies (interview: CRE).

Centralized, State-Centered Incorporation

In comparison with Switzerland and Britain, incorporation in France is a centrally structured operation. The tasks that local public and private organizations perform in liberal polities are part of a much more centralized and bureaucratic administration in France. Most aspects of migrant policy are organized and managed by central state agencies connected to local structures.[12] This is not surprising if we consider the French administrative system, which is a hierarchical bureaucracy that encompasses the localities and every sector of public life (Ashford 1982). In France, where the individual and the state are highly differentiated (Birnbaum 1988), intermediary structures that address collective identities are conspicuously deemphasized.

The Ministry of Social Affairs and Integration[13] is the governmental unit in charge of policy on migrants. Within the ministry, the Directorate of Migrant Populations has the task of proposing and evaluating policies and measures that concern the integration and status of migrants in French society. In 1991, upon the recommendation of the High Council for Integration, an advisory body of nine experts, the government established a new state secretary for integration to expedite the process of integrating migrants.

A number of centralized state agencies are responsible for different aspects of immigration and migrants' affairs (see appendix B, table 5). The International Migration Office (OMI), founded as a liaison between employers and prospective immigrants in the recruitment process, is now mainly involved with the reception of family members, and their orientation to French society (ONI 1986; OMI 1988). The mission of the

Agency for the Development of Intercultural Relations (ADRI) is to facilitate communication between foreigners and French society through cultural activities, including television broadcasting for and about migrants. The Association of Social Assistance for Migrants (SSAE) organizes the delivery of social services to migrants through its local branches. In addition, migrants are expected to take advantage of services that municipalities and local state agencies offer the general public.

The Social Action Fund (FAS), acting under the auspices of the Ministry of Social Affairs and Integration, is the central state agency with the specific purpose of integrating migrants into French society. In general, the FAS is a funding agency for "social action on behalf of migrants" (interview: FAS).[14] It manages the state funds allocated to initiatives and programs designed to advance integration. The FAS has the task of facilitating a policy of integration that is national in scope but implemented largely at the local level. Most of the projects subsidized by the FAS are carried out by private associations, municipalities, or local administrators, but also by commercial or industrial firms. The number of migrant organizations that receive grants within this scheme is relatively small. A governing council, made up of representatives from ministries, trade unions, business associations, and other social service institutions, determines the FAS's national strategy and allocates grants. Since 1984, foreigners have also been represented on the council; their position as full members of an administrative body is an anomaly for French public institutions, considered generally.

In France, as in liberal polities, intermediary structures that provide for the collective participation of migrants are not institutionalized. However, since 1980 there have been efforts to involve migrant groups in different levels of decision making. Between 1984 and 1986, the National Council for Immigrant Populations included representatives from certain migrant groups; but the Council itself did not have much legitimacy among migrant organizations (interview: Council of Associations of Immigrants in France [CAIF]). In 1989, the government reinstated the Council, charging it to make a more explicit effort to involve migrant representatives (OMI 1989c). More interestingly, in 1990, the Ministry of Interior created an advisory council composed of French and foreign Muslims, thus recognizing that group's collective representation. Also, in the late 1970s, as part of a Europewide trend, some municipalities established immigrant councils, with representatives chosen by local authorities, to advise them on migration issues (Miller 1981). In all of these cases, however, state (local or central) authorities appoint the representatives. As Sophie Body-Gendrot and Martin Schain point out "it is still the state that chooses its negotiating partners, and the state itself takes the initiative to generate these partners if they do not yet exist" (1992:435). Moreover, despite recent arrangements that tacitly recognize the specificity and collectivity of migrant communities, government integration discourse continues to emphasize strongly the principle of treating migrants as individuals within the general collectivity of "citizens."[15]

Statist-Corporatist Incorporation

In Germany, centralized, semi-public institutions play an important role in the organization of incorporation. A centralized corporate pattern is especially apparent in the organization of services specific to migrants. Certain semi-public institutions that function as part of German state bureaucracy, organize and manage social or educational activities for migrant groups. In the social service area, three major welfare organizations—associated with the Catholic Church, the Protestant Church, and the Social Democratic Party—cater to migrants according to their religious orientation. Social services to Italians and Spaniards are delivered by the organization Caritas, and to Greeks by Diakonisches Werk. Turks, predominantly Muslims, do not fit into this religious fractioning, so they become the responsibility of the Arbeiterwohlfahrt, a social democratic welfare organization.[16] In addition, numerous publicly funded projects target the needs of specific migrant groups. Specialized educational services, such as language classes and vocational training, are provided by institutions fully subsidized through the federal or local state budgets.

Although the state, federal or local, is the major sponsor of migrant-specific measures and programs, no federal agencies are specifically designed to administer migrant-related tasks.

Within the Ministry of Labor and Social Affairs, there is a committee designated to coordinate integration measures taken by the states, local authorities, and semi-public institutions. This coordination committee is made up of representatives from a wide range of governmental and public organizations, federations of trade unions and business associations, welfare agencies, and churches; but it does not include migrant groups.

The Office of the Federal Commissioner for Foreigners' Affairs has the specific function of developing guidelines for integration policy. When similar agencies in other countries are considered, the Federal Commissioner has a much weaker position vis-à-vis both the state and migrant groups. The Commissioner's office does not have a specialized budget to spend on measures for the integration of foreigners.[17] A former commissioner complained publicly on several occasions about the "lack of resources and attention from the government" (*Cumhuriyet Hafta*, 5–11 April 1991). The Commissioner's office has an advisory status; however, no formal mechanisms have been established to consult with migrant groups.

At the local level, more specific administrative resources and powers have been allocated to state offices that specialize in the integration of foreigners. The Berlin Senate, for example, has a special Commissioner for Foreigners' Affairs.[18] The Commissioner has the task of formulating basic issues and measures concerning the Berlin Senate's policy on foreigners and integration, and coordinating the action of the various departments in this field (Commisioner for Foreigners' Affairs of the Senate of Berlin 1992). The commissioner's office is also responsible for funding migrant organizations in order to promote migrants' cultures and enhance their participation in Berlin's social life.

At the local level, a network of advisory councils with migrant-group representation has evolved. In 1983, 40 percent of all local municipalities, a total of about 300, had some such consultative body (Andersen 1990). Most of the migrants who participate are either trade union representatives or individuals chosen by migrant organizations. In some cases, the foreign representatives are regularly elected. In recent years, as in other host countries, more deliberate efforts have been made to establish contact with migrant organizations as representatives of their communities. In 1984, the Berlin Senate set up a council that entitles registered migrant organizations a voice in senate hearings. Also, during the 1990 federal debates in parliament on the new Foreigners' Law, migrant leaders were invited to give their opinions.

State Incorporation Patterns

In chapters four and five, I have shown not only that incorporation varies across host states but also that it varies systematically. When states encounter the incorporation of postwar migrants as a new issue area, they draw upon existing institutional repertoires and resources, that is, their predominant models and organizing principles of membership. These models and principles constitute bases for different modes of state action, and generate different incorporation patterns. Table 5.1

Table 5.1. Summary of Incorporation Patterns

	Corporatist	Liberal	Statist
Unit of incorporation	Collective group	Individual	Individual
Goal of incorporation	Equality between groups	Equal opportunities for individuals	Equal standing of individuals vis-à-vis the state
Instruments of incorporation	Group-specific programs and institutions	Existing institutions (especially labor markets and education)	Existing institutions
Organization of incorporation	Centrally organized, through formal structures	Decentralized, through local voluntary or public agencies	Centralized, bureaucratized
Formal participation (through consultative arrangements)	As collective groups at national and local levels	As individuals mostly at local levels	As individuals at national and local levels
Location of incorporation	National level, central	Local level	National level, central

summarizes the three patterns of incorporation that I have delineated.

In the corporatist pattern, the primary unit of incorporation is the collective group. Policy defines migrant groups as ethnic minority communities, and gives them a clear position vis-à-vis the state. This pattern aims at equality between ethnic groups, while emphasizing separate existences and collective identities.

In contrast, the liberal pattern targets the individual migrant, rather than migrant groups, as the primary unit of incorporation, even in the case of policies addressing ethnic and racial categories (e.g., race relations acts in Britain). In the liberal context, existing opportunity structures, especially labor markets and education, along with legal strategies to facilitate equal participation of individual migrants, become the means of incorporation.

In the statist pattern, as in the liberal, migrants do not constitute collective categories. But statist policy aims to give individual migrants equal standing with other residents vis-à-vis the state, which means a formal assurance of access to the host country's institutions. Again, labor markets and education are emphasized; however, the central state takes a more interventionist position to strengthen the opportunity structures of migrants.

In accord with their perception of migrants as separate corporate entities, corporatist polities are more inclined to produce specifically group-oriented policies, programs, and institutions. In these polities, incorporation takes place mainly at the national level through vertical, bureaucratic organizational structures. Intermediary bodies provide formal channels for migrant participation.

Liberal and statist polities, which perceive migrants as individuals, privilege non-group-specific, general (public or private) institutions. In the liberal pattern, incorporation occurs mainly at the societal level through private and voluntary associations. Formal intermediary structures linking migrants and the state do not exist. The statist pattern also lacks intermediary organizations, but in this case the central state, with its bureaucracy, is the major agent of incorporation.

Despite these pronounced differences, incorporation regimes

Table 5.2. Central State Agencies or Commissions Directly Responsible for the Incorporation of Migrants

Country	National Agency	Year Established
Sweden	National Immigration Board (SIV)	1969
Netherlands	Directorate for the Coordination of Minorities Policy (Ministry of Home Affairs)	1981
Switzerland[a]	Federal Commission for Aliens (EKA)	1970
Britain	Commission for Racial Equality (CRE) (formerly Race Relations Board, 1966)	1976
France	State Secretary for Integration	1991
	Directorate of Migrant Populations (Ministry of Social Affairs and Integration)	1981
Germany[a]	Federal Commissioner for Foreigners' Affairs	1978

[a]Mainly an advisory body without any administrative capacity.

are becoming increasingly standardized and institutionalized. In the 1960s, international migrants were not acknowledged in state categories; state systems were oblivious to these populations except insofar as they constituted a temporary labor force in certain programs. Over time, the host states' obligations toward migrants have expanded from the accommodation of "immediate needs" (information, orientation, housing, and translation services) to a broader set of social, economic, and cultural provisions like vocational training, child support, welfare, and mother-tongue education. Consequently, new bureaucracies, policy schemes, and budgets have emerged, amounting to an extensive network of public, semi-public, and voluntary organizations concerned with the incorporation of migrants.

By the 1990s, all of the major European host countries had established some form of central agency that specifically focuses on the incorporation of migrant populations (see table 5.2). In addition, they all have interministerial committees and/or special ministers to coordinate and organize policy for relevant ministries and central and local state agencies. Furthermore, migrants are increasingly incorporated into their host country's political structures through consultative arrangements, although the extent and form of consultation differ from one country to another (see table 5.3).

Even those European states that have become destinations for migratory flows only in the last decade are already developing similar organizational and policy schemes for the incorporation of migrants. In Italy, for example, legislation passed in 1990 to regulate the hiring and treatment of migrant workers

Table 5.3. Channels for the Consultative Participation of Migrants

Country	Central	Local
Sweden	Immigrants' Advisory Council; National Immigration Board (SIV) (representation by national federations)	Municipal advisory councils (local migrant organizations represented)
Netherlands	National Advisory Council for Ethnic Minorities (LAO) (representation by national federations)	Municipal advisory councils (local migrant organizations represented)
Switzerland	Federal Commission for Aliens (EKA) (migrants represented on an individual basis since 1988)	Foreigners commissions (migrants represented on an individual basis)
Britain	Commission for Racial Equality (CRE) (individual members from ethnic minorities, appointed by the government)	Race Equality Councils; Race Relations Units (representatives appointed on an individual basis by local governments)
France	Social Action Fund (FAS); National Council for Immigrant Populations (migrants represented on an individual basis, appointed by the government)	Immigrant councils (representation on an individual basis, by appointment or election)
Germany	None (on occasion, migrant representatives invited to solicit their opinions)	Foreigner Advisory Councils (representatives nominated by migrant organizations or elected by migrants)

provides for social and health services and housing, and recognizes the right to family reunification. It also proposes the creation of a committee for "migrant workers' problems" at the Ministry of Labor and Social Affairs, with representation from the migrant groups themselves—an increasingly common organizational feature in many European countries. In 1991, a Ministry for Expatriates and Immigration was established whose responsibilities include education and training of migrants, along with assistance to Italian communities abroad (SOPEMI 1992).

All of these trends affirm that "international migrant" has become a salient category and incorporated into the European policy fields, budgets, and legal and organizational structures. Incorporation of migrants is now a requisite domain of state responsibility and intervention—a "problem" to be managed by expanding organization and policy. A growing web of bureaucrats, experts, consultants, researchers, pedagogues, social workers, and migrant organizers further legitimize incorporation as a proper policy area. In that, incorporation has become a dominant theme in European host polities, with differences in policy discourse and organization persisting as variations upon that theme.

CHAPTER SIX

The Collective Organization of Migrants

Although migrants arrive with an organizational repertoire of their own, through interaction with host polity institutions their practices acquire new forms and characteristics. How migrants are incorporated affects their organizational discourses, strategies, and identities. My main assertion is that the rules of membership that define the forms of participation in particular polities also configure the collective patterns of migrant organization.

Migrant organizing also takes on new forms and functions in response to changes in the international arena. Intensifying global discourses on rights and pluralistic conceptions of identity, as celebrated by the UN, UNESCO, and the like, provide impetus for social movements and penetrate their vocabularies of action. Accordingly, migrant organizations adopt these discourses in their claims and strategies and negotiate new modes of belonging beyond the confines of national boundaries.

There is no comprehensive body of literature on the collective action or organization of migrants in Europe. Although studies of migrant associations in individual countries have been conducted, focusing especially on questions of ethnic community formation and identity, there have been few attempts to provide a comparative framework within which to understand emerging organizational forms and patterns.[1] Existing studies primarily consider the migrants' cultural, religious, and political backgrounds (elements that they bring from their homelands), failing to examine how the host society's institutions shape the organizational incorporation of migrants.[2]

The most common variables in these studies are the social and cultural characteristics of migrant groups. For example, the concentration of migrants and their home-country-based social networks are viewed as crucial to their organizing on the basis of ethnic attributes. The literature also emphasizes the organizational skills that migrants bring with them; migrant populations with a more established "tradition of organization" are expected to generate more associational activity than other groups. The only aspect of the host society considered relevant is the "insecure and restricted political universe," that is, the limited set of political-legal rights that inhibits migrants' political expression and organizing (Miller 1981).

These group-level variables may explain why, in individual cases, migrant groups organize or why some are more organized than others (in other words, they constitute control variables), but they do not explain why distinct organizational patterns emerge in particular countries of destination. Even with similar social networks and "organizational traditions," migrants' collective organization takes different forms in different host countries. In other words, Turks in Sweden are organized differently than Turks in France or Switzerland, in ways that reproduce the predominant organizational models of the particular host country.

My analyses suggest that the organizing principles and incorporation styles of the host polity are crucial variables in accounting for the emerging organizational patterns of migrants. Host societies shape the collective organization of migrants by providing (or not) certain resources for and models of organizing. Some host polities afford explicit channels for the participation and organization of migrant populations, thereby affecting their self-organization. Certain host-society institutions and policies encourage collective identity and organization, by means of categorization and the provision of resources to ethnic groups. Migrant organizations, in turn, define their goals, strategies, functions, and level of operation in relation to the existing policies and resources of the host state. They advance demands and set agendas vis-à-vis state policy and discourses in order to seize institutional opportunities and further their claims. In that sense, the expression and organization of migrant collective identity are framed by the institutionalized forms of the state's incorporation regime.

The sections that follow map patterns of collective organizing among migrants in relation to host society institutions and policies. I concentrate on organizational forms, goals, and level of operation as the major constituents of migrant organizational patterns. My analysis draws primarily on data about the organizations of Turkish migrants, collected between 1988 and 1991.[3] It focuses on organizational structures as collective forms rather than on the actual participation of individual migrants in these structures. Moreover, I analyze organizational goals and functions as they are formulated, not as they are performed; in that sense, it is an analysis of collective forms and discourses, rather than of collective action.[4]

Patterns of Collective Organization

As we have seen, host societies differ in their policies and organization with respect to the incorporation of migrants. Those differences affect the ways in which migrant populations organize collectively. Corporatist regimes assume that migrants integrate best through their own organizations and in a collective framework. To this end, instruments of state policy encourage migrants to organize. Migrant organizations are funded by the central government and local authorities, and afforded formal channels of participation at the national level.

Because each migrant group is expected to be represented by its own national organization, migrant associations with differing political orientations are compelled to organize under one umbrella federation. Recognition by the state as a legitimate ethnic category, a prerequisite for access to funding and participatory mechanisms, becomes an animating goal for migrant organizations. The functional tasks assumed by these organizations are primarily interest representation and policy formulation, with the goal of promoting the rights and status of their particular ethnic constituencies. Their formal membership is generally large; most organizations envision everyone from their "national group" as part of their natural constituency.

In liberal polities, where the incorporation regime is structured in reference to the individual, state policies are less likely to promote centralized, ethnically based migrant organizations. Furthermore, the links between the state and migrant organizations—participatory structures that might facilitate their collective representation—are less institutionalized. The pattern that emerges is a dispersed and localized one. Migrant associations function mainly as social service and advising organizations, rather than as interest or advocacy groups, and undertake tasks not performed by the central government. Most such associations are founded by local initiative and are not federated at the national level.

As in the liberal case, statist incorporation lacks institutionalized support for collective ethnic identity and organization. The state does give some financial support to migrant organizations; however, there is no systematic representation of or consultation with migrant groups, such that would promote a unified organizational structure. Migrant organizations are small, but much more centralized and politicized than those in liberal polities. Within a centrally structured political system, migrants orient their action and organizing to the national plane, so as to target the state. Their activities are directed toward public authorities, not to gain recognition as such, but to redefine and reestablish political categories at the national level. Organizations take the form of advocacy or action groups, usually coalitions mobilized around specific issues or goals.

Table 6.1, which shows the distribution of migrant organi-

Table 6.1. Percentage of Migrant Organizations Performing Selected Functions in Sweden, Britain, and Germany

	Cultural Recreational	Advice Social Service	Advocacy Interest Representation	Education
Sweden (N = 161)	84	33	72	—
Britain (N = 316)	37	70	10	47
Germany (N = 298)	75	44	18	24

Note: Because the table was constructed from different sources, the categories may not be always identical. Advice and social services usually involve general social assistance as well as service to specific groups (the elderly, women, and youth) and service in specific areas (housing, employment, and health care). Advocacy and interest representation is a broad category, mainly comprising activities directed toward broad policy issues and interests of the migrant communities. In Britain, for example, it includes activities opposing race discrimination. The figures for Germany were calculated using a survey of migrant associations conducted by the Federal Commissioner for Foreigners' Affairs in 1987. For Britain, I used the Directory of Ethnic Minority Organizations (CRE 1985), which is based upon a questionnaire administered to the migrant organizations by the CRE. The Swedish data are restricted to the local Finnish organizations and are taken from Jaakkola (1987:211), who carried out a study of these associations between 1982 and 1986.

zations according to their self-proclaimed functions, confirms these general patterns. It is apparent that the overall majority of migrant organizations undertake cultural and recreational activities. Otherwise, the percentages indicate clear differences in the corporatist (Swedish) and liberal (British) patterns. In Sweden, only 33 percent of migrant associations carry out social service projects, whereas in Britain the number amounts to an overwhelming 70 percent. On the other hand, while interest representation in Sweden is a major task that 72 percent of the migrant organizations perform, in Britain only 10 percent of associations are involved in such activity. Germany, where the state does more in terms of the welfare of migrants but lacks formal channels for migrant interest representation, ranks in between. Dutch data show a similar corporatist pattern. According to a 1985 survey of 2,158 local migrant organizations conducted by the Ministry of Welfare, Health, and

Cultural Affairs, the majority of associations ranked their sociocultural and recreational activities as the most important. Interest representation ranked second. Providing information came in third, and a mere 10 percent of associations considered social services an important aspect of their activities (de Graaf 1985; de Graaf, Penninx, and Stoové 1988:219–22). The sections that follow detail these organizational patterns as well as those of Switzerland and France.

Sweden

In Sweden, the idea of collective organization as the natural response to the question of how migrants can influence the Swedish society and improve their lives is put forth in every possible way, even in the handbook distributed to migrants upon their arrival. There are around 1,200 migrant associations (with a total membership of about 175,000) and more than half of them are united under 34 umbrella organizations, on the basis of nationality (see table 6.2). This unified and centralized structure conforms to the general Swedish organizational model which is "unifying, national, polity-wide, and absorbing" (Boli 1991).[5]

Most of the national migrant federations came into being in the late 1970s; twenty-two were founded after 1977 when the Swedish state began to offer subsidies to migrant groups to help them organize. The Popular Movements Section of the National Immigration Board was established in 1975 to support migrant organizing.[6] It provides organizational training and advice to assist new migrant groups in building up their own organizational structures. Migrant federations participate in the consultative councils of the Ministry of Labor and the National Immigration Board, the major state agencies concerned with migrant affairs. Furthermore, there are two working groups of the national migrant federations, formed as "common platforms" to respond to various government proposals and address issues that affect migrants generally.[7]

As table 6.3 indicates, the majority of federations report that their main objectives are to represent the interests of their own "community," negotiate with the authorities, and promote their cultural identity. Social services and related activities

Table 6.2. State Funding of National Organizations of Migrants in Sweden, 1987/88 (Swedish crowns, in thousands)

National Federation	Associations	Membership	Financial Aid
National Federation of Finnish Associations	176	41,163	1,339
National Yugoslav Federation	124	18,863	1,133
National Greek Federation	46	11,761	900
National Syrian Federation	27	9,335	824
National Turkish Federation	27	9,087	824
National Federation of Assyrians	23	5,432	669.5
Estonian Committee	42	8,650	412
National Croatian Federation	13	3,569	412
National Federation of Swedish-Speaking Finns	25	4,313	412
National Italian Federation	18	4,002	412
Central Latvian Council/Latvian Aid Committee		3,800	257.5
Estonian Representation	18	11,001	257.5
National Federation of Immigrants	25	5,279	257.5
National Federation of Polish Associations	12	1,305	257.5
National Hungarian Federation	16	3,125	257.5
National Icelandic Federation	7	3,332	257.5
National Kurdish Federation	24	4,150	257.5
National Portuguese Federation	8	1,382	257.5
National Spanish Federation	8	2,137	257.5
Polish Refugee Council	19	2,000	257.5
National Federation of International Associations of Immigrant Women	19	1,884	124.2
National Eritrean Federation	12	1,484	100

Source: SIV, Popular Movements Section; SIV 1988/89.

Note: The following organizations also have a national scope and operate according to "democratic principles," but because of their small membership are not eligible for SIV funding: Central Federation of Finnish-Ingrians, Central Organization of Salvadorian Associations, Democratic Association of Iranians, Gambian Association, Immigrant Cultural Center, Korean Association, National Chilean Federation, National Federation of Czechoslovakian Associations, National Japanese Federation, Nordic Gypsy Council, Palestinian Workers Association, Ukrainian Association.

Table 6.3. Organizational Goals and Functions of National Federations in Sweden (N = 28)

Cultural function (preservation of the original culture)	19	68%
Interest representation	17	61%
Relationship with Swedish authorities	10	36%
Political activity vis-à-vis the country of origin[a]	8	28%
Adaptation function (individual services to migrants)	5	18%

Source: Bäck 1983:111.
[a] Asked of refugee organizations.

amount to only a small part of their agenda.[8] This pattern mirrors the host country's organizational model, from which charitable associations are strikingly absent, since social welfare is the exclusive responsibility of the Swedish state (Boli 1991).

Sweden has a comprehensive funding scheme that aims at strengthening migrant self-organization and to further contact and cooperation between migrants and Swedish institutions (interview: SIV). All national-level migrant organizations receive grants for such working expenses as rent and salaries, and funding for activities like publishing, training, cultural events, and conferences. Criteria for state funding are as follows. An association has to be organized nationwide, with local chapters and at least 1,000 members, the majority of which must be migrants; it must promote migrant interests and orient its organizational activities toward Sweden; and it must have a "democratic structure," an elected board, an annual meeting open to general membership, and formal by-laws. The amount of funding is determined in proportion to membership.[9] The direct correlation between number of members and funding makes size of membership a central concern of migrant organizations (interviews: National Turkish Federation; the Swedish Muslim Association). Enlarging membership, without necessarily broadening the active participation of members, thus becomes a goal in itself.

From 1976 to 1987, state funding of national migrant federations rose from 4.5 million SKr ($729,000) to 12 million SKr ($1.94 million; interview: SIV). (See table 6.2 for the distribution of central state funding among migrant organizations in the fiscal year 1987/88.) Government funding constitutes an important part of the budgets of the national migrant federations. In the early 1980s, 73 percent of the total budget of the federations (16.8 million SKr, or $2.72 million) came from state subsidies. Only 26 percent (6.3 million SKr, $1.02 million) derived from self-financing, fees, festivals, and other contributions (Bäck 1983:55).

In addition, the state subsidizes specific projects in high-priority areas, in accord with the emphases of the governmental policy. In 1987, fifty-seven projects conducted by migrant or Swedish organizations and concerning various aspects of the incorporation of migrants received around 2 million SKr ($324,000; SIV 1988/89). Since the mid-1980s, issues specifically concerning migrant women and youth have received a high priority, upon which have been immediately incorporated into the activities of the federations. In 1987, for example, the National Turkish Federation received 433,000 SKr ($70,146) for its youth-related activities, and in 1988, 15,000 SKr ($2,430) for programs directed toward women. In their eighth annual congress, the federation decided to form a women's committee, and to elect at least one woman to all executive councils of the member associations.

Since organizational activity is seen as a main conduit for incorporation, migrant associations are supported financially and consulted formally at the local level as well (interview: City of Stockholm Immigration Board). Public funding in the form of local and regional subsidies accounts for almost half the total budget of local associations (14 million SKr, or $2.27 million; Bäck 1983:53). Financial support to migrant organizations accounts for one-third of the budget of the City of Stockholm Immigration Board. The beneficiaries of this support have increased from 8 organizations in 1971 to 98 organizations in 1987, when they received a total of 6 million SKr ($972,000; City of Stockholm 1987).

In accord with the Swedish model, associations of Turkish migrant workers in Sweden are united under one federation. The National Turkish Federation, founded in 1977, had 27 member associations nationwide and about 9,000 individual members when I conducted my research in 1988. The federation adopts verbatim the principles of the Swedish official

Table 6.4. 1987 Revenues of the National Turkish Federation (Swedish crowns and U.S. dollars)

Basic SIV funding	737,000 SKr	$119,394
State Youth Organization Grants	433,051	70,154
Subscription and advertisement fees	103,855	16,825
Membership fees	16,414	2,659
Grants for personnel costs	127,542	20,662
Project grants	280,154	45,385
Other	92,450	14,975
Total	1,790,466 SKr	$290,054

Source: *Yeni Birlik* 1988:12.

policy as its own objectives: "equality between migrants and Swedes, freedom of cultural choice, and cooperation and solidarity between the Swedish and migrant populations" (Turkiska Riksförbundet 1987). As stated in the federation's bylaws, these aims involve advocating the social, economic, and political rights of the Turkish community, securing its cultural development, and maintaining contact with Swedish authorities and institutions by representing the community at different governmental and administrative levels. The federation organizes seminars and courses for the cadres of the member associations in order to "make them competent in organizational functioning" (interview: National Turkish Federation). Such activities contribute significantly to the reproduction of similar organizational structures and goals at local levels.

In 1988, the federation had a budget of 2 million SKr ($324,000), more than half of which came from direct state funding, as can be seen in table 6.4. Federation officials I interviewed made a point of informing me that the state funding they received has increased, as they have "learned to plan their activities ahead of time and apply for funding from various available sources."

The migrants' religious associations also have adopted a centralized, unifying organizational model.

In Sweden, all religious groups outside the state church are considered free churches, and have received financial support from the state since 1972. Free churches act as interest organizations, participating in advisory commissions related to their sphere of activity, and help their constituencies to maintain their cultural identities (Boli 1991). The religions of migrant groups, including Islam, are given the same status.[10]

The Swedish Muslim Association, founded in 1982, is organized as a congregation; in 1988, it had five local branches and a list of 12,000 members, with an active membership of 1,500.[11] It belongs to the Swedish Association of Free Churches and participates in meetings at the National Immigration Board, which has a special subsection for religious organizations.

The Swedish Association of Free Churches is the formal body that represents all free churches, and is responsible for distributing state funds granted to free churches. This financial support is available to all religious communities of above a certain membership. Between 1976 and 1982, the amount of funding allocated to religious organizations multiplied by more than ten: from 3 million SKr ($486,000) to 36 million SKr ($5.83 million) (interview: SIV). As of 1988, the total amount of funding the religious organizations got was around 33 million SKr ($5.35 million). Of this amount, a basic sum of 150,000 SKr ($24,300) is given to every religion that qualifies as a free church, and the rest is distributed according to membership.

In 1987, Islamic organizations received about 800,000 SKr ($129,600); in 1988 the amount grew to 2 million SKr ($324,000).[12] In addition to their religious functions, these organizations engage in social, cultural, recreational, and educational activities that bring in additional funding on a project basis. In 1988, the Swedish government introduced a new funding source to promote the establishment of local branches of religious organizations. This "establishment fund" is given to certain projects for a period of three years to defray infrastructural costs. Since other churches already have established stable bases, priority is given to the Islamic organizations. Hence, the Muslim Association was able to obtain an additional 280,000 SKr ($45,360) in 1988 to found branches in three new districts.

The Netherlands

Dutch policy also establishes collective categories and supports migrant organizations as important agents of "integration" and "emancipation" (interview: Directorate for the Coordination of Minorities Policy [DCM]). In the Netherlands, as in Sweden, the government's support for "ethnic minority organizing" fosters the assertion of collective identity. In the mid-1980s, there were between 2,000 and 2,500 local migrant associations, founded for the purpose of supporting religious and cultural activities, promoting interest, or serving political ends (Ministry of Welfare, Health, and Cultural Affairs 1984). Most of these associations are federated at the national level, under about 25 umbrella organizations (see table 6.5). The goals of

Table 6.5. State Funding of National Organizations of Migrants in the Netherlands, 1988 (in Dutch florins)

National Organization	Financial Aid	
National Cooperation of Foreign Workers' Organizations (LSOBA)[a]	550,000	
Turkish Islamic Cultural Federation	120,000	
Federation of Yugoslavian Associations	85,000	
Dutch Islamic Center	60,000	
Federation of Associations of Spanish Migrants (FAEEH)	35,000	
Federation of Social Democratic Associations (DSDF)	30,000	
Union of Laborers from Turkey (HTIB)	30,000	
Federation of Italian Migrant Workers and their Families (FILEF)	25,000	
Federation of Democratic Workers Associations (DIDF)	23,000	
Committee of Moroccan Workers (KMAN)	22,000	
Greek Federation	20,000	
National Organization of Arabic Women	20,000	
TICF	10,000	
Siciliani nel Mondo	4,000	
Total	1,034,000	($537,680)

Source: The Ministry of Welfare, Health, and Cultural Affairs.

Note: The following groups are also nationally organized, but did not receive state funding in 1988: Union of Women from Turkey (HTKB), Federation of Islamic Associations and Communities, Federation of Turkish Sports Associations, Union of Moroccan Muslim Organizations (UMMON), Christian Association of Italian Workers (ACLI), Recreational Center of Italian Workers (CRLI).

[a]The LSOBA is an umbrella organization of 20 migrant associations of Moroccans, Turks, Greeks, Spaniards, Yugoslavians, Italians, and Tunisians.

these nationality-based organizations are generally specified as "community development" and "emancipation activities."

As in the Swedish case, central administrative bodies play an active role in configuring the organizational life of migrants. The National Advisory Council for Ethnic Minorities (LAO), a consultative body set up by the Dutch government, brings together migrant organizations with diverse political and functional orientations. The main purpose of the LAO is defined as providing migrant groups with a channel for participation at the national level through subcouncils that represent nationality and minority groups. The subcouncils are structured as umbrella organizations and are financed by the Dutch government; in 1988, an annual amount of 173,000 Fl ($89,960) was allocated for their permanent offices and staff (interview: DCM).

The Turkish subcouncil (IOT), founded in 1985 upon an initiative from the Dutch government, consisted at that time of delegates from six organizations: the Turkish Islamic Cultural Federation, the Union of Laborers from Turkey, the Turkish Islamic Center, the Federation of Turkish Sports Associations, the Federation of Social Democratic Associations, and the Union of Women from Turkey. Officials of the IOT recalled that when the subcouncil was formed, the Dutch government insisted that groups with different political orientations should cooperate. It is clear from interviews that the leaders of the member organizations themselves consider "compromise and cooperation" crucial to the "representation of a larger section of the Turkish community" and "improvement of the legal and social status of Turkish migrants" in the Netherlands (see also IOT 1986/87).

In practice, cooperation requires the collaboration of Turkish Islamic organizations and left-oriented Turkish political associations that would otherwise be rivals. However, such cooperation is mainly limited to the leadership; there is little interaction to further unity of interest and action between the members of different associations (Rath 1988). Neither is there much interaction between the groups of migrants who form the nationality-specific federations and advisory subcouncils recognized by the LAO. This island-like organizational style contrasts with the French scheme, in which migrant groups frequently unite and mobilize to carry out political action programs.

The organizations that compose the IOT are themselves federations. Two of them had a wide membership and activity range among the Turkish community at the time of my research. The Union of Laborers from Turkey, founded in 1974, had 6 local associations and 12 working groups, with a membership of 600 in 1988. The Union is politically on the left, but has, according to its leadership, an agenda that represents the interests of the Turkish community as a whole. In 1987, it received 47,000 Fl ($24,440) from the government toward its working expenses and activities.

The Turkish Islamic Cultural Federation, founded in 1979, has been very active and influential in the Turkish community and vis-à-vis the Dutch authorities. The federation had 80 local member associations in 1988 and an established formal structure, that is, elected officials and annual meetings. According to the leaders of the federation, fostering "Islamic identity and organization" is a step toward the "emancipation" of the Turkish migrant community. This stance echoes the official Dutch discourse that emphasizes strengthening minority group members' sense of identity and belief in their own value as a necessary condition for their participation in Dutch society (Ministry of Home Affairs 1983:3). Moreover, the leadership of the federation sees no conflict in integrating the "Islamic way of living" into Dutch society (cf. Rath 1988). To this end, the federation trains bicultural and bilingual Islamic clergy to act as liaisons between migrants and the Dutch. In 1987, the federation received 145,500 Fl ($75,660), half of which was allocated for the training of volunteers and clergy. The federation also founded an Islamic Broadcasting Organization (IOS) to "seek a visibility and place in Dutch society." The IOS has a public status and is funded by the state.

In the Netherlands, as in Sweden, criteria for funding encourage migrant organizations to form federations and to assume the task of interest representation. Migrant organizations become eligible for state subsidies if they operate at the national level and if they perform the following functions: promoting migrants' interests; providing informational, cultural, and "emancipation activities" for their national constituencies;

and training volunteers as professional organizational leaders (interview: Ministry of Welfare, Health, and Cultural Affairs).

The state is a major source of funding for migrant organizations. For example, in 1988, the Ministry of Welfare, Health, and Cultural Affairs had a budget of 1 million Fl ($520,000) for organizations of migrants from Mediterranean countries. In 1987, 22 percent of state funding was used to develop training programs for volunteers and organizational leaders. Thirty-five percent was allocated for funding meetings, seminars, cultural activities, and activities of specific benefit to youth and women. Another 44 percent went to organizational costs including salaries. Local organizations are subsidized separately by municipalities. Seventy percent of the total number of migrant associations (over 2,000) receive some sort of support from local government (de Graaf, Penninx, and Stoové 1988).

In addition to funding, the state provides organizational support. A major responsibility of the Dutch Center for Foreigners (NCB) is to give professional assistance to national-level migrant organizations and set up training programs for their cadres. Such activities seek to create a pool of expert organizational leaders and staff, capable of functioning self-sufficiently as representatives of their constituencies. Dutch policy emphasizes training, with the idea that it is crucial for migrant organizations "to be competently staffed and in a position to train future administrative staff" (Ministry of Welfare, Health, and Cultural Affairs 1986b:2). The Government Grant Scheme explicitly provides for the training of migrant women, since, as reasoned in the official papers, "at present too few women in minority groups possess the appropriate training to set up organizations of their own in the short term" (Ministry of Home Affairs 1983:16). Accordingly, in 1988, the NCB held meetings to train women of different migrant groups, from 25 local women's centers and associations, to set up a nationwide organization to represent them (interview: NCB). The NCB also offers special support for the activities of organizations set up by migrant youth.[13]

In both Sweden and the Netherlands, the predominant organizational model prioritizes formal participation and state support, in the process creating institutionalized and centrally defined categories. The organizational language of the host states is appropriated and reproduced by migrant leaders, and the aims of state policies are similarly articulated in the agendas of migrant organizations. As an example, all the associations I interviewed, including the religious ones, mentioned some activity involving migrant women and youth—two priority areas of Swedish and Dutch policy.

Moreover, through formal participatory mechanisms and state-provided training, there emerges a professional cadre of migrant activists with a knowledge of possible resources and experience in dealing with the bureaucracy. This translates into a convenient channel for the propagation of organizational forms. The relatively unquestioned status of participatory structures and funding arrangements indicates that the migrant communities themselves accept and internalize these models. New migrant groups, like Chinese and Pakistanis in the Netherlands, vie for the state recognition that would give them access to resources available to other ethnic groups (Rath 1988). This mode of organizational incorporation is quite different from the cases I discuss next, in which the legitimacy of formal consultative arrangements and direct state funding is contested. Most migrant organizational leaders I interviewed in Switzerland and Britain were skeptical of state subsidation, viewing it as a form of cooptation—to the extent that they appeared disturbed when I inquired about government funding of their organizations.

A related outcome of professionalized and formalized migrant organizing in Sweden and the Netherlands is a low level of membership mobilization. In fact, studies indicate that individual participation in migrant organizational activity in these countries is indeed insignificant (Bäck 1983; de Graaf, Penninx, and Stoové 1988). Migrant leaders in Sweden sometimes complain of a lack of incentive for participation: "We cannot mobilize the Turkish population around any real demands. . . . Most rights and freedoms are already given by the state, and there is already an organization for every problem that migrants face in this country" (interview: Solidarity Association, Stockholm; also expressed by the president of the Association of Women from Turkey in Sweden).

Although the organizational forms adopted may not always be consequential, they are nevertheless perceived as important links between migrants and the host state authorities.[14] These organizational modalities are seen as productive ways of interacting with and influencing host societies. This view was expressed with great assurance by the president of the National Turkish Federation in Sweden, who, in an interview, said, "Our organizational model, that is, the Swedish model, which allows for the participation and representation of organizations with diverse political backgrounds, and creates a network of cooperation among them, is the most effective step towards resolving the problems of Turkish migrants in Europe."

Switzerland

In Switzerland, most migrant associations are small-scale operations sharing a goal that is generally stated as "furthering the integration of migrants." Organizational discourse and activities commonly center on "successful integration of migrants into Swiss society," in contrast to the emphasis on collective emancipation or interest representation in the Dutch and Swedish cases. The 1987 foreigners' platform on the problems and demands of migrants, cosigned by the Italian, Portuguese, Spanish, and Turkish associations, declares that "for better relations with the Swiss society, integration is both necessary and urgent" (FCLIS 1987).

In 1988, there were about 70 local Turkish associations in Switzerland, all fairly small, to assist Turkish migrants in their localities—43 support and cultural associations, 22 mosque organizations, and 5 sports clubs. Although there had been previous attempts to gather these associations under one umbrella organization, those attempts had failed, in the main. At the time of my research, two weakly organized federations existed: The Federation of Turkish Associations in Switzerland, founded in 1976, a left-oriented federation with 15 member associations; and the Federation for Solidarity among Turkish Associations in Switzerland, founded in 1984, with 22 member associations. In my interviews, the leaders of both federations stressed their role in helping the Turkish migrant community with their legal and social problems and with integration. Both organizations work primarily to resolve migrants' immediate needs, in areas such as retirement planning, visa applications, and military service. Large-scale policy formulation and advocacy are a negligible part of their agenda. Compared to counterparts in Sweden and the Netherlands, they have little prominence vis-à-vis Swiss authorities or the migrant community. Only since 1987 have two representatives from the Federation for Solidarity among Turkish Associations participated on the EKA, the federal advisory commission.

The Swiss government has no special budget to subsidize migrant organizations. Neither of the Turkish federations receive regular funding for their activities; occasional funds are generated through personal contacts, usually from general welfare agencies. The Federation for Solidarity was able to obtain 4,500 SFr ($3,123) from ProHelvetia in 1988 for the language training of the religious clergy sent from Turkey; in 1987, the Dutch government gave about 70,000 Fl ($36,270), nearly ten times as much, to the Turkish Islamic Cultural Federation for the same purpose. Most organizations depend on membership fees, which usually do not even cover the cost of publishing newsletters. At the local level, some indirect public support is available, such as allocation of space by social service organizations for particular activities. However, activities that would foster collective identities or structures do not commonly receive support, direct or indirect. In particular, the state does not promote religious activity or organization, the idea being that such activity may hinder the integration of individual migrants into Swiss society. This perspective seems counter to Swedish and Dutch policies, which emphasize ethnic/national organizing as the framework for better integration of migrants.

An important deviation from the generally scattered and localized pattern of migrant organizing in Switzerland is the case of Italian and Spanish organizations. In contrast to the Turkish associations, they are highly coordinated and for the most part centrally federated. As Heisler (1985, 1986) argues, a lack of active policy and support on the part of the Swiss state creates space for the sending country governments to get involved in matters related to the lives of their citizens. Both the Italian and the Spanish states have created a network of formal offices and agencies to initiate, coordinate, and finance voluntary associations of their nationals. In this case, the policies and organizational capacities of the sending governments significantly affect migrants' organizational activity in the host society (see also Miller 1981).

Britain

In Britain, large federations or national organizations of migrant groups are also exceptional. Existing ones are fairly weak and do not have a significant presence in the migrant communities (FitzGerald 1988). In the 1980s, in response to the establishment of direct consultative channels, such as the Race Relation Councils, there were efforts to organize alliances, forums, and umbrella organizations, at least at the local level. However, as in Switzerland, these attempts did not succeed in creating overarching organizations to represent migrants' wider interests (see Rath and Saggar 1987). This is true even for Asians and Afro-Caribbeans, the two earliest migrant groups, whose organizations are more prominent at the national level.[15] Overall, organizational activity remains locally oriented.

There are an estimated 2,000 migrant organizations throughout Britain (Anwar 1991), most of which are involved in welfare and cultural functions. Others include religious, political, and professional organizations. Among these, the organizations of immigrants from Bangladesh, India, Pakistan, and the West Indies are particularly active in local electoral and racial politics (see Werbner and Anwar 1991). In the 1990s, Islamic associations have become visible pressure groups, as they intensify their demands for provisions for Islamic education.

In Britain, government financial aid schemes provide funding primarily for specific educational and social service functions of migrant associations. One of the sources for public funding of migrant organizations is the Commission for Racial Equality (CRE), which offers financial or other assistance under the provisions of the Race Relations Act. In 1988, the CRE assisted 136 organizations with a total amount of £1,557,670 ($2,702,557). However, only 31 of the recipients were migrant associations with national or ethnic bases. They received one fourth of the total aid; the rest went to the voluntary organizations (RECs), which aim to further the goals of the CRE at the local level. All but four of the migrant associations were funded for welfare services, primarily to pay the salaries of administrative, social, and legal advice workers. As in Switzerland, it is more difficult to get funding for projects or activities that directly promote collective identities or ethnic organizing (interview: Home Office, Research and Planning Unit; see also Cheetham 1988).

Within the framework of a number of schemes such as the Urban Program and Inner City Partnership, local authorities may provide funding for welfare, educational, cultural, and recreational projects. During the 1986/87 budget year, for example, the Birmingham City Council allocated £4.5 million ($7.8 million) to voluntary associations, £2.2 million ($3.8 million) of which went to migrant associations (Joly 1988b:58). Financial aid policy varies significantly among municipalities. However, since the 1980s, increasing numbers of local authorities have financed cultural activities of ethnic groups (see also Werbner 1991). In Birmingham and Manchester, Islamic organizations have received subsidies for mother-tongue instruction (such as Urdu and Hindi), while other local authorities may be less willing to give money to religious groups.

As I discussed in chapter 4, welfare provisions that specifically target migrant groups are limited in Britain. In this context, migrant organizations orient themselves toward social services. The migrant organizations' self-understanding reflects strong reliance on "community care" without public involvement. In an interview at Tamil Refugee Action Group, one executive officer told me with certain pride: "It is better for us to take care of our own problems in our own community." Most migrant associations function as social service agencies for their local constituencies. Some focus on specific tasks, such as managing housing projects (e.g., the Tamil Refugee Action Group Housing Association), administering training programs for the youth, or helping the elderly or the handicapped. Others are community centers that combine social service and cultural and recreational activities. When I was conducting my research, the Turkish Community Center served as a hostel for migrants who had just arrived from Turkey. In the other countries I studied, such functions are generally performed by public agencies.

The Turkish Community Center in London, which had 1,000

members in 1989, receives subsidies from the Hackney municipality and other public funds reserved for migrants. The other Turkish migrant organization in London is the Turkish Education Union, which organizes language courses for migrant children funded by the municipality and by parents. No Turkish organization is involved in large-scale policy advocacy or formulation. This is true as well for other recent immigrant groups—Filipinos and Latin Americans—whose associations are also small local organizations that concentrate on social service activities (Runnymede Trust 1984a). Joly (1987) and Josephides (1987) make similar observations about Pakistani and Cypriot associations in Britain. They are almost all local initiatives, serving the needs of their own groups; only a very few are part of a Britain-wide organizational structure. Even those migrant organizations that define themselves as political and whose agenda includes advocacy provide some form of social service, as in the case of the Joint Council for the Welfare of Immigrants (JCWI).[16]

France

In France, legal restrictions on migrant organizing in effect until 1981, coupled with the lack of policy instruments and incentives to promote the collective organization of immigrants, have resulted in relatively limited and dispersed organizational activity among migrants. The same conditions also led to the formation of a high number (around 3,000) of "solidarity associations" established by French nationals (Pillard 1986). The most important ones are the Federation of Associations of Solidarity with Immigrant Workers (FASTI), the Information and Support Group for Immigrant Workers (GISTI), and Accueil et Promotion, all of which work as information, social help, and legal aid organizations, and advocate the rights and legal status of immigrants. With the extension of full associative rights to noncitizens in 1981, the initiatives undertaken by relatively new migrant groups (Maghrebians and Turks, for instance) have increased.[17] These initiatives are primarily characterized by their mobilization around political positions and demands. By the mid-1980s, there were about 4,200 migrant organizations. Large federations of migrants based on ethnicity or nationality, however, are few, and those that do exist are weak and do not represent a united front.[18]

Nevertheless, most associations operate at the national level; associational activity is concentrated in Paris, the political center. One organizational leader at FASTI asserted that "in order to make the government understand certain problems, you need a central political force to take a position against the authorities." Judicially, all registered associations have national status, whether or not their activities in fact take place at the national level.

The Social Action Fund (FAS), the central state agency responsible for integration, subsidizes organizations that cater to migrants. And, since the late 1980s, policy has favored the initiatives of migrants themselves (FAS 1989b). Still, the state does not directly support collective ethnic identity and organizing. According to officials at the FAS, the amount of funding that goes to migrants' self-associations is minimal. In 1988, there were about 200 migrant associations, which together received about 23 million francs ($756,800) from that agency; although migrant associations made up 7 percent of the organizations funded by the FAS, they received only 2 percent of its funding. More than half of these associations only obtained small grants, ranging from 5,000 to 50,000 francs ($165–$1,650) for social and cultural activities (FAS 1988a).

In 1988, the FAS subsidized only 13 of the 100 associations of migrants from Turkey for their services. Eight of these were provincial sports and cultural associations, with small subsidies of between 5,000 and 30,000 francs ($860 to $5,160). The other organizations are located in Paris. Elele, which provides social services and legal advice, received 120,040 F ($20,647) for its activities. Elele was founded in 1984 on the initiative of French activists, and currently has both French and Turkish members. That same year, the FAS provided 216,064 F ($37,163) to the Association of Workers from Turkey (ATT), for services to migrants similar to those Elele offers. In 1989, ATT received 500,000 F ($86,000) for language classes and special activities for women.

Of these associations, ATT has a broader agenda and set of

activities. Founded in 1980 as a result of a series of actions around the legalization of illegal workers, the ATT defines itself as "a platform to advocate the rights of migrants and to enable migrants to express themselves politically" (ATT 1987:4). It works with a small but very active membership cadre, who organize festivals, seminars, and workshops in order to build a common platform with other migrant organizations. The ATT also belongs to the executive body of the Council of Associations of Immigrants in France (CAIF), which consists of 17 migrant organizations from different nationalities.

One particular characteristic of migrant organizational life in France is mobilization and unification with respect to single political issues. The main form of organized migrant activity is political—not very systematic or regular, but always mobilized with regard to such national political issues, as the debate on citizenship or campaigns for family reunification and legalization. Activities include large-scale political projects, protests, expositions at conferences, marches, and festivals, aimed at attracting national attention. The most publicized examples of such actions include the 1983 March for Equality from Marseille to Paris, involving 100,000 people; the 1984 March for Convergence; and the 1985 March for Equal Rights and Against Racism. This spontaneous and nationally focused pattern of organizing differs strikingly from Swedish and Dutch models, which assign predefined functions to migrant organizations, and where systematic interest representation and consultation with different organs of the state are routine. Mobilization against the state is the general form that collective action takes in France (Birnbaum 1988), and migrant organizational activity conforms to the dominant mode of expression. Migrant organizations do not act as partners of the state; instead, they challenge its categories.

The *Memoire Fertile* movement, in which ATT also has taken part, is a good example of this oppositional dynamic. The main goals of the movement, which involves about 20 different migrant organizations (Moroccan, Tunisian, Algerian, Turkish, and French) as well as individuals, are "to reclaim the history of immigrants" and "to negotiate a new belonging in the nation-state" (interview: Memoire Fertile). In accord with these goals, the movement exerts pressure on the state, by means of nationwide political action, to "redefine citizenship and the social contract" to take different national and cultural backgrounds of migrants into account (de Wenden 1988a). Memoire Fertile works to legitimize immigrants and immigration as part of French history and citizenship, and thus enlarge the boundaries of the polity. To this end, Memoire Fertile seeks to assemble a "collective memory" for the migrant communities and to construct a "new citizenship" (*nouvelle citoyennété*). During the bicentennial of the French Revolution, Memoire Fertile made a special effort to mobilize and incorporate "the immigrant" into discussions of the Revolution and citizenship held concurrently with the official celebrations (Memoire Fertile 1988).

In France, mention of ethnic categories is to a large extent absent both from state policies, which refuse to recognize collective identities, and from the ways that migrants organize and formulate their positions. The preoccupation with citizenship and nationality that shapes the predominant discourse undermines ethnic politics. Despite its pronounced identification with Muslim Maghrebi culture, *France Plus*, an organization of second-generation immigrants of Maghrebi origin founded in 1985, clearly situates itself within the secular ideals of republican citizenship (Feldblum 1993). Even the Memoire Fertile movement emphasizes, not the cultural dimension ("multiculturalism" or "emancipation"), but rather the collective participation and insertion of migrant groups in the French political citizenship. Migrant (Islamic or Franco-Maghrebian) identity is expressly formulated as a step toward penetrating French politics; it is a political identity rather than a cultural one. Thus, by embracing citizenship as the "normal" frame of reference, migrant organizations both question and appropriate the very categories of the state in their discourse and practice.

Germany

In Germany, migrant organizations are not given a special role in incorporation policy, and formal links to guestworker organizations are much less established. At the federal level, there are no special provisions for the collective participation of migrants, but, at the municipal level, several advisory councils have been formed. Compared to similar arrangements in Sweden and the Netherlands, these councils receive less recognition from both the German authorities and migrant organizations. The federal budget for the integration of migrants does not include any special item for migrant organizations. Funding at the local level is left to the discretion of local authorities, who distribute it mainly on a project basis. In localities like Berlin and Hamburg, migrants' cultural, youth, and women's organizations do receive substantial support.

Although there is a high level of organizational activity among migrants, existing organizations lack the centralized, representative character of their Dutch and Swedish counterparts. For instance, there are no national federations of Portuguese or Yugoslavs, although, respectively, they have 120 and 350 local associations. The organizational life of Turkish migrants is similarly fragmented. Before 1980, there were four major Turkish federations organized nationwide (not including religious ones), all representing different political stances.[19] Various groups have made attempts, especially after 1980, to establish overarching organizations to overcome the divisions among the Turkish population. In 1983, two umbrella organizations were founded in Berlin, both claiming to represent the broad interests of Turkish migrants. The first, the Turkish Community of Berlin, had 13 member associations in 1990. It gets some degree of recognition from the Berlin city government and is invited to various meetings and hearings of the Senate. The other organization, the Turkish Union of Berlin, which no longer exists, had a more leftist orientation and included professionals, trade-unionists, social workers, and intellectuals. In 1990, another initiative, the Union of Turkish Associations in Berlin, was formed to create a common action platform against the new German Foreigners Law.

Similar organizations have come into being in other parts of Germany as well. The Hamburg Union of Migrants from Turkey, founded in 1985, is composed of various migrant associations and representative individuals with different political inclinations, including Islamic ones. The Union calls for the recognition of "minority rights for migrants" and dual citizenship, and emphasizes the need for "multicultural policies" (*Cumhuriyet Hafta*, 5–11 October 1990). In addition, some older organizations have changed direction, adopting new functions and goals. For instance, the Federation of Progressive People's Associations, which formerly acted as an extension of the social democratic movement in Turkey, has reoriented itself mainly to address migrant issues in Germany. Another development is the growing number of professional associations. Examples from Berlin include the Association of Health Personnel, the Science and Technology Center, the Union of Turkish Parents, and the Turkish Chamber of Commerce. Modeled after German counterparts, these organizations seek to represent and further the interests of their particular groups, and to provide help and advice in their subject areas. They are all recognized and supported financially by the Berlin Senate.

The Turkish Islamic community in Germany has also been politicized and fragmented. Three different associations control the majority of mosque organizations: The National Vision Organization, the Islamic Cultural Centers, and the Directorate of Religious Affairs' Turkish Islamic Union. These organizations all attempt to gather Islamic associations under one roof and compete to represent Turkish Muslims. The Islamic Federation of Berlin was established in 1980 as a local initiative, claiming to represent all Muslims, and thus seeking official recognition from the German authorities.[20] The Islamic Federation resembles the other umbrella organizations that have emerged in Berlin, in terms of its charter and organizational structure—the difference being that its president is called *imam*. The Federation is accepted as a "democratic organization" by the Berlin Senate and has the right to be heard before the Senate, along with other organizations, on migrant issues.

It is interesting to note that all of these organizational reconfigurations have taken place concurrently with the development of more participatory policies by local states. The city governments of both Berlin and Hamburg adopted a more "multiculturalist" discourse in the late 1980s, and have made deliberate efforts to establish contacts with migrant organizations and to fund their activities. A proliferation of organizational activity is especially evident among migrant youth, who increasingly assert membership in their localities and situate their identities in the public space.

The foregoing cases demonstrate how the institutions and incorporation styles of particular host polities shape the configurations of migrants' collective organization and participation. Much organizational activity arises from interaction with the host society's institutions, and migrant organizations appropriate and mobilize the predominating models.

In Sweden and the Netherlands, the central state, through funding and formal participatory structures, legitimizes the demands of and provides an institutional framework for collective organization along ethnic or national lines. State-allocated functions—interest representation and consultative participation—create unified and bureaucratic organizations that act as spokepersons for their respective ethnic constituencies. Even spontaneous or oppositional organizational movements are incorporated into the funding and consultative structures. The National Cooperation of Foreign Workers' Organizations (LSOBA), an organization critical of government policies, is subsidized by the Dutch state "because it provides an oppositional stance" (interview: Ministry of Welfare, Health, and Cultural Affairs).

In contrast, in the absence of an institutional system that officially prescribes and supports centralized organizing based on collective identity, migrant organizational patterns are either fragmented or localized, as in Germany, Switzerland, and Britain. In cases where the central state does not take a direct role in the welfare and incorporation of immigrants, such as Switzerland and Britain, migrant organizations tend to focus on social and welfare services or local politics. In cases like France, where politics are primarily determined at the national level, the resulting forms are centralized action groups and organizations with larger ideological programs.

The existence of these different patterns of migrant organizing in different host countries warrants the conclusion that a common organizational tradition or form attributable to the "Turkish" or "Islamic" origins of immigrants cannot be assumed. Migrants respond to the institutional environments of host societies and draw upon resources and models available to them. The institutional structures and policy patterns of host states are essential factors in accounting for the organizational incorporation of migrants into European societies.

New Actors, New Strategies

Migrant organizations in Europe, over time, have developed new forms and adopted new strategies of participation. They have redefined their discourse in accord with the intensification of pluralistic concepts of identity and membership at European and global levels. What were once simply represented as "guestworker problems" have been recast as issues of rights and belonging, justified by global ideologies of human rights. Whereas the immediate problems of international migrants, such as housing and language training, were of primary concern to organizations in the early 1970s, by the end of the decade, issues of equal rights and legal equality predominated. The late 1980s then saw the emergence of newly defined migrant identities and collective existences.

Identity politics, as it permeates the repertoire of migrant organizing, is not a simple revitalization of "ethnic identities" or "traditions." It serves as a means by which to partake in politics and to negotiate belonging. It is a new way of relating to membership in host countries, without a necessary reference to shared nationhood, as witnessed by demands for dual citizenship, voting rights for foreign residents, and the recognition of different immigrant cultures. This new politics also asserts migrants' identities and claims at the European level, as a way of making space for themselves within the emerging categories of the European Community.

The following sections reflect on these trends by discussing two aspects of migrant organizing: the elevation of migrants' activities to the European level, and the visibility of organized "Islam."

The Internationalization of Migrant Organizing

As supranational political institutions emerge and expand their scope of jurisdiction and action in Europe, migrant activity and interests get linked to wider institutional frameworks. Once authority over particular domains and issues is concentrated in supranational structures—immigration is increasingly one such domain—then it becomes more of a "rational strategy" for migrant organizations to address and lobby these structures in order to influence decision making. In this vein, politics at the European level is crucial, since rules regarding the flow of labor and population, social policies, and rights are increasingly defined and coordinated by the European Community. Thus, more and more, migrant associations elevate their operations to the European level, establishing umbrella organizations and forums to coordinate their activities and to pursue a Europewide migrant policy.

Let me substantiate this trend by citing some organizational indicators. As one type of international activity, organizations concerned with similar issues attempt to form a common platform and program of action. Such coordination involves international conferences and meetings and other networking activities. For example, in 1988, the Society of Swiss Women Who Are Married to Foreigners met with similar organizations from other countries to constitute a common agenda. There is also the European Immigrant Women's Organization (EIWO), founded in 1980 as an international network of migrant women in Europe. The organization holds annual European conferences to deal with specific issues that concern migrant women.

A parallel development involves the coordination of nationality-specific organizations at the European level. Examples are the European Council of Moroccan Associations (CEDAM), the Coordination of Associations of Spanish Immigrants in Europe (CEAEE), the Assembly of Portuguese Communities in Europe (ACPE), and the European Federation of Associations of Italian Immigrants (FILEF).

A third development is the emergence of supranational organizations that work explicitly to redefine the identity and status of migrants at the European level. The Council of Associations of Immigrants in Europe (CAIEUROPE) comprises 2,530 associations Europewide, including thirteen European host countries and forty nationalities. In 1986, it became a permanent council for coordination, dialogue, and concerted action (CAIF 1988). CAIEUROPE tries to expand the socioeconomic, legal, political, and cultural status of international migrants within the framework of the Universal Declaration of Human Rights and the European Convention of Human Rights. To this end, it has established contacts with and lobbied related agencies of UNESCO, the Council of Europe, and the European Community. It has proposed initiatives concerning the rights of migrants for inclusion in the European Social Charter and the harmonization of migrant rights at the European level. Accordingly, two European campaigns were held during the 1984 and 1988 European Parliament elections to promote the political, social, and cultural rights of migrants (FASTI 1989).

Another supranational effort is *SOS Racisme,* a movement with widespread recognition and a broad network. SOS Racisme was founded in France in 1983 to take an antiracist stand, specifically addressing the worldwide solidarity of youth. It included both French nationals and migrants. Since 1985, with the acceleration of efforts to realize the European Community, SOS Racisme has begun organizing in other European countries, including Belgium, Germany, Italy, and Sweden. In 1986, SOS Racisme Europe prepared an immigrants' bill of rights that declares the following principles:

> • The right of everyone to love and live in freedom
> • The right to travel freely and to be treated with equality and respect by the police and other authorities
> • The right to choose one's place of residence
> • The right to freedom of speech and a vote in elections
> • The right to work without discrimination. (Spectre of Organized Racism 1986)

In a similar vein, France Plus drafted and promoted a Eurocharter during the 1989 European parliamentary elections as the basis of its election platform. Along with SOS Racisme, the group explicitly emphasizes two identities for migrants: an immigrant identity within France and a French identity in Europe; in other words, a pluralist national and an international identity.

Parallel to these efforts, various European host state agencies responsible for the integration of migrants have intensified their activity at the European level. For example, in Britain in 1990, the Commission for Racial Equality, with the participation of 40 other migrant organizations, established a Standing Conference on Race Equality (SCORE) in Europe, specifically to address the issues of racial and ethnic discrimination in the European Community (CRE 1990). The Commission has also undertaken initiatives to form alliances with similar agencies in other EC countries, such as the Dutch Bureau against Discrimination and the Belgian Royal Commission on Policy for Immigration, to promote EC-level legislation prohibiting racial discrimination and improve the rights of non-EC migrants.

Finally, the European Community itself has formed an umbrella organization of migrant groups as part of an initiative to generate dialogue between migrant communities and Community institutions. The Migrants Forum, which brings together over 100 associations from twelve EC states, was formally launched in 1991, with a budget from the Commission of the European Community.

Through such organizational activity, conferences, conventions, campaigning, and lobbying at the level of the European Community, migrant organizations forge a transnational status and identity—an identity that is enacted as a symbol in communicating with host societies and supranational authority structures, to redefine and expand the boundaries of belonging in Europe.

A Note on Organized "Islam"

A related outcome of postwar labor migration has been the increasing organization and institutionalization of Islam in Europe. Whether European host states recognize Islam as an official religion or not, Islamic groups are allowed to organize under public law as regular associations. One consequence of this has been the proliferation of religious organizations that practice and advocate Islam in its most radical forms. Another consequence, however, has been the recasting of Islam as an ethnicized political identity through exchange with host societies' institutions, and through attempts to foster a collective existence within the categories of the host states. This transformation is reflected in the organizational practices of Islamic groups and the discourse they employ.

Rationally defined goals and functions, and systematic management are considered modern organizational forms and as such are assumed to be alien to "Islamic cultures." The underlying assumption is that Islam cannot combine European organizational categories with its religious order, which does not provide for an autonomous, hierarchical structure.[21] However, the organizational experience of Islamic groups within the secular order of European polities speaks to the contrary. They organize and function as ethnic interest groups, making claims and demands not only for the right to religious life, but also for the political, social, and economic rights of their members. They have explicit goals and agendas (whose style, arguments, and formulations mirror the host society's forms) and take steps to obtain support from the state and other agencies. They adopt the predominant organizational models, communicate with the host society's institutions, and are not shy about framing their activities in secular structures.

Although they can operate through informal congregations or, simply, unofficial places for prayer, Islamic groups opt to organize formally. To obtain grants for their activities, secure allowances for their particular religious practices, and assert their collective identity, Islamic organizations become active participants in local and national politics. In the process, these organizations acquire other than strictly religious functions and take stands on such migrant issues as racism, discrimination, and integration. Like their secular counterparts, they adopt statutes or by-laws that state the objectives of the association, its area of functioning, its modes of constituting a general assembly, and the functions and responsibilities of the general assembly and administrative board. They commonly have member registers, produce annual reports, and convene annual congresses. They work hard on their image as representatives of the Turkish migrant population.[22] This image consciousness, manifest in their publications, came out repeatedly in the interviews I conducted. Many Islamic groups get involved in economic activity, usually small-scale enterprises such as local broadcasting stations, travel or insurance agencies, driving schools, import-export shops, cafes, bakeries, butcher shops, and grocery stores (Gitmez and Wilpert 1987; de Wit 1988). They also operate as social clubs, and are involved in nonreligious cultural activities, such as courses, gatherings, and sports activities for women and children (Doomernik 1988).

More important, Islamic migrant associations employ a new discourse—not a particularly religious one, but one that appropriates human rights and the rights of the individual as its central theme. They locate their demands within "Western" categories, most of which speak to "modern individuals' needs," acting as advocates for the rights of Muslim women, the psychological needs of Muslim individuals, and the educational rights of Muslim children (see the closing statement of the fourth European Muslims Conference, *Kirpi,* July 1990, p. 15).

Furthermore, the Islamic identity claimed by migrant groups is a political one, rather than a traditional religious identity. Many of the young Maghrebis in France organize around a "Muslim Maghrebi" identity, yet follow a secular course; they are more concerned with gaining religious rights than practicing them (Leveau 1988). Migrants of the younger generation who still identify with Islam do not view it as irreconcilable with a French or Western societal organization or lifestyle; nor do they see any contradiction between an Islamic identity and French republican, secular values (Kepel 1987). Membership in the Muslim community is used in quest of political participation and mainly "serves as a functional entry into the sphere of French politics" (Feldblum 1993:60). Islamic activists redefine and reconstruct religious symbols, such as veiling, as cultural or political expression, and defend them on the grounds of human rights, thereby reproducing and contributing to the host society and global discourses.

With this discussion, I aim to show that the expression and understanding of Islamic identity among migrants in Europe is necessarily modern, as opposed to traditional, and is framed in universalistic, rather than particularistic arguments. This view accords with Handler's (1988:195) assertion that "the desire to appropriate one's own culture, to secure a unique identity, places one in the mainstream of a modern, individualistic culture to which national boundaries are irrelevant."

Along with the general trend toward a secular/political Islamic identity, the country-specific differences in organizational practice discussed earlier in the chapter also pertain to how Islam is organized and exercised in particular polities. A more centrally organized Islam emerges in countries where the state actively incorporates and defines Islam as a functional group. In Sweden and the Netherlands, Islam has the same status as other religions. In 1983, changes in the Dutch constitution granted equal protection to religious and nonreligious convictions, thus giving the same political and legal position to Islamic, Hindu, Jewish, and also Humanist organizations (Rath, Groenendijk, and Penninx 1991). In both Sweden and the Netherlands, the state has stimulated Islamic groups to form umbrella organizations within the terms of its incorporation policy. In turn, Islamic organizations have partaken in the structures of the host states; they have established close relationships with Swedish and Dutch authorities, who recognize them as representatives of their respective communities, and the leaders of the federations act as mediators in negotiations between migrants and the state.

France and Britain, on the other hand, do not recognize Islam as an official religion, despite the high numbers of Muslims in their countries—2.5 million and 1.5 million, respectively. The centralist orientation and secularist principles of the French state mark the way it handles religious matters. In general, the state does not provide special exemptions for migrants on religious grounds. Neither does it make allowances for their particular religious practices. The most publicized example of this unitary, secular orientation was the *foulard* affair of 1989. The issue of Islamic scarves provoked a national crisis and debate when three North African students were expelled from school for insisting on wearing their veils in class (*Washington Post*, 23 October 1989). The affair accentuated concerns about the "laicism principle" of the French state, the definition of freedom of religion in the public school system, and even issues of integration. Not surprisingly, the state attempted to resolve the crisis by a circular regulating the use of religious symbols in schools.[23]

Islam does not have an official status in the United Kingdom either. But in Britain, as opposed to France, most conflicts about religious issues are dealt with at the local level, by the initiative of local governments and organizations. Many school authorities, in response to local requests, have accommodated such Islamic requirements as rules about dressing, food, separate physical education classes for girls, and so on. Religious education, a required component of the public curriculum, usually has as its basis a locally agreed upon multifaith syllabus (Nielsen 1986). In Birmingham, *helal* food, prepared according to Islamic codes, has been made available in schools in response to pressure from local migrant organizations; and Muslim girls are either excused from sports classes or allowed to wear "appropriate Islamic dress," including head coverings, as long as they wear the school colors. Also in Birmingham, the city council allows the central mosque to make prayer calls, having compromised with the Muslim associations on two (instead of the requisite five) calls at fixed hours, so as not to inconvenience local residents (Joly 1988a, 1988b).

These examples illustrate the variety of ways different states define and manage religious matters. Issues that turn into national debates and conflicts in France are matters of local politics in Britain. In Sweden and in the Netherlands, the same issues are resolved through formalized interaction and consulting between migrant organizations and the state.

CHAPTER SEVEN

The Membership Rights and Status of Migrants

So far, I have addressed the institutional and organizational framework through which migrants are incorporated. In this chapter, I turn to another aspect of incorporation: the extent to which noncitizen migrants are incorporated into the rights and privileges that conventionally define citizenship status. In it I examine the membership status of postwar migrants, drawing on information about their rights in a broader set of countries in Europe and North America: Austria, Belgium, Canada, Denmark, Germany, Great Britain, France, the Netherlands, Sweden, Switzerland, and the United States. My analysis reveals that the scope and inventory of noncitizens' rights do not differ significantly from those of citizens, and that the rights of noncitizens are increasingly standardized across host polities. Further, the order in which rights are extended to guestworkers reverses T. H. Marshall's way of organizing rights historically, much reflecting the development of the global context of rights in the postwar period.

Entry and Residence: Protecting Membership

Citizenship in a nation-state is an exclusive status that confers on the individual rights and privileges within national boundaries. Nation-states try to protect this exclusive status through immigration and aliens' laws. Regulating population movements is considered elemental to the very existence of the modern nation-state system and to national sovereignty (Zolberg 1981). In principle, states have the right to refuse entry to citizens of other states, on the grounds of national security, public order, or public health (Niessen 1989). The major legal constraints on state action regarding population movements are imposed by international or bilateral treaties and arrangements. Such is the case with the European Community and the Common Nordic Labor Market,[1] under which nationals of the member states are free from restrictions regarding free movement and gainful activity. They hold a privileged position in terms of entry and residence rights. Similarly, international rules that apply to asylum seekers impose limitations on states' exercise of control over their national borders.[2]

For entry and residency, aliens generally need some form of permit or authorization, the granting of which depends primarily on the labor market, or on such human rights considerations as family reunification or political refugee status. Residence permits are initially given for temporary periods, usually one year, with the possibility of yearly extensions. Permanent residency (residency for an unlimited period) can be obtained after residing lawfully in the host country for a period of time, varying from two to ten years (see table 7.1). Political migrants, once granted refugee status, are entitled to unlimited residence and work permits (in Britain, Switzerland, and the United States, permanent residence is given after a certain period of time). Seasonal workers are normally excluded from residency rights. In Switzerland, seasonal workers become eligible for annual permits after working in the country for thirty-six

Table 7.1. Duration Required for Permanent Residency

Country	Duration
Austria	4 years (in effect, 6–10 years)
Belgium	5 years
Britain	4 years
Denmark	2 years
Germany	8 years
France	3 years
Netherlands	5 years
Sweden	2 years
Switzerland	10 years

Source: Niessen (1989:34).

Note: Other rules may apply to the citizens of the European Community or Common Nordic Labor Market countries.

months of the previous four years; until then, they are not allowed to bring their families or change jobs and residence.

Although guestworker programs were initially designed for single, temporary workers, family reunification for aliens is now an established right. Restriction of family immigration is generally viewed as an infraction of the basic rights of individuals. Throughout the 1970s, constitutional and administrative courts in many European countries repealed limitations on reunification (Hollifield 1992; O'Brien 1990).[3] The period of time family members have to wait before reunification differs among countries. "Family" refers to spouse and dependent children; however, in most countries, parents may be included on humanitarian grounds (see table 7.2). A sufficient income and suitable housing are required, especially for migrants with temporary residence, except in Denmark and Sweden. In the case of refugees, family reunification is given high priority.

A common feature in European immigration legislation has been its increasing restrictiveness. Since 1974, the formal end of labor migration in Europe, there have been two restrictive waves, one in the early 1980s (the Netherlands 1979; France 1980; Britain 1982), and the other by the end of the decade (Britain 1988; Germany 1990 and 1993; and France 1993).[4] Currently all western European countries formally prohibit economic migration, except for European Community citizens, seasonal workers, and people with special skills (e.g., man-

Table 7.2. Family Reunification Requirements

Country	Family Definition	Time Period
Austria	parents, spouse, children	no waiting period
Belgium	spouse and children	no waiting period
Britain	parents, spouse, children	no waiting period
Denmark	parents, spouse, children	no waiting period
Germany	spouse and children	no waiting period[a]
France	parents, spouse, children	1 year[b]
Netherlands	parents, spouse, children	no waiting period
Sweden	parents, spouse, children	no waiting period
Switzerland	spouse and children	1 year

Source: Niessen (1989:41).

Note: Other rules may apply to the citizens of the European Community or Common Nordic Labor Market countries.

[a]Since 1991.

[b]A government bill introduced in 1993 proposes a waiting period of 2 years.

agers of multinational companies, computer engineers, and other high-technology professionals).

However, measures that restrict entry coincide with a more secure legal status for resident foreigners. Since 1973, many European host states have introduced legislation guaranteeing the rights and status of migrants and their families. By the 1980s, well over half the foreigners in Europe already had permanent residency in their host countries—a virtually irrevocable status carrying with it varying rights and privileges of membership (Miller 1981).

Rights of Membership: Social, Economic, and Political

When the guestworker programs first began, migrants were conceived of as temporary, and their existence was defined by the constraints of economic cycles. Guestworkers were denied many of the basic civil rights, such as family unification, freedom of assembly and association, and freedom of movement.[5] The German Foreigners Law of 1965, for example, declared that "foreigners enjoy all basic rights, except the basic rights of freedom of assembly, freedom of association, freedom of movement and free choice of occupation, place of work and place of education, and protection from extradition abroad" (quoted in Castles 1985:522). The extension of rights to guest-

Table 7.3. Social Rights: Factors Determining Noncitizens' Access to Social Service Programs

Factor	Relative Significance
Physical presence	usually important
Legal status	usually important
Specific noncitizen status	sometimes important
Nation of origin	sometimes important
Passage of time	rarely important
Common-market citizenship	rarely important
Citizenship	rarely important

Source: Adapted from North, de Wenden, and Taylor (1987:5).
Note: Data for Austria, Belgium, Denmark, Switzerland, and the Netherlands come from my own research.

workers and the removal of statutory obstacles to equal status have occurred gradually (Layton-Henry 1990a). The first rights granted, early on, were trade-union and collective bargaining rights, and some social benefits. Other economic and social rights followed, not long after guestworkers had established themselves in the host countries. Since the 1980s, the extension of political rights, especially that of voting in local and, in some cases, even national elections has been on the agenda.

Tables 7.3 through 7.6 summarize the access of noncitizens to social, economic, and political rights. My analysis follows North, de Wenden, and Taylor (1987), who examine various factors that affect aliens' access to social programs in six Western countries and conclude that citizenship is not a significant factor determining eligibility for social services. The ten factors that they consider pertinent are the existence of a program, nature of service, zeal of enforcing eligibility, and passage of time, together with the foreigners' physical presence, legal status in the nation, specific noncitizen status, nation of origin, state or province of residence, and citizenship. Among these factors, my analysis concerns those listed in tables 7.3 and 7.4, which are directly related to the arguments developed in this chapter.[6]

The factors that determine noncitizens' access to social rights—such government programs as education in public schools, health benefits, and welfare and social insurance schemes—are listed in table 7.3. The foreigners' legal status and physical presence are the most important factors, whereas formal citizenship is the least. Being a common-market citizen does not make much difference, either. In other words, legal aliens have access to a set of social services almost identical to those available to citizens. In certain cases, even legal status is unnecessary. In the United States, for example, public education and certain social security pensions are available to all noncitizens, irrespective of their legal status. Similarly, U.S. medical programs for the elderly and disabled do not differentiate patients with regard to their immigration status (Schuck 1987). Moreover, a 1985 United States federal law requires general hospitals to treat all critically ill and emergency patients, including noncitizens, thus providing illegal migrants with limited access to health care.[7]

Residency is not always a requirement for social benefits, either. Migrants in certain states receive family allowances even for children who do not reside in the host country. Through bilateral arrangements, many host states pay retirement benefits to migrant workers even after they return to their country of origin (Austria and the United States are notable exceptions). Moreover, migrants who have earned benefits under national insurance schemes generally do not lose it by moving to a different country. Asylum seekers in western European countries are usually entitled to free housing, health benefits, education, and a small cash assistance while their application is pending, before achieving resident status. In many countries, after their refugee status is approved, migrants gain welfare and educational benefits equal to those of nationals.

Other factors may have a bearing on access to social rights. For certain social benefits, the migrant's specific noncitizen status (temporary or permanent residency) can make a difference. In Germany and Denmark, temporary residents have the right to receive welfare money, although doing so may result in a loss of the right of residence. Differences in welfare provisions may also depend on the nation of origin, when there are bilateral treaties between sending and host countries. Germany, for instance, has a preferential treatment agreement with Turkey, under which being unemployed or receiving welfare does not jeopardize Turkish migrants' resident status in Germany. Finally, the passage of time can be important to the dependents of migrants, who may be excluded from welfare benefits until they satisfy certain residency requirements, especially in the United States.

Overall, however, the array of social rights accorded to nationals are similarly extended to resident aliens. Even those with temporary permits have many social rights. Seasonal workers in Switzerland, for instance, can receive unemployment compensation (Hoffmann-Nowotny 1985).

Obviously, the substance of welfare rights differs considerably from country to country, reflecting variations in national social systems. Sweden's is the most comprehensive, while in Switzerland the welfare system is rather recent and less elaborate (Esping-Andersen 1990; Katzenstein 1980). Differences among national social systems make the availability of social provisions to migrants unequal across host countries. The more extensive the service structure, the more open it is to noncitizens. Once certain definitions and categories of social rights are created and institutionalized, it is hard to deny them, even to newcomers.

In regard to economic activity, the factors that determine migrants' access are closely related to immigration laws (see Brubaker 1989c and Plender 1987). As table 7.4 shows, a person's specific legal status as a noncitizen is the most important

Table 7.4. Economic Rights: Factors Determining Noncitizens' Access to Economic Activity and Labor Markets

	Relative Significance		
Factor	Civil Service	Professions and Trade	Labor Markets
Specific noncitizen status	—	almost always important	almost always important
Legal status	—	usually important	usually important
Common market citizenship	—	usually important	usually important
Nation of origin	—	sometimes important	sometimes important
Passage of time	—	sometimes important	sometimes important
Citizenship	almost always important	sometimes important	rarely important

Sources: Plender (1987); Brubaker (1989c); and my own research.

Table 7.5. Requirements for Work Permits

Country	Type of Permit	Unlimited Permission
Austria	specific occupation	after 8 years, no permit needed
Belgium	time/work limited	after 3 or 5 years
Britain	time/work limited	after 4 years, no permit needed
Denmark	time limited	after 2 years
Germany	time/work limited	after 8 years
France	included in residence	after 3 years, no permit needed
Netherlands	time/work limited	after 3 years
Sweden	time limited	after 2 years, no permit needed
Switzerland	included in residence	after 10 years

Source: Niessen (1989:51).

Note: Other rules apply to the citizens of the European Community or Common Nordic Labor Market countries.

one. Status categories, which are normally distinguished by details of work or residence permits, impose the principal constraints on migrants' exercise of economic rights. They determine the scope of noncitizens' engagement in professions and trades and their access to labor markets. This factor is also what most differentiates non-common-market migrants from nationals of the European and Nordic common markets, who are exempted from such restrictions at the outset. Migrants from non-common-market countries, after staying and/or working legally for a certain period of time, do not need work permits or become eligible for time-unlimited permits (see table 7.5). In Denmark, Switzerland, and Britain, dependents joining their families may not be allowed to work until after they have been in the country for a length of time. In 1991, Germany lifted all waiting requirements for dependents, except dependents of temporary residents, who have to wait for a year before being granted a work permit.

Constraints related to noncitizen status and waiting periods are designed to control the inflow of foreign labor. But, once migrants are in and established as legal permanent residents, they are entitled to take up any gainful activity. There may be some restrictions on the extent of their involvement in business—for example, in Sweden citizenship is required in order to start a company with shareholders. In most countries, however, after receiving permanent residency, noncitizens can start their own business. Thus, in terms of economic rights, credentials and the appropriate legal status count more than formal citizenship status.

A major exception is civil service employment, which is often reserved for citizens. In Canada, Denmark, and the United States, noncitizens may hold certain public service jobs; citizens have priority in Canada. Professions that involve public authority, such as being a judge or a lawyer, may not always be open to noncitizens, either. (Neither can they work as chimney sweeps in Germany, thanks to highly institutionalized rules dating back to the Imperial era, when mutual associations of privileged workers were modeled on the old guild system of membership.) Since European Community law requires the recognition of professional credentials regardless of where they were earned, restrictions on professional employment are gradually being eliminated, at least for Community nationals. Recent trends also indicate that more and more host countries are opening their civil service, military, and police force to aliens (e.g., Britain, the Netherlands, and the United States) and employing them as "contractual" members of public offices (in France, Germany, and the Netherlands; Plender 1987).[8]

Table 7.6 exhibits the political rights of noncitizens. For full participation in political activity, formal citizenship is crucial. None of the countries listed allow noncitizens to participate in national elections, except Britain, where Commonwealth and Irish Republic citizens have a special status. National voting rights for aliens are, in fact, very rare. New Zealand is the only country other than Britain where migrants (citizen or noncitizen) are allowed to vote in national parliamentary elections (Hammar 1985b).[9]

Local voting rights, on the other hand, were extended to noncitizens in the following countries, beginning in the 1970s.

Ireland	1973 (local, after 6 months' residence)
Sweden	1975 (local and regional, after 3 years' residence)
Denmark	1981 (local and regional, after 3 years' residence)
Norway	1983 (local, after 3 years' residence)
Netherlands	1983 (local, after 5 years' residence)

Table 7.6. Political Rights: Participation of Noncitizens in Various Forms of Political Activity

	National Elections	Local Elections	Alien Advisory Committees	Work Council and/or Union Elections
Denmark	no	yes	yes	yes
Netherlands	no	yes	yes	yes
Sweden	no	yes	yes	yes
Belgium	no	no	yes	yes
France	no	no	yes	yes
Austria	no	no	no	yes[a]
Germany	no	no	yes	yes
Switzerland	no	no[b]	yes	yes
Britain	no[c]	no[c]	yes	yes
Canada	no	no[d]	no	yes
United States	no	no	no	yes

Sources: Miller (1981, 1989), and my own research.

[a]Noncitizens are ineligible to stand for elections as shop stewards.

[b]Noncitizens may vote in the cantons of Jura and Neuchatel.

[c]Citizens of Commonwealth countries and the Republic of Ireland may vote after establishing residency in Britain.

[d]British and Commonwealth citizens may vote in some provinces.

Certain classes of aliens are entitled to vote in local elections in Spain and Portugal as well.

In Denmark and Sweden, noncitizens can vote and stand for office in both local and regional elections. In the Netherlands, this right applies only on the local level. Similarly, in Switzerland, the cantons of Neuchatel and Jura allow their noncitizen residents to vote and be elected locally. In Germany, the states of Berlin, Hamburg, and Schleswig-Holstein adopted bills allowing foreigners who have resided in Germany more than five years to vote in local elections. In 1990, however, the Federal Constitutional Court ruled local voting rights for foreigners unconstitutional, thus prohibiting the enactment of these bills. In other European countries, especially Belgium and France, local voting rights have been a topic of public debate since the 1980s, and such controversies gain momentum locally as the debate intensifies at the European Community level. Both the Commission of the European Community and the Council of Europe have endorsed resolutions to grant local voting rights to noncitizens (Reuter 1990). Sweden and the Netherlands have also considered extending the national franchise to foreigners, as advocated by the social democratic and other leftist parties, trade unions, and migrant associations (Rath 1990).

Still, the main avenues of political participation for noncitizens are indirect ones—foreigners' advisory committees, national and local, and unions and work councils in the workplace.[10] With the exceptions of Canada and the United States, all of the countries included in this study have some form of consultative arrangement for noncitizens. The role, functioning, perception, and reception of such arrangements are by no means uniform across countries (see table 5.3).

Finally, noncitizens are entitled to full civil rights, as guaranteed either by constitutions (as in Canada, the Netherlands, and Sweden) or by statutory extension to foreigners. Article 1 of the Dutch constitution declares that fundamental rights do not differ according to nationality; foreigners have an equal claim to basic constitutional rights (Swart 1987). The Swedish constitution includes similar provisions. The German Basic Law and the Belgian constitution define most rights and freedoms as equal for everyone, citizens and foreigners alike (Hammar 1990b). In all of the countries under study, noncitizens are granted equality before the law and have full legal rights, including those of due process and appeal. The right to appeal may also cover decrees of deportation and expulsion, although, in Britain filing an appeal does not postpone the decision itself. In general, noncitizens may acquire property on an equal footing with citizens; in Canada, Denmark, Switzerland, and Sweden, a special permit is needed to buy real estate unless the person has resided in the country for a certain period of time. Foreigners enjoy freedom of religion, expression, assembly, and association, though sometimes constrained by "national security" considerations.[11] They can participate in public affairs and politics by setting up or joining organizations that promote their collective interests and demands, such as migrant associations, trade unions, and political parties. This is significant when we consider that, until as recently as the mid-1950s, foreigners in most European countries were not allowed to take part in any political activity (Hammar 1990b).

In 1965, the first Foreigners Law that the Federal Republic of Germany instituted after the Nazi period specifically excluded noncitizens from all domains of civil rights. Similarly, until the 1980s, both France and Belgium restricted the associational rights of foreigners. These restrictions have gradually been revoked in accordance with international human rights standards as well as domestic constitutional principles.[12]

Membership of Guestworkers

Contrary to what the national model of citizenship projects, it is no longer a simple task to differentiate permanent noncitizen residents of Western nation-states in terms of the rights and privileges they hold. This is more and more the case even for temporary residents, particularly with regard to civil and social rights. Although nation-states still protect their membership by controlling the inflow of foreigners, an expanding range of rights and privileges is being granted to the migrants, blurring the line between citizen and noncitizen.

My discussion is confined to membership rights, but foreigners are clearly incorporated into the duties of citizenship as well. They are obliged to perform the most basic duties—being lawful, respecting other people's rights and public property, paying taxes, "properly" raising and complying with the compulsory education of children, and so on. They are excused from one special form of duty, namely, loyalty to the state demonstrated through military service, although the meaning and practice of this duty is frequently contested by citizens themselves.

Let me now highlight two crucial points regarding the incorporation of guestworkers into the rights of membership. First, the order in which rights are extended to guestworkers challenges Marshall's (1964) theory of the formation of citizenship. According to Marshall's model, based on his reading of the British case, rights are extended in stages to members of social entities that had previously been excluded from the polity, thus gradually transforming them into citizens. Marshall argues that citizenship rights evolve sequentially: civil, then political, then social. In Marshall's framework, each step is a prerequisite for the next set of rights (Giddens 1985:198–

221). The eighteenth century witnessed the formation of civil rights and liberties of the individual. Civil liberties were, in turn, "the necessary foundation for the emergence of political rights [in the nineteenth and the early twentieth centuries]; for only if the individual is recognized as an autonomous agent does it become reasonable to regard that individual as politically responsible" (Giddens 1985:203). Consequently, the advancement of political rights, especially universal franchise, enabled the organized working class to achieve welfare and social rights in the twentieth century.[13]

In the case of guestworkers, the acquisition of membership rights reverses the Marshallian sequence. According to Marshall's model, political rights precede, and are instrumental in securing, social rights. In fact, however, economic and social rights were the first ones to be fully granted to migrant workers in European host countries. Political rights became part of the agenda much later. In general, host states find it much harder to deny social and civil rights—those directly linked to the person, such as individual liberties and a minimum standard of living—to new groups of people, even if they do not belong to the formal national polity. The right to vote, which has more to do with the national collectivity, still carries a symbolic meaning in terms of national sovereignty. Thus it is more strictly protected, and largely reserved for nationals. Since political rights, as enacted in the principles of suffrage and popular sovereignty, were codified at a time when the nation-state was at its ideological apex, they came to be equated exclusively with national citizenship. The notion of social rights, on the other hand, emerged in the twentieth century, when most Western states had already completed their nation-building process. Social rights are hence more expandable, both in scope and content, and are less exclusive than political rights.

My second point has to do with the trend toward international standardization of the rights and status of noncitizens. Not only does the array of rights improve over time, but also the categories of populations that they cover expand. Even illegal workers are granted the right to appeal deportation, to be treated humanely, and, in the United States, to receive education and some social services. Furthermore, host countries tend to regularize the status of illegal aliens through official amnesties, rather than expel them. For example, Belgium regularized 12,000 illegals in 1974; the Netherlands, 15,000 in 1975; France, 140,000 in 1981; Spain, 44,000 in 1986 and 104,000 in 1991; Italy, 118,000 in 1988; and, the United States, about 3 million in 1989 (SOPEMI 1989, 1992).[14] In France, periodic amnesties have come to be regarded as a right, de Wenden (1990) points out, which has resulted in several political campaigns and strikes since the 1970s. Moreover, Carens (1989) asserts that regularization of illegal aliens manifests an implicit recognition of claims to membership, legal status notwithstanding. The changing status of illegal residents is also reflected in the vocabulary used to refer to them. Such terms as *undocumented immigrants* or *irregular aliens* have come to replace *illegals* or *clandestines,* "focusing on the situational context, rather than on the individual migrant" (Niessen 1989:57).

All of these changes testify to the decreasing importance of formal citizenship status in determining the rights and privileges of migrants in host polities. Formal citizenship is not a prerequisite for granting individuals many rights and duties with respect to the national polity and the state. In ascendance, rather, is the well-defined category and status of the individual migrant with rights and entitlements independent of national citizenship.

This trend is the more striking when we compare the status of contemporary migrants with that of migrants at the turn of the century. Although this book cannot give a complete account of the status of those earlier migrants, even a cursory look can be telling. For one thing, deportation was much more common; foreigners could be deported because they were sick, or poor, or because their presence jeopardized perceived national interests; in short, they were deprived of most basic rights (Hammar 1990a). Poles who worked in Germany during the nineteenth century, mainly in agriculture and the mines, had "low wages, . . . no claim to poor relief, and could be deported for the slightest insubordination" (Burgdörfer 1931, quoted in Rhoades 1978:556). In 1886, at the height of Bismarckian efforts to build the national state, 30,000 Polish workers were expelled. By 1890, to prevent their permanent settlement, the German authorities forced Polish workers to report to the police and only allowed them to stay during the agricultural work season (Dohse 1981). In 1908, a law was introduced in the Ruhr region forbidding public use of the Polish language (Castles and Kosack 1973). Compare this with current policy trends that emphasize the right to one's own language and provide for instruction in the mother-tongue.

In France, an 1890 law aimed at guarding against accidents in the workplace applied only to French nationals, excluding large numbers of industrial workers from Belgium (Silverman 1991). During the First World War, workers recruited from China and Algeria were organized and supervised in "military fashion" by the French colonial office (Singer-Kérel 1991:285). During the same period, the recruitment of industrial labor from the southern European countries of Italy, Portugal, and Spain involved contracts between France and the sending countries that entailed equal wages, insurance against accidents, and medical treatment for the workers. Even then, a 1917 government decree required the workers to carry special identity cards in order to ensure strict police control (Singer-Kérel 1991). In 1935, the French government passed a law limiting foreigners' mobility and settlement without official permission. However, in the postwar era, similar measures enacted in various host countries were rescinded by court decision.

In the United States, where immigration is glorified as part of the national myth, restrictive legislation targeting migratory groups was quite customary. Between 1850 and 1920 a series of laws regarding employment, civil rights, and education were enacted to define specific populations as "outside" the polity:

- In 1850, a foreign miners' tax required all miners who were not native-born citizens of the United States to pay a tax of $20 a month in order to work in the mines.
- In 1860, by a California Statute, Asian immigrants were barred from the public school system.
- In 1870, a Peddling Ordinance prohibited persons from walking on the sidewalk while carrying baskets suspended from poles across their shoulders.
- In 1879, Chinese were prohibited from employment in state, city, county, municipal, and other public works.

- In 1906, a California law prohibited Chinese from marrying whites (declared void in 1948).
- In 1913, by the Alien Land Act, aliens were forbidden to own real estate (declared void in 1947).
- In 1924, Chinese wives of American citizens were declared ineligible to enter the United States. (Wong 1978:183–87)

Obviously, the rights of Chinese immigrants differed from those of white immigrants, who were eligible for naturalization and were expected to assimilate through public schools and labor markets (Brumberg 1986). But this is exactly my point: certain immigrant groups who were categorically defined as aliens were not entitled to the rights that they are accorded today. In the classical immigration model, states either accepted foreigners as "future citizens," and made efforts to mold them along with the rest of the national population, or dubbed them "foreigners" and left them out. Although contemporary migrants are also defined as foreign, as is shown in chapter 2, unlike their earlier counterparts, they are incorporated into the host country's system of membership rights and privileges. As "incorporated foreigners," international migrants constitute a legitimate category addressed by a wide array of organizational and administrative structures, state instruments, and budgets.

With these observations, I do not mean to project an evolutionary scheme for the expansion of membership rights—one similar to Marshall's sequence of citizenship rights, but reordered. The development of migrants' rights does not display an immanent linear progressive (or regressive) logic. The rights of noncitizens, as well as citizens, can be contested and undermined by various sets of political and economic factors, as history has witnessed. In response to the global recession of the 1990s, many Western states have moved to cut the range and disbursement of social benefits, among them, Sweden and Germany, the states with the largest welfare budgets in Europe. Furthermore, the existence of a complex of legal rights and privileges may not dissolve discrimination and empirical inequalities. There is always an "implementation deficit,"[15] a discrepancy between formal rights and their praxis. Various market and social indicators consistently show discrimination against migrant workers and their families, but also against citizens of the polity who happened to be women or people of color.

Though empirical inequalities of race, gender, and class persist, the existence of formally encoded rights has rendered the unequivocal exclusion of migrants from membership unjustifiable and unsustainable (cf. Turner 1986a). The transformation of "national" rights into more universalistic entitlements that include noncitizens undermines the categorical dichotomies patterned after the national citizenship model. Yet, ironically, as guestworkers are increasingly incorporated into the membership schemes of European host polities, the debate over how well they "adjust" intensifies, and their cultural otherness is accentuated. Guestworkers become *symbolic* foreigners.

CHAPTER EIGHT

Toward a Postnational Model of Membership

In the preceding chapters I discussed the membership status of guestworkers in Western nation-states, concluding that, even without formal citizenship status, they are incorporated into various legal and organizational structures of the host society. In this chapter, reflecting upon guestworker membership, I analyze the changing structure and meaning of citizenship in the contemporary world. I introduce a new model of membership, the main thrust of which is that individual rights, historically defined on the basis of nationality, are increasingly codified into a different scheme that emphasizes universal personhood. I formalize the model by comparing it with the national model of citizenship and specifying its distinctive elements. The articulation of this model sets the stage for the further elaboration of dualities in the rules of the postwar global system, which, while insisting on the nation-state and its sovereignty, at the same time, legitimate a new form of membership that transcends the boundaries of the nation-state.

Guestworkers and Citizenship: Old Concepts, New Formations

The postwar era is characterized by a reconfiguration of citizenship from a more particularistic one based on nationhood to a more universalistic one based on personhood. Historically, citizenship and its rights and privileges have expanded in waves, with changes in how the national public is defined in relation to class, gender, and age (Marshall 1964; Ramirez 1989; Turner 1986a, 1986b). Each wave has represented the entry of a new segment of population into the national polity; workers, women, and children were eventually included in the definition of citizenship.[1] This universalizing movement has made exclusions based on any criteria of ascribed status incompatible with the institution of citizenship (Turner 1986a:92–100). The expansion, however, was limited from within: the rights of men, women, and children, as individuals, were defined with respect to their membership in a particular nation-state. In that sense, the expansion of rights protracted and reinforced particularities ordained by national attributes. In contrast, in the postwar era, an intensified discourse of personhood and human rights has rent the bounded universality of national citizenship, generating contiguities beyond the limits of national citizenry. Accordingly, contemporary membership formations have superseded the dichotomy that opposes the national citizen and the alien, by including populations that were previously defined as outside the national polity. Rights that used to belong solely to nationals are now extended to foreign populations, thereby undermining the very basis of national citizenship. This transformation requires a new understanding of citizenship and its foundation.

Recent studies recognize the disparity between the national citizenship model and the membership of postwar migrants in European host countries. Tomas Hammar (1986, 1990a), for instance, argues that foreigners who are long-term residents of European states, and who possess substantial rights and privileges, should be given a new classification, and suggests the term *denizen.* In the same vein, Brubaker (1989a, 1989c) maintains that the membership forms generated by postwar immigration deviate from the norms of classical nation-state membership, which he views as "egalitarian, sacred, national, democratic, unique, and socially consequential." In acknowledging these deviations, he offers a model of "dual membership" organized as concentric circles: an inner circle of citizenship, based on nationality, and an outer circle of denizenship, based on residency. Both Hammar and Brubaker contend that, in regard to rights of immigrants, the crucial determinant is residence, not citizenship. Similar versions of the denizen model have been discussed in Heisler and Heisler 1990, Layton-Henry 1990c, Fullinwider 1988, and d'Oliveira 1984.

Heisler and Heisler (1990) attribute the emergence of the denizenship status to the existence of a "mature" welfare state. They suggest that the elaborate redistribution machinery and the "ethos of equality" of the welfare state have led to the widening of the scope of citizenship in European societies. As I showed in chapters 4 and 5, states of Europe have indeed expanded their comprehensive welfare apparatuses to guestworkers and their families. However, there is nothing inherent about the logic of the welfare state that would dictate the incorporation of foreigners into its system of privileges. Welfare states are also conceived as "compelled by their logic to be closed systems that seek to insulate themselves from external pressures and that restrict rights and benefits to members" (Freeman 1986:51; see also Leibfried 1990). Not that this logic of closure is empirically realized in the world of welfare states. Many of the most advanced welfare states, especially those that are small in size and trade-dependent, have open economies that operate as part of an increasingly integrated global economy (Katzenstein 1985; Cameron 1978).[2] Nevertheless, welfare states are expected to operate with the assumption of closure: the effective distribution of welfare among citizens and maintenance of high standards of benefits and services require the exclusion of noncitizens (see Schuck and Smith

1985; Walzer 1983). As such, the welfare state is universal only within national boundaries.

The denizenship model depicts changes in citizenship as an expansion of scope on a *territorial* basis: the principle of domicile augments the principle of nationality. Denizens acquire certain membership rights by virtue of living and working in host countries. Within this framework, denizenship becomes an irregularity for the nation-state and its citizenry, that should be corrected in the long-run (see Heisler and Heisler 1990, and the articles in Brubaker 1989 and Layton-Henry 1990).

In construing changes in citizenship as territorial, these studies remain within the confines of the nation-state model. They do not recognize the changing basis and legitimacy of membership or the recent, fundamental changes in the relationship between the individual, the nation-state, and the world order. As I see it, the incorporation of guestworkers is no mere expansion of the scope of national citizenship, nor is it an irregularity. Rather, it reveals a profound transformation in the institution of citizenship, both in its institutional logic and in the way it is legitimated. To locate the changes, we need to go beyond the nation-state.

A Model for Postnational Membership

This section introduces a model of membership that delineates the contemporary restructuring and reconfiguration of citizenship. The summary in table 8.1 compares this model, which I call *postnational,* with the classical model of national citizenship as conceptualized in political sociology. The two models differ in various dimensions, some of which are mentioned in the discussion of guestworker membership in chapter 7. A comparative discussion, in terms of each dimension, follows.

Time Period

The modern history of citizenship begins with the French Revolution. Although the idea of national citizenship emerged at the time of the Revolution, the realization of this particular form of membership occurred much later. Only quite recently has national citizenship become a powerful construct. The

Table 8.1. Comparison of National and Postnational Models of Membership

Dimension	Model I: National Citizenship	Model II: Postnational Membership
Time period	19th to mid-20th centuries	Postwar
Territorial	Nation-state bounded	Fluid boundaries
Congruence between membership and territory	Identical	Distinct
Rights/privileges	Single status	Multiple status
Basis of membership	Shared nationhood (national rights)	Universal personhood (human rights)
Source of legitimacy	Nation-state	Transnational community
Organization of membership	Nation-state	Nation-state

classical instruments for creating a national citizenry, the first compulsory education laws and universal (male) suffrage acts, were not enacted before the mid-nineteenth century (Ramirez and Soysal 1989; Soysal and Strang 1989). Moreover, construction of the dichotomy between national citizens and aliens, through the first immigration and alien acts, and made visible in the introduction of passports, identity cards, and visas, did not take place until as late as the First World War.[3]

The reconfiguration of citizenship is mainly a postwar phenomenon. Even as the nation-state and its membership became authorized and taken-for-granted, its classificatory premises were beginning to be contested. By the 1960s, the classical model of nation-state membership was loosening its grip on the Western world, while consolidation of national polity and citizenship was an impassioned item on the agenda of many countries in Africa and Asia. The increasing flow of goods and persons and the large magnitude of labor migrations after World War II have facilitated this process.

Territorial Dimension

The classical model is nation-state bounded. Citizenship entails a territorial relationship between the individual and the state (Bendix 1977; Weber 1978). It postulates well-defined, exclusionary boundaries and state jurisdiction over the national population within those boundaries. The model thus implies a congruence between membership and territory: only French nationals are entitled to the rights and privileges the French state affords—nobody else.

In the postnational model, the boundaries of membership are fluid; a Turkish guestworker can become a member of the French polity without French citizenship. By holding citizenship in one state while living and enjoying rights and privileges in a different state, guestworkers violate the presumed congruence between membership and territory. The growing number of dual nationality acquisitions further formalizes the fluidity of membership.[4]

The fluid boundaries of membership do not necessarily mean that the boundaries of the nation-state are fluid. Neither does it imply that the nation-state is less predominant than before.[5] Indeed, the nation-states, still acting upon the national model—since their existence is predicated on this model—constantly try to keep out foreigners by issuing new aliens laws and adopting restrictive immigration policies. However, these continued attempts testify that European states have not succeeded in controlling the influx of foreigners. In particular, such measures have failed to prevent migratory flows justified on humanitarian grounds—political asylum and family unification, two major sources of persisting immigration to European countries discussed in chapter 2.

Rights and Privileges

The classic order of nation-states expresses formal equality in the sense of uniform citizenship rights. Citizenship assumes a single status; all citizens are entitled to the same rights and privileges. The postnational model, on the other hand, implies multiplicity of membership—a principal organizational form for empires and city states. As we have seen in the case of guestworkers, the distribution of rights among various groups and citizens is not even. In the emerging European system, certain groups of migrants are more privileged than others: legal permanent residents, political refugees, dual citizens, and nationals of common market countries.[6]

In earlier polities, multiplicity of membership was also a given, but inequality was considered a "natural" characteristic of social order. Differential membership status, such as that of slaves, was thus constructed as part of the formal definition of the polity. Modern polities, however, claim a uniform and universal status for individuals. As Turner (1986a:133) comments, in the modern polity "the particularistic criteria which define the person become increasingly irrelevant in the public sphere." What makes the case of the guestworker controversial is that it violates this claim for unitary status.[7] Rendering differential status unjustifiable within the framework of universalistic personhood, the modern polity encourages a climate for diverse claims to and further expansion of rights.

Basis and Legitimation of Membership

In the classical model, shared nationality is the main source of equal treatment among members. Citizenship invests individuals with equal rights and obligations on the grounds of shared nationhood. In that sense, the basis of legitimacy for individual rights is located within the nation-state.

However, guestworker experience shows that membership and the rights it entails are not necessarily based on the criterion of nationality. In the postnational model, universal personhood replaces nationhood; and universal human rights replace national rights. The justification for the state's obligations to foreign populations goes beyond the nation-state itself. The rights and claims of individuals are legitimated by ideologies grounded in a transnational community, through international codes, conventions, and laws on human rights, independent of their citizenship in a nation-state. Hence, the individual transcends the citizen. This is the most elemental way that the postnational model differs from the national model.

Universal personhood as the basis of membership comes across most clearly in the case of political refugees, whose status in host polities rests exclusively on an appeal to human rights. Refugees are in essence stateless (some carry a United Nations passport) but are nonetheless still protected and granted rights as individuals.[8] Similarly, the most universalized aspects of citizenship are those immediately related to the person—civil and social rights—which are often the subject of international conventions and discourse. These rights are more commonly secured in international codes and laws, and they permeate national boundaries more easily than universal political rights that still imply a referential proximity to national citizenship.

Organization of Membership

While the basis and legitimation of membership rights have shifted to a transnational level, membership itself is not really organized in a new scheme. In both models, the responsibility of providing and implementing individual rights lies with national states. In other words, one still has to go through, for instance, the German, British, or French welfare system. The state is the immediate guarantor and provider, though now for "every person" living within its borders, noncitizen as well as citizen. Actually, the very transnational normative system that legitimizes universal personhood as the basis of membership also designates the nation-state as the primary unit for dispensing rights and privileges (Meyer 1980).

This is critical to explaining why residency in a state is consequential in securing various rights. The world is still largely organized on the basis of spatially configured political units; and topographic matrixes still inform the models and praxis of national and international actors. Hence the nation-state remains the central structure regulating access to social distribution. The material realization of individual rights and privileges is primarily organized by the nation-state, although the legitimacy for these rights now lies in a transnational order.

Transnational Sources of Membership

How can we account for the manifest changes in national citizenship, that celebrated and stubborn construction of the modern era? As it stands, postnational membership derives its force and legitimacy from changes in the transnational order that defines the rules and organization of the nation-state system. I regard two interrelated lines of development as crucial in explaining the reconfiguration of citizenship.

The first one concerns a transformation in the organization of the international state system: an increasing interdependence and connectedness, intensified world-level interaction and organizing, and the emergence of transnational political structures, which altogether confound and complicate nation-state sovereignty and jurisdiction (Abu-Lughod 1989a, 1989b; Boli 1993; Meyer 1980; Robertson 1992). I refer not only to growth in the volume of transactions and interactions, which, in relative terms, has not changed significantly over the last century (Thomson and Krasner 1989). More important are qualitative changes in the intensity of these interactions, and their perception by the parties involved.

In the postwar era, many aspects of the public domain that used to be the exclusive preserve of the nation-state have become legitimate concerns of international discourse and action. The case of guestworkers clearly demonstrates this shift. The host states no longer have sole control over migrant populations. The governments of the sending countries and extranational organizations of various kinds also hold claims vis-à-vis these populations, in regard to their lives, education, welfare, family relations, and political activities.[9] A dense set of interactions facilitated by inter- and transnational market and security arrangements (NATO, the EC, and the UN system) constrain the host states from dispensing with their migrant populations at will. In fact, this system not only delegitimizes host state actions that attempt to dispense with foreigners; it obliges the state to protect them.

This is a different picture than that of nineteenth-century conceptions of the international system, which assume a world of discrete nation-states with exclusive sovereignty over territory and population. In the postwar period, the nation-state as a formal organizational structure is increasingly decoupled from the locus of legitimacy, which has shifted to the global level, transcending territorialized identities and structures. In this new order of sovereignty, the larger system assumes the role of defining rules and principles, charging nation-states with the responsibility to uphold them (Meyer 1980, 1994). Nation-states remain the primary agents of public functions, but the nature and parameters of these functions are increasingly determined at the global level.

The intensification and connectedness of the global system do not necessarily signal that nation-states are organizationally weaker or that their formal sovereignty is questioned. Rather, it refers to the explicitness of global rules and structures, and the increasing invocation of these rules. In that sense, nation-states, as authorized actors, function concurrently with inter- and transnational normative structures, ordering and organizing individuals' lives.

The second major development is the emergence of universalistic rules and conceptions regarding the rights of the individual, which are formalized and legitimated by a multitude of international codes and laws. International conventions and charters ascribe universal rights to persons regardless of their membership status in a nation-state. They oblige nation-states *not* to make distinctions on the grounds of nationality in granting civil, social, and political rights. The Universal Declaration of Human Rights (1948) unequivocally asserts that "all beings are born free and equal in dignity and rights, independent of their race, color, national or ethnic origin." The International Covenant on Civil and Political Rights (1966) further imposes a responsibility on the state to respect and ensure the rights of "all individuals within its territory and subject to its jurisdiction" (Goodwin-Gill, Jenny, and Perruchoud 1985:558). The European Convention on Human Rights (1950) expounds almost identical provisions, with further protection against the collective expulsion of aliens. Both the Universal Declaration of Human Rights and the European Convention have been incorporated into the constitutions and laws of many countries.[10]

In addition to these principal codes of human rights, many aspects of international migration, including the status of migrant workers and their particular rights, have been elaborated and regularized through a complex of international treaties, conventions, charters, and recommendations. Some of these instruments originated in the early 1950s, at the onset of large-scale labor migration. Over time, their span has expanded to include entry and residence, the rights to choice and security of employment, working conditions, vocational training and guidance, trade-union and collective bargaining rights, social security, family reunification, education of migrant children, and associative and participatory rights, as well as individual and collective freedoms. These conventions differ in scope. Some have universal application; others are country-specific. Nonetheless, they all aim to set standards for the "equitable" treatment of migrants and the elimination of disparities between nationals and migrants of different categories.

The conventions concluded under the aegis of the International Labor Office (ILO) and the Council of Europe are especially noteworthy.[11] According to the ILO Convention of 1949, the contracting states agree to treat migrant workers "without discrimination in respect of nationality, race, religion, or sex" regarding employment, conditions of work, trade union membership, collective bargaining, and accommodation (ILO n.d.:2). The 1975 convention goes further, promoting the social and cultural rights of migrant workers and their families, in addition to provisions strictly concerned with labor. It explicitly states that the participating countries will take all steps to assist migrant workers and their families "to maintain their own culture" and to provide for their children "to learn their own mother tongue" (ILO 1986:7).

In a similar vein, the 1955 Convention of the European Council on Establishment requires the contracting parties "to treat the nationals of the other contracting states on a basis of equality and to secure for them the enjoyment of civil rights . . . [and] the same economic rights as are possessed by nationals of the state in which the alien is established" (Plender 1985:3). Later conventions of the Council (1961, 1977) introduce provisions regarding freedom of association and information, residence and work permits, social security, social and medical assistance, and family reunification. More recently, the Council has given priority to extending the lists of individuals' rights, specifically to include further rights in the cultural and political spheres. The Council organizes meetings and conferences to promote cultural rights and make national and local authorities aware of "specifities" of minorities, both native and foreign.

More generally, the United Nations has produced a series of instruments with implications for international migration and migrants. The UNESCO Declaration on Race and Racial Prejudice (1978) extends provisions for the cultural rights of migrants—the right to be different, to have one's cultural values respected, and to receive instruction in one's mother tongue. The United Nations convention on the Protection of the Rights of All Migrant Workers and Their Families, adopted in 1990, aims to establish universal standards that transcend national definitions of foreigners' status. The convention guarantees minimum rights to every migrant, including women and undocumented aliens and their families (see *International Migration Review* 1991). In doing so, it constructs the category of "migrant worker," including such subcategories as "seasonal worker" and "frontier worker," as a universal status with legitimate rights. The ILO and the European Council also have provisions dealing specifically with illegal aliens and their protection (Niessen 1989).

Lastly, political refugees are protected by a set of international legal instruments designed to ensure their rights. According to the Geneva Convention on the Legal Status of Refugees (1951), persons shall not be forced to return to their country of origin if they have a "well-founded fear of persecution" for reasons of race, religion, nationality, membership of a particular social group or political opinion. The Convention further guarantees treatment in the country of asylum equal with that of nationals in regard to religious freedom, acquisition of property, rights of association, and access to courts and public education (Plender 1985).

The multitude and scope of these instruments are impressive. The rights defined and codified assure not just the economic, civil, and social rights of individual migrants—membership rights, in Marshall's terms—but also the cultural rights of migrant groups as collectivities. Within this context, the collective rights of foreigners—the right to an ethnic identity, culture, and use of one's native tongue—emerge as a locus of international legal action.[12] Appendix C provides a selected list of the conventions applicable to international migrants,[13] and appendix D cites the inter- and nongovernmental organizations that deal with them.

The most comprehensive legal enactment of a transnational status for migrants is encoded in European Communities law. Citizenship in one EC member state confers rights in all of the others, thereby breaking the link between the status attached to citizenship and national territory. The provisions specify a migrant regime under which European Community citizens are entitled to equal status and treatment with the nationals of the host country. The basic tenets of this regime are as follows:

- Citizens of member states have the right to free movement, gainful employment, and residence within the boundaries of the Community.
- Community law prohibits discrimination based on nationality among workers of the member states with regard to employment, social security, trade union rights, living and working conditions, and education and vocational training.
- Community law obliges host states to facilitate teaching of the language and culture of the countries of origin within the framework of normal education and in collaboration with those countries.
- The Commission of the European Community recommends full political rights in the long run for Community citizens living in other member states. Under current arrangements, they have the right to vote and stand as candidates in local and European elections.[14]

These rights are protected by a growing body of directives, regulations, and laws that locates them within a human rights context (Commission of the European Communities 1989b). Moreover, the 1991 Maastricht treaty has created the status of citizen of the Community, to "strengthen the protection of the rights and interests of the nationals of its member states." The treaty foresees a multilevel citizenship structure that guarantees rights independently of membership in a particular state. Thus, the Community as a supranational organization establishes a direct relationship with individuals in the member nation-states. As such, "European citizenship" clearly embodies postnational membership in its most elaborate legal form. It is a citizenship whose legal and normative bases are located in the wider community, and whose actual implementation is assigned to the member states.

At the present, the new Community citizenship and the free-movement provision do not apply to nationals of non-EC countries, who constitute the majority of the migrant populations in Europe. For non-EC migrants, the Community has issued guidelines toward the equalization of their status with that of nationals of EC countries. In 1989, for example, the Community adopted the Charter of the Fundamental Rights of Workers, which requires the member states to guarantee workers and their families from non-member countries living and working conditions comparable to those of EC nationals. More directly, with its authority to engage in international treaties, the Community has made agreements with several non-EC sending countries. These bilateral agreements incorporate the rights of non-EC foreign workers into the legal framework of the Community with provisions in regard to social security, working conditions, and wages, under which workers and their families from signing countries can claim benefits on equal terms with community citizens (Callovi 1992).[15]

My intention in citing all of these instruments and regimes is to draw attention to the proliferation of transnational arrangements, grounded in human rights discourse, that address the rights and interests of migrants and refugees. These instruments and regimes provide guidelines as to the management of migrant affairs for national legislation, by standardizing and rationalizing the category and status of the international migrant. Like other transnational instruments, the charters and conventions regarding guestworkers do not for the most part entail formal obligations or enforceable rules. This does not mean that they do not effect binding dispositions. By setting norms, framing discourses, and engineering legal categories and legitimate models, they enjoin obligations on nation-states to take action. They define goals and levels of competence, and compel nation-states to achieve specific standards. They form a basis for the claims of migrants shaping the platforms of migrant organizations as well as other public interests. They generate transnational activity and stir up publicity regarding migrant issues.

One of the ways international instruments affect nation-state action on migrants is through the construction of migrants as a legal category. Statutes on aliens, migrant workers, and refugees, which entitle migrants to claim legal protection on the basis of human rights, are now established branches of international law (Perruchoud 1986). In the case of the European Community and the European Council, extragovernmental bodies have been established, to interpret and give meaning to international codes and laws, thereby both constraining and enabling nation-state jurisdiction in many ways. One such example is the European Court of Human Rights. According to the European Convention of Human Rights, individual citizens of the European Council countries, as well as nongovernmental organizations or groups, can appeal directly to the European Court, whose decisions are binding on member states. In the last two decades, the caseload of the European Court has increased drastically, with some 5,500 complaints filed each year (Lester 1993). The Court has given a significant number of rulings on individual rights in recent years, including decisions on immigration and family unification.

Corresponding to this growth in the activity of the European Court, national courts increasingly invoke the European Human Rights Convention. The resulting panoply of human rights arrangements generates interesting cases. For example, in 1992, a Sudanese political refugee in Germany fled to Britain for asylum, fearing racial persecution in Germany. The British government decided to send him back to Germany, his first port of entry; however, a British high-court judge ordered the government to halt the deportation in accord with the European Convention on Human Rights, acknowledging that in Germany he might be in danger of attack by neo-Nazis (*The Economist,* 15 February 1992). In an earlier case, some East-African Asians, by appealing to the European Convention of Human Rights, were able to contest their exclusion from the United Kingdom under the 1968 Commonwealth Immigrants Act, which subjected the populations from the New Commonwealth to immigration controls (Plender 1986). Thereby, an international human rights instrument superseded the decision of the British Parliament.

The Court of Justice of the European Community, another supranational legal arrangement, oversees individual or state-level complaints that fall within Community Law. The Court has the task of harmonizing national laws with those of the Community. Fourteen percent of the cases brought before the European Court of Justice between 1953 and 1986 were related to the free movement of workers and their dependents, the right of abode and work, and other social issues (Commission of the European Communities 1987). The European Convention on Human Rights has been cited frequently by the Court of Justice in elaborating the general principles of Community Law and making decisions (Brown and McBride 1981).

In addition to their effect in the realm of legal rights, transnational laws, rules, conventions, and recommendations also directly influence nation-state policy and action. Let me cite some examples to illustrate this point. The inspiration for foreigners' assemblies and advisory councils came from a directive of the fifth session of the European Conference on Local Powers in 1964 (Sica 1977). Acting upon this directive, European host governments established several such assemblies and councils between 1968 and 1978 (Miller 1981). In creating specialized social service centers for migrants, the EC Commission's recommendation of 1962 constituted the basis upon which many national governments acted (Dumon 1977). In the early 1970s, the participation rights for foreigners in the workplace were mainly introduced by the expansion of the European Community law and practice. Similarly, the European Community General Directive on Education of Migrant Workers (1977) afforded a backdrop for national provisions for teaching migrant children their own language and culture. In collaboration with sending countries, many European host states have established arrangements for such instruction.

Existing national policies are also sometimes revised in response to transnational instruments. In Sweden, limitations on the political activity of aliens were rescinded in 1954 as an effect of the European Convention on Human Rights and Fundamental Freedoms (Hammar 1985c). Similarly, in 1985 the Austrian Supreme Court ruled the Foreigners Police Law unconstitutional, "since it did not accord with Article 8 of the European Convention on Human Rights, . . . interfering with private and family life" of migrants (Bauböck and Wimmer 1988:664). This decision resulted in an amendment of the law, requiring the foreigners police to take into account an individual's family situation and length of residence before making a decision about deportation.

All of these examples substantiate the impact of transnational instruments in the rationalization of the status of international migrant. Migrants' rights increasingly expand within the domain of human rights, supported by a growing number of transnational networks and institutions. The crucial point is that this intensified transnational modus operandi very much determines the discourse of membership and rights on the national level. The universalistic conceptions of rights and personhood become formally institutionalized norms through the agency of an array of collectivities—international governmental and nongovernmental organizations, legal institutions, networks of experts, and scientific communities. These collectivities, by advising national governments, enforcing legal categories, crafting models and standards, and producing reports and recommendations, promote and diffuse ideas and norms about universal human rights that in turn engenders a commanding discourse on membership.[16] The same discourse is adopted by states, organizations, and individuals in granting and claiming rights and privileges, thereby reenacting the transnational discourse.

Human rights discourse is widely evoked in national policy language and government rhetoric pertaining to the rights of international migrants. As Catherine de Wenden remarks, since 1981, French immigration policies have been transformed from "a mere body of laws dealing with labor" to legislation and governmental guidelines that prescribe "equal treatment of foreigners and nationals, and human rights." Over the years, the basic rights of migrants, including "the fundamental right to a family life" and the "expression and representation of migrants in a multicultural France," have become part of policy discourse (de Wenden 1987). After the electoral victory of conservative and centrist parties in 1993, the French parliament passed a series of restrictive laws concerning the nationality code, family unification, and illegal immigration. The restrictions were criticized not only by civil rights groups and opposition parties, but also by prominent cabinet members, expressing concerns about human rights (*New York Times*, 23 June 1993).[17] The French Constitutional Council ruled against the legislation concerning family unification on the grounds that it would violate the rights of migrants as individuals. The Council reasoned that "foreigners are not French, but they are human beings" (*Le Monde*, 16 August 1993).

Germany's policy language and official rhetoric have also

changed over time. In 1981, Richard von Weizsaecker, then the mayor of West Berlin, insisted that foreigners must decide between repatriation and becoming Germans (Castles 1985). In the 1990s, however, Berlin offers its foreign residents a "multicultural society" and "no forced integration," as was noted in the official address of the secretary of the Berlin City State at a conference at the Free University in June 1990. The term *multicultural society* is invoked in public debates and has gained currency among experts on foreigners' issues and government officials responsible for implementing policies of integration.

As attacks on migrants and asylum seekers have risen, the debate about easing Germany's restrictive nationality law and allowing dual citizenship has intensified. The argument of the Social Democratic Party for extending dual citizenship was that "it would send a signal to our foreign residents that we fully recognize them as human beings" (Reuter news agency, 4 June 1993).[18] The major rally organized by the government to protest the killings of three Turkish migrants by neo-Nazis convened under a banner proclaiming that "Human Dignity is Inviolable" (*Boston Globe,* 8 November 1992). In addressing another such protest, Richard von Weizsaecker, the president of Germany, reasserted the theme of human dignity: "The first article of our constitution does not say 'the dignity of Germans is inviolable' but 'the dignity of man is inviolable' " (United Press International, 3 June 1993).

In much official debate, arguments for furthering the rights of migrants are typically presented in terms of the inalienable right of personhood. For example, the Belgian delegation to the 1981 Conference of European Ministers, in making a case for multicultural policies, reasoned that "any attempt to deprive a people of its history, culture, and language produces human beings who are incomplete and incapable both of forming plans for the future and of participating in community life and politics. It is to prevent alienation of this kind that any initiative permitting multilingual and multicultural education and a well-developed community life must be encouraged" (Council of Europe 1981:205). Claims for the political rights of migrants are framed within the same discourse: "The migrant's integration—apart from economic, social, and cultural aspects—involves the question of political participation, since the migrant has a political dimension, as does any other human being; his status in the receiving country cannot be divorced from this fundamental dimension" (*International Migration* 1977:78, citing the conclusions of the seminar on Adaptation and Integration of Permanent Immigrants of the Intergovernmental Committee for Migration [ICM]). Such an understanding of political rights clearly contradicts the construction of the individual's political existence as a national citizen.

Migrants themselves repeatedly urge the universalistic concept of personhood as the grounding principle for membership rights. Claims for membership become publicly coded as human rights, as is clearly discernible from the platforms and action programs of foreigners. In its sixth congress in Stockholm, the European Trade Union Confederation called for a more "humanitarian European unity," referring to the rights of migrant workers, especially those from the non-EC countries (*İkibin'e Doğru*, 29 January 1989). Debates about local voting rights invariably center on the universal/humanistic versus national/particularistic controversy. The most notable argument put forth is that "the right to take part in the political process of one's country of residence is an essential aspect of human life" (Rath 1990:140). In their manifesto for local voting rights, the foreigners' organizations in Switzerland explicitly referred to humans' "natural right" of self-determination. The motto of the 1990 voting rights campaign of migrants in Austria was "Voting Rights Are Human Rights" (*Milliyet*, 10 October 1990). All these claims portray suffrage not only as a participatory right, but as an essential aspect of human personhood.

Human rights discourse dominates calls for cultural rights, as well. Multiculturalism, the right to be different and to foster one's own culture, is elementally asserted as the natural and inalienable right of all individuals. What is ironic is that the preservation of particularistic group characteristics—such as language, a customary marker of national identity—is justified by appealing to universalistic ideas of personhood. The Turkish Parents Association in Berlin demands mother-tongue instruction in schools on the grounds that "as a human being, one has certain natural rights. To learn and enrich one's own language and culture are the most crucial ones" (from the 1990 pamphlet of the association). In the same vein, the Initiative of Turkish Parents and Teachers in Stuttgart publicized its cause with the slogan "Mother Tongue is Human Right" (*Milliyet*, 4 October 1990).

Urging Islamic instruction in public schools, migrant associations also assert the natural right of individuals to their own cultures. During the 1987 national elections, Islamic associations in Britain justified their demands for the observance of Islamic rules in public schools and the recognition of Muslim family law by invoking the Declaration of Human Rights and the Declaration on the Elimination of All Forms of Intolerance based on Religion or Belief (Centre for the Study of Islam and Christian-Muslim Relations 1987). In May 1990, when the local authorities refused to permit the opening of another Islamic primary school, the Islamic Foundation in London decided to take the issue to the European Court of Human Rights. As part of the debate over the *foulard* affair in France, the head of the Great Mosque of Paris declared the rules preventing the wearing of scarves in school to be discriminatory. He emphasized personal rights, rather than religious duties: "If a girl asks to have her hair covered, I believe it is her most basic right" (*Washington Post*, 23 October 1989). Accordingly, the closing statement of the fourth European Muslims Conference made an appeal for the rights of Muslims as "human beings" and "equal members" of European societies (*Kirpi*, July 1990, p. 15).

In all of these examples, the prevalence of transnational discourse is evident. Membership rights are recast as human rights; governments, organizations, and individuals recurrently appeal to this "higher-order" principle. The changes I have delineated indicate, not only the empirical extension of rights, but the existence of legitimate grounds upon which new and more extensive demands can be made. The dominance of human rights discourse, and the definition of individuals and their rights as abstract universal categories, license even foreign populations to push for further elaboration of their rights. The fact that rights, and claims to rights, are no longer confined to national parameters, supports the premise of a postnational model of membership.

One caveat: Although my discussion draws on cases from

western Europe, the arguments I develop are not exclusive to Europe. As the transnational norms and discourse of human rights permeate the boundaries of nation-states, the postnational model is activated and approximated world-wide. However, in countries where the nation-building efforts are still underway, or are contested by alternative groups or ideologies, national citizenship constitutes a significant category and has important organizational consequences. In such cases, the boundaries between citizens and noncitizens are sharply constructed, without much space for ambiguity. The expulsion of hundreds of thousands of Ghanaian laborers from Nigeria in 1983 is an example (Plender 1985). Similarly, during the 1990 Gulf war, when the Yemeni government sided with Iraq, Saudi Arabia deported about a half-million Yemeni workers, some of whom were long-time residents (Esman 1992). In most of these countries, definitions and categories of foreign labor and their rights are not as elaborately codified and institutionalized as they are in the West. In several of the Gulf countries, for example, there are few labor codes, and international labor conventions have not been ratified (Nakhleh 1977).[19] Foreign workers in these systems are generally excluded from most forms of participatory rights and entitlements. Obvious examples are Turks in Libya, Indians and Pakistanis in Saudi Arabia, and Filipinos and Sinhalese in other Gulf states—but, note also the Palestinians in Israel and Iranians and Koreans in Japan.

The Dialectics of Postnational Membership and the Nation-State

Unfolding episodes of world politics in the 1990s may seem to contradict my assertions about postnational membership and the declining significance of national citizenship. Consider the reinventions and reassertions of national(ist) narratives throughout the world: fierce struggles for ethnic or national closure, in former Yugoslavia, Somalia, India, and Ireland; the violent vocalization of anti-foreigner groups throughout Europe, accompanied by demands for restrictive refugee and immigration policies.

How can we account for these seemingly contradictory propensities? In order to untangle such trends from the perspective of this book, let me return to the dialectical dualities of the global system with which I began.

The apparent paradoxes reflected in postwar international migration emanate from the institutionalized duality between the two principles of the global system: national sovereignty and universal human rights. The same global-level processes and institutional frameworks that foster postnational membership also reify the nation-state and its sovereignty.

The principle of human rights ascribes a universal status to individuals and their rights, undermining the boundaries of the nation-state. The principle of sovereignty, on the other hand, reinforces national boundaries and invents new ones. This paradox manifests itself as a deterritorialized expansion of rights despite the territorialized closure of polities. The postwar period has witnessed a vast proliferation in the scope and categories of universalistic rights. Human rights have expanded beyond a conventional list of civil rights to include such social and economic rights as employment, education, health care, nourishment, and housing. The collective rights of nations and peoples to culture, language, and development have also been recodified as inalienable human rights. Women's rights have become "women's human rights" of freedom from gender violence and "certain traditional or customary practices, cultural prejudices and religious extremism" (from the draft document of the 1993 World Conference on Human Rights, cited in the *New York Times*, 16 June 1993).[20]

Incongruously, inasmuch as the ascription and codification of rights move beyond national frames of reference, postnational rights remain organized at the national level. The nation-state is still the repository of educational, welfare, and public health functions and the regulator of social distribution. Simply put, the exercise of universalistic rights is tied to specific states and their institutions. Even though its mode and scope of action are increasingly defined and constrained by the wider global system, the sovereign nation-state retains the formally and organizationally legitimate form venerated by the ideologies and conventions of transnational reference groups such as the UN, UNESCO, and the like.

Expressions of this duality between universalistic rights and the territorially confined nation-state abound. Faced with a growing flux of asylum seekers in 1990s, Western states have defensively reconsidered their immigration policies. Regulation of immigration is often articulated as indispensable to national sovereignty, and several host countries have initiated restrictions.[21] On the other hand, the category of refugee has broadened to encompass new definitions of persecution. For example, Canada's Immigration and Refugee Board has begun to grant asylum to women persecuted because of their gender; cases involving rape, domestic violence, and states' restrictions on women's activities qualify for asylum (*New York Times*, 27 September 1993). France recognized "genital mutilation" as a form of persecution in granting asylum to a west African woman (*New York Times Magazine*, 19 September 1993). In the United States, an immigration judge in San Francisco granted asylum to a gay Brazilian man, as a member of a "persecuted social group" in his home country (*New York Times*, 12 August 1993). So, even as Western states attempt to maintain their boundaries through quantitative restrictions, the introduction of expanding categories and definitions of rights of personhood sets the stage for new patterns of asylum, making national boundaries more penetrable.

A parallel dynamic is also manifest in the German government's attempts to control the flow of refugees. At the end of 1990, a significant number of Gypsies from Yugoslavia was denied asylum, but nonetheless allowed to stay after much public debate concerning human rights (*Süddeutsche Zeitung*, 23 November 1990). In 1992, the German government again decided to repatriate Gypsies, "who do not qualify for asylum," to Romania. This time, to "compensate" for human rights, Germany pledged financial aid to assist the Gypsies "reintegrate" into Romanian society (*Boston Globe*, 1 November 1992).[22] Thus, while acting in its "national interest" by denying entry to potential refugees, the German state simultaneously extends its responsibilities beyond its national borders by "providing for the welfare" of deportees.

The European Community, as an emerging political entity, is not immune to the dualities of the global system either. The doctrine of human rights is frequently invoked in European Community texts and provisions. For instance, the Maastricht treaty and other EC conventions declare that immigration policies will comply with "international commitments" to human rights and the "humanitarian traditions" of EC states. Concurrently, the Community is engaged in boundary-maintaining activities through arrangements such as "European citizenship" and the Schengen agreement. While the latter aims at drawing the borders of a supranational entity through common visa and immigration procedures, the former reconstitutes an exclusionary membership scheme at a supranational level. However, constrained by its own discourse, conventions, and laws, the Community establishes, and compels its member states to provide, an expanding range of rights and privileges to migrants from both EC and non-EC countries.

These seemingly paradoxical affinities articulate an underlying dialectic of the postwar global system: While nation-states and their boundaries are reified through assertions of border controls and appeals to nationhood, a new mode of membership, anchored in the universalistic rights of personhood, transgresses the national order of things.

The duality embedded in the principles of the global system is further reflected in the incongruence between the two elements of modern citizenship: identity and rights. In the postwar era, these two elements of citizenship are decoupled. Rights increasingly assume universality, legal uniformity, and abstractness, and are defined at the global level. Identities, in contrast, still express particularity, and are conceived of as being territorially bounded. As an identity, national citizenship—as it is promoted, reinvented, and reified by states and other societal actors—still prevails. But in terms of its translation into rights and privileges, it is no longer a significant construction. Thus, the universalistic status of personhood and postnational membership coexist with assertive national identities and intense ethnic struggles.

Indeed, the explosion of nationalism can be construed as an exponent of the underlying dialectic of the postwar global system. More and more collectivities are asserting their "national identities" and alleging statehood on the basis of their acclaimed "nationness." These claims are fed and legitimated by the highly institutionalized principle of political sovereignty and self-determination, which promises each people an autonomous state of its own. As political practice, national sovereignty may be contested (as in the case of Kuwait and Iraq during the Gulf war), but as a mode of organization, it is yet to have an alternative. Sovereignty provides a protected status in the international realm, authenticated by membership in the United Nations. Thus, even when previous nation-states are dissolving (e.g., the Soviet Union and Yugoslavia), the emerging units aspire to become territorial states with self-determination, and the world political community grants them this right. The new (or would-be) states immediately appropriate the language of nationhood, produce anthems and flags, and, of course, pledge allegiance to human rights.

The principle of self-determination further reinforces expressions of nationalism, since, for sovereign statehood, a nationally bounded and unified population is imperative. Therefore, collectivities that have been previously defined simply as ethnicities, religious minorities, or language groups, reinvent their "nationness," accentuate the uniqueness of their cultures and histories, and cultivate particularisms to construct their "others" (see Hobsbawm 1990).[23]

At another level, the collective right to self-determination and to political and cultural existence, is itself increasingly codified as a universal human right.[24] Claims to particularistic identities, cultural distinctiveness, and self-determination are legitimated by reference to the essential, indisputable rights of persons, and, thus, are recast as world-level, postnational rights. This recodification is, in fact, what Roland Robertson (1992:100) calls "the universalization of particularism and the particularization of universalism." What are considered particularistic characteristics of collectivities—culture, language, and standard ethnic traits—become variants of the universal core of humanness. In turn, as universal attributes and human rights, they are exercised in individual and collective actors' narratives and strategies.

Framing political self-determination and collective cultural rights as universalistic prerogatives occasions ever-increasing claims and mobilizations around particularistic identities. An intensifying world-level discourse of "plurality" that encourages "distinct cultures" within and across national borders contributes to this new dynamism. An identity politics, energized by narrations of collective pasts and accentuated cultural differences, becomes the basis for participation, and affords the means for mobilizing resources in the national and world polities. If one aspect of this dynamism is relegitimization and reification of nationness, the other is its fragmentation, displacement of its meaning, and hence its delegitimization.

A growing tendency toward regionalisms (sometimes separatisms) and their recognition by the central states, fragments existing nations and nationalities into infinitely distinct ethnicities and cultural subunits. In Europe more and more groups seek economic and linguistic autonomy on the basis of their regional identities—Bretons, Corsicans, Basques, and Occitans in France; Scots and Welsh in Britain; Lombards and Sardinians in Italy. And European states, even those that have long resisted linguistic and cultural diversity, increasingly accommodate autonomous entities (as in Spain) and provide for regional languages (as in France and Italy).[25] The multiplication of particularisms and subsequent fragmentation disrupt the presumed contiguities of nationness and undermine the territorial sanctity of nation-states.

Furthermore, as particularistic identities are transformed into expressive modes of a core humanness, thus acquiring universal currency, the "nation" looses its charisma and becomes normalized. The idea of nation becomes a trope of convenience for claims to collective rights and identity. Even groups that may not fit the classic definitions of a nation refer to themselves as such: gays and lesbians claim a "Queer Nation"; the Deaf define themselves as a national subgroup with its own cultural peculiarities and language; and indigenous peoples request to be called, not tribes, but nations, and seek a vote in the United Nations. In this universalizing flux, "the ways of 'doing' identity" (Robertson 1992:99) become standardized exercises, with common themes and modes of presentation. At the center of this activity lies the construction of official taxonomies, with reference to routine markers and attributes of culture; that is, the placid images of cuisines, crafts, life-styles, religious symbols, folklores, and customs.

In the context of this normalizing trend, national identities that celebrate discriminatory uniqueness and naturalistic canonizations of nationhood become more and more discredited. It is, for instance, increasingly difficult to protect and practice a code of nationality that inscribes "blood" or "lineage" as its primary principle. Note the widespread reaction to Germany's blood-based citizenship and naturalization laws, and the German government's decision to overhaul these "outdated" laws (Reuter news agency, 12 June 1993). Similarly, national canons that valorize ancestral warmaking and symbols of patriarchy are increasingly less enticing as vehicles for doing identity. It has been truly amazing to observe the remaking of the "Vikings," from warrior forefathers to spirited long-distance traders.[26]

All of these recontextualizations of "nationness" within the universalistic discourse of human rights blur the meanings and boundaries attached to the nation and the nation-state. The idea of the nation persists as an intense metaphor, at times an idiom of war. However, in a world within which rights, and identities as rights, derive their legitimacy from discourses of universalistic personhood, the limits of nationness, or of national citizenship, for that matter, become inventively irrelevant.

CHAPTER NINE

Conclusion

This book is about the reconfiguration of the institution of citizenship in the postwar era. The modern construction of citizenship affords a framework for sociological analyses of membership in contemporary polities. The predominant conceptions of political sociology posit that populations are organized within nation-state boundaries by citizenship rules that acclaim national belonging as the legitimate basis of membership in modern states. This study, however, finds that the classical formal order of the nation-state and its membership is not in place. The state is no longer an autonomous and independent organization closed over a nationally defined population. Instead, we have a system of constitutionally interconnected states with a multiplicity of membership. The stubbornness in current sociological praxis that assigns the nation-state an impervious agency as a unit of action, even when conversing about global processes and transnational networks, renders invisible emerging forms of membership and obscures their manifest multiplicities in national binarisms. Thus, we have anomalies in existing paradigms, models that do not work, and incongruences between "official" rhetoric and institutional "actualities."

My analysis of the incorporation of guestworkers in Europe reveals a shift in the major organizing principle of membership in contemporary polities: the logic of personhood supersedes the logic of national citizenship. This trend is informed by a dialectical tension between national citizenship and universal human rights. Individual rights and obligations, which were historically located in the nation-state, have increasingly moved to a universalistic plane, transcending the boundaries of particular nation-states. Originally, individual rights were defined and codified within schemes of national citizenship. After all, the first compilation of a comprehensive list of individual rights was called the Declaration of the Rights of Man and of the Citizen (1789). The rights of man were inextricable from the substance of citizenship, feeding the nationalistic ideology associated with it.

Today, however, individual rights, expansively redefined as human rights on a universalistic basis and legitimized at the transnational level, undercut the import of national citizenship by disrupting the territorial closure of nations. The same human rights that came to be secured over the centuries in national constitutions as the rights and privileges of a proper citizenry have now attained a new meaning and have become globally sanctioned norms and components of a supranational discourse. It is within this new universalistic discourse that the individual, as an abstract, human person, supplants the national citizen. And it is within this universalized scheme of rights that nonnationals participate in a national polity, advance claims, and achieve rights in a state not their own. The expanse and intensity of concepts of personhood predicate a broadened, postnational constellation of membership in the postwar era.

As a world-level index of legitimate action, human rights discourse provides a hegemonic language for formulating claims to rights above and beyond national belonging. The same discourse also fortifies the nation-state and its authority by assigning the responsibility of maintaining human rights to the nation-states. Thus, as it hegemonically encompasses new domains, human rights discourse generates its own ironies: the human rights mission of the United Nations to alleviate starvation in Somalia "requires" waging a war for peace against people in the streets of Mogadishu; Iraq's civilian population suffers from inadequate humanitarian aid under provisions of an embargo to punish "Iraq" for human rights violations. Human rights discourse is, then, a commanding apparatus that legitimizes a collection of incoherent outcomes. In its powerful pervasiveness, it contests and confounds its own agency.

Although, under a mantle of institutionalized human rights discourse, the rights of the person transcend those of the citizen, they are still realized through membership in a state. It is through the agency of the state that rights are enacted and implemented. This structural constraint predicates the incorporation of individuals in a polity in the role of citizen; in the modern order of political organization, individuals are identified by their existence as "citizens" vis-à-vis the state and its institutions. However, as implied by formations of postnational membership, national belonging, or a formal nationality, is no longer imperative for this role of citizen. Rights, participation, and representation in a polity, are increasingly matters beyond the vocabulary of national citizenship. Neither is "nation" a meaningful definer of the contemporary state, given the intensification and interconnectedness of the global system and the penetration of national dominions by supranational discourses (see Hobsbawm 1990; Meyer 1994; Tilly 1990). The nation-state becomes an implementer of a multitude of, at times conflicting, functions and responsibilities, derived from world-level discourses rather than from its territorialized identity. And the link between the individual and the state becomes more and more instrumental and routine rather than charismatic and sentimental.

The dissociation of nationness from the state and identity from rights within a postnational scheme projects multiple levels of participation in a polity. I am not invoking a simple world-citizen/local-citizen duality, or some version of the aphorism "think globally, act locally." My intention is to highlight the emergence of membership that is multiple in the sense of spanning local, regional, and global identities, and which accommodates intersecting complexes of rights, duties, and loyalties. Turkish migrants in Berlin represent an example of this emerging form of membership (so, for that matter, do Moroccans in Paris, Pakistanis in London, and Surinamese in Amsterdam). As foreign residents of Berlin, Turkish migrants share a social space with foreigners from other countries and with German citizens. They pay taxes, own businesses and homes, work in factories and in the service sector, receive welfare, rent government-subsidized apartments, and attend schools. They form political associations, join unions and political parties, organize protests, formulate platforms, and advance claims. Either selectively or concurrently, they invoke, negotiate, and map collective identities as immigrant, Turk, Muslim, foreigner, and European.

What makes them rightful members of the host polity? What is the basis of their participation and claims? Not common blood, lineage, or some other imagined attachment from time immemorial. Neither is their membership founded on loyalty and allegiance to a state, or commitment to a common national interest or ideal. Rather, it is grounded in a shared public, social space; a set of abstract principles and responsibilities (such as human rights, respect for justice, protection of the environment, expectations of a "better future" and a "productive life"); and the rationalized organization and routine of everyday praxis, independent of the specificities of the locale in which they live. Perhaps the motto, *Wir sind Berlin*, promoted by Berlin's Foreigner's Office and invoked by migrants themselves, best captures the way the migrants live their lives and interact with the host polity, within which their membership is realized. The trajectory of "being part of Berlin" precludes national fixities and allows for shifting categories and fluid confines, and thus can traverse multiple borders.

Obviously, all this is not to suggest that the formal categories of alien and citizen have withered away or that their symbolic intensity has eroded. The citizen/noncitizen dichotomy persistently reappears in scholarly readings of the immigration experience, in policy debates, and in the popular imagination. National citizenship, the "invented tradition" of the nineteenth century (Hobsbawm 1983), and the customary sentiments it signals may be with us for some time. However, it is essential to recognize that national citizenship is no longer an adequate concept upon which to base a perceptive narrative of membership in the postwar era. Postnational formations of membership challenge us to refurbish our definitions and theoretical vistas of and about citizenship and the nation-state.

APPENDIX A

State Agencies, Organizations, and Migrant Associations at which Interviews Were Conducted

Britain

State Agencies

Commission for Racial Equality (CRE) (9 June 1989)
Home Office, Research and Planning Unit (13 June 1989)
United Kingdom Immigrants Advisory Service (UKIAS) (9 June 1989)

Trade Unions

Trades Union Congress (TUC) (14 June 1989)

Migrant Associations

Tamil Refugee Action Group (TRAG), London (June 1989)
Turkish Community Center (Halk Evi), London (June 1989)
Turkish Education Union (Türk Eğitim Birliği), London (June 1989)

France

State Agencies

Agence de le Développement des Relations Interculturelles (Agency for the Development of Intercultural Relations; ADRI) (June 1988)

Direction de la Population et des Migrations, Ministère des Affaires Sociales et de l'Emploi (Directorate of Migrant Populations, Ministry of Social Affairs and Employment; since 1991, Ministry of Social Affairs and Integration) (20 June 1988)
Fonds d'Action Sociale pour les Travailleurs Immigrés et leurs Familles (Social Action Fund for Immigrant Workers and Their Families; FAS) (16 May 1989)
Office des Migrations Internationales (International Migration Office; OMI) (19 May 1989)

Social Service and Solidarity Organizations
Accueil et Promotion (26 May 1989)
Association de Solidarité avec les Travailleurs Immigrés du 14e et 15e Arrondissement (Association of Solidarity with Immigrant Workers; ASTI), Paris (20, 22 May 1989)
Fédération des Associations de Solidarité avec les Travailleurs Immigrés (Federation of Associations of Solidarity with Immigrant Workers; FASTI) (23 May 1989)
Groupe d'Information et de Soutien des Travailleurs Immigrés (Information and Support Group for Immigrant Workers; GISTI) (22 May 1989)

Migrant Associations
Association des Travailleurs de Turquie (Association of Workers from Turkey; ATT), Paris (July 1988; 9, 15, 21 May 1989)
Conseil des Associations Immigrés en France (Council of Associations of Immigrants in France; CAIF), Paris (June 1988)
Maison des Travailleurs de Turquie—Elele, Paris (21 June 1988)
Memoire Fertile (20, 24 May 1989)
SOS Racisme (June 1988)

Germany

Federal Agencies
Beauftragte der Bundesregierung für Ausländerfragen (Federal Commissioner for Foreigners' Affairs) (9 June 1988)
Bundesministerium für Arbeit und Sozialordnung (Federal Ministry of Labor and Social Affairs) (9 June 1988)

Local Agencies

Ausländerbeauftragte des Senats beim Senator für Gesundheit und Soziales (Commissioner for Foreigners' Affairs of the Senate of Berlin, Senate Department of Health and Social Affairs) (10 May 1988; 30 April 1991; 7 September 1992)

Social Service Organizations

Otur-Yaşa, Wohnen und Leben e.V., Berlin (May 1988)

Türk-Danış, Beratungsstelle der Arbeiterwohlfahrt, Berlin (May 1988)

Trade Unions

Deutscher Gewerkschaftsbund (German Trade Union Federation; DGB) (13 May 1988)

Industriegewerkschaft Metall (Metal Industry Trade Union; IGM) (13 May 1988)

Migrant Associations

Berlin Türk Cemaati (Turkish Community of Berlin; BTC) (10 May 1988)

Berlin Türk Topluluğu (Turkish Union of Berlin; BTT) (11 May 1988)

Berlin Türk Veliler Birliği (Union of Turkish Parents in Berlin) (6 May 1988; 14 March 1991; 4 September 1992)

Türkiye Halkçı Devrimci Federasyonu (Federation of Progressive People's Associations in Europe; HDF) (11 May 1988)

The Netherlands

State Agencies

Inspraakorgaan Turken (National Advisory Council for Turks; IOT) (6 June 1988)

Ministerie van Binnenlandse Zaken (Ministry of Home Affairs, Directorate for the Coordination of Minorities Policy; DCM) (6 June 1988)

Ministerie van Justitie (Ministry of Justice, Department of Alien Affairs) (7 June 1988)

Ministerie van Welzijn, Volksgezonheid en Cultuur (Ministry of Welfare, Health, and Cultural Affairs) (13 June 1988)

Sociaal en Cultureel Planbureau (Social and Cultural Planning Office; SCP) (3 June 1988)
Wetenschappelijke Raad voor het Regeringsbeleid (Netherlands Scientific Council for Government Policy; WRR) (31 May 1988)

Local Agencies
City of Amsterdam, Bureau for Ethnic Minority Affairs (2 June 1988)

Public Organizations
Landelijk Buro Racismebestrijding (National Bureau Against Discrimination; LBR) (13 June 1988)
Nederlands Centrum Buitenlanders (Dutch Center for Foreigners; NCB) (7 June 1988)
Vereniging van Nederlandse Gemeenten (National Organization of Dutch Municipalities; VNG) (3 June 1988)

Trade Unions
Federatie Nederlandse Vakbeweging (Federation of Dutch Trade Unions; FNV) (13 June 1988)

Migrant Associations
Hollanda Türkiyeli İşçiler Birliği (Union of Laborers from Turkey; HTIB), Amsterdam (June 1988)
Landelijke Samenwerking van Organisaties van Buitenlandse Arbeiders (National Cooperation of Foreign Workers' Organizations; LSOBA), Utrecht (June 1988)
Türk İslam Kültür Federasyonu (Turkish Islamic Cultural Federation), Rotterdam (6 June 1988)

Sweden

State Agencies
Delegationen för Invandrarforskning (Swedish Commission for Immigrant Research; DEIFO) (21 April 1988)
Statens Invandrarverk (National Immigration Board; SIV) Information, Citizenship, and Popular Movements Sections (28 April, 2 May 1988)

Local Agencies
City of Malmö Immigration Board (3 May 1988)
City of Stockholm Immigration Board (29 April 1988)

Trade Unions
Landsorganisationen (National Federation of Workers; LO) (19 April 1988)

Migrant Associations
Dayanışma Derneği (Solidarity Association), Stockholm (24 April 1988)
İsveç Türkiyeli Kadınlar Derneği (Association of Women from Turkey in Sweden), Stockholm (23 April 1988)
Riksförbundet Internationella Föreningen för Invandrarkvinnor (National Federation of International Associations of Immigrant Women; RIFFI), Stockholm (25 April 1988)
Sveriges Muslimska Förbund (Swedish Muslim Association), Stockholm (26 April 1988)
Turkiska Riksförbundet (National Turkish Federation), Stockholm (25 April 1988)
Türk Kültür ve Spor Derneği (Turkish Culture and Sports Association), Malmö (3 May 1988)

Switzerland

Federal Agencies
Bundesamt für Ausländerfragen, Eidgenössisches Justiz- und Polizeidepartement (Federal Aliens Office, Federal Department of Justice and Police) (24 May 1988)
Bundesamt für Industrie, Gewerbe und Arbeit (Federal Office of Industry, Small Business, and Labor; BIGA) (26 May 1988)
Eidgenössische Kommission für Ausländerprobleme (Federal Commission for Aliens; EKA) (18 May 1988)
Zentrales Ausländerregister, Bundesamt für Ausländerfragen (Central Register for Aliens, Federal Aliens Office) (24 May 1988)

Local Agencies
Kantonale Fremdenpolizei Zürich (Canton of Zurich Foreigners Police) (30 May 1988)

Städtische Koordinationsstelle für Ausländerfragen, Zürich (City Coordination Office for Foreigners' Affairs, Zurich; KSA) (27 May 1988)
Städtisches Arbeitsamt Zürich (City of Zurich Employment Bureau) (30 May 1988)
Stadtzürcherische Ausländerkomission (City of Zurich Foreigners Commission) (27 May 1988)

Social Service Organizations
Berner Informationstelle für Ausländerfragen (City of Bern Information Office for Foreigners' Affairs; ISA) (18 May 1988)
Kirchlicher Sozialdienst Zürich (Social Service Office of the Evangelical Churches; KSD) (20 May 1988)
Zentralstelle für Flüchtlingshilfe (Central Office for Refugee Help), Zurich (27 May 1988)

Trade Unions
Christlicher Holz-und Bauarbeiterverband der Schweiz (Catholic Construction Workers Union; CHB) (20 May 1988)
Christlichnationaler Gewerkschaftsbund der Schweiz (Catholic Trade Union Federation; CNG) (20 May 1988)

Migrant Associations
İsviçre Türk Dernekleri Dayanışma Federasyonu (Federation for Solidarity among Turkish Associations in Switzerland; ITDDF) (May 1988)
İsviçre Türk Dernekleri Federasyonu (Federation of Turkish Associations in Switzerland; ITDF) (May 1988)

International Organizations

European Community (EC), Division of Freedom of Movement, Migration Policy and Social Security for Migrant Workers, Brussels (8 June 1989)
International Labor Organization (ILO), Geneva (25 May 1988)
International Social Service (ISS), Geneva (25 May 1988)

Research Centers and Libraries

Centre d'Information et d'Etudes sur les Migrations Internationales (Center for Information and Research on International Migration; CIEMI), Paris

Centre National de Recherche Scientifique (National Center for Scientific Research, Documentation; CNRS), Paris

Centre for Research in International Migration and Ethnic Relations (CEIFO), Stockholm

European Center for Work and Society, Maastricht, the Netherlands

European Migration Centre, Berlin

Forschungszentrum für schweizerische Politik, Universität Bern (Research Center for Swiss Politics), Bern

Library of the Advisory Committee on Minorities Research (ACOM), Leiden, the Netherlands

Library of the National Immigration Board (SIV), Norrköping, Sweden

Runnymede Trust, London

Scientific Documentation Center on Ethnic Minorities (WEDEM), Leuven, Belgium

Système Bibliographique et Documentaire relatif à l'Immigration (Documentation and Bibliography System on Immigration; SYBIDI), Brussels

Zentrum für Türkeistudien (Center for Turkish Studies), Bonn

APPENDIX B

The Organizational Structure of Incorporation

Table 1. Organization of Incorporation in Sweden

Ministerial level	Ministry of Justice	Ministry of Labor	Ministry of Health and Social Affairs	Ministry of Education
		Minister of Immigrant Affairs		
		Ad hoc interministerial committee for the coordination of immigration policy		
Ad hoc/permanent commissions	Immigrants' Advisory Council			Commission on legislation concerning aliens
	Commission on racial discrimination	Swedish Commission on Immigrant Research (DEIFO)		Commission on the teaching of Swedish to immigrants
Central agencies	National Immigration Board (SIV)	National Labor Market Board (AMS)	National Office for Health and Social Welfare	National Education Office
Local level	Immigration Board or Council (Immigrant Service Bureau)	Employment Office	Municipal Social Service	

Note: See Widgren (1982:159) for a full chart of the administrative structure of Swedish immigration policy.

Table 2. Organization of Incorporation in the Netherlands

Ministerial level	Ministry of Justice	Ministry of Home Affairs	Ministry of Social Affairs and Employment	Ministry of Welfare, Health, and Cultural Affairs	Ministry of Housing, Physical Planning and the Environment	Ministry of Education and Science
		Directorate for the Coordination of Minorities Policy				
		Interministerial Coordinating Committee on Minorities Policy				
Ad hoc/ permanent commissions		National Advisory Council for Ethnic Minorities (LAO)	Advisory Committee on Minorities Research (ACOM)		Scientific Council for Government Policy (WRR)	
Central agencies		Dutch Center for Foreigners[1] (NCB)	Dutch Center for Surinamese[1] (SSA)	Dutch Center for Antilleans[1] (POA)	National Bureau Against Discrimination[1] (LBR)	
		Social and Cultural Planning Office (SCP)		National Organization of Dutch Municipalities[1] (VNG)		
Local level		Municipal Bureau for Ethnic Minority Affairs	Employment Office	Municipal Social Services	Municipal Council for Foreigners	Foreign Workers Assistance Units[1]

[1] Autonomous organizations, but fully subsidized by the state.

Table 3. Organization of Incorporation in Switzerland

Ministerial level (federal)	Federal Department of Justice and Police		Federal Department of Economic Affairs	
Ad hoc/permanent commissions	Federal Commission for Aliens (EKA)			
Central agencies	Federal Aliens Office Central Register for Aliens		Federal Office of Industry, Small Business, and Labor (BIGA)	
Cantonal level	Foreigners Police	Commission for Foreigners' Affairs[1]	Cantonal Office of Industry, Small Business, and Labor (KIGA)	
Community level (gemeinde)	Coordination or Contact Office for Foreigners' Affairs	Foreigners Commission[1]	Employment Office	Information Contact Centers[2]

[1]The status and organization of these commissions differ among cantons and communes, usually consultative bodies.

[2]Voluntary associations, mainly funded by municipalities and/or churches, as well as donations from corporations.

Table 4. Organization of Incorporation in Britain

Ministerial level	Home Office Junior minister with special responsibility for immigration and race relations	Department of Employment		Department of Education
Ad hoc/permanent commissions		Commission for Racial Equality (CRE)		
Central agencies		Immigrants Advisory Service (UKIAS)[1]		
Local level	Race Equality Councils (RECs)[2]	Race Relations Units	Municipal Social Services	Community Centers[3]

[1] Autonomous organization, but fully subsidized by the state.

[2] Autonomous, voluntary organizations, but work closely with the CRE.

[3] Voluntary associations, some receiving subsidies from local authorities.

Table 5. Organization of Incorporation in France

Ministerial level	Ministry of Interior	Ministry of Labor	Ministry of Social Affairs and Integration		Ministry of National Education and Culture
			State Secretary for Integration		
			Directorate of Migrant Populations		
Ad hoc/permanent commissions	Commission on Nationality (1987–88)		National Council for Immigrant Populations		High Council for Integration
Central agencies	International Migration Office (OMI)	National Society for Housing (SNCL)	Social Action Fund (FAS)	Association of Social Assistance for Migrants (SSAE)[1]	Agency for the Development of Intercultural Relations (ADRI)
Local level (provinces)	Employment office		Regional Commission for the Insertion of Migrant Populations (CRIPI)		
(municipalities)	Immigrant Councils	Municipal Social Service Bureau		Local SSAE offices and other social service organizations	

[1] Autonomous organizations, but funded by the state.

Table 6. Organization of Incorporation in Germany

Ministerial level (federal)	Ministry of Interior	Ministry of Labor and Social Affairs Coordination Committee for Foreigners Policy		Ministry for Youth, Family, and Health	
Ad hoc/permanent commissions		Federal Commissioner for Foreigners' Affairs			
Central agencies		Federal Employment Office		Semi-public welfare agencies	
State level	Ministry of Interior	Ministry of Labor	Ministry of Education	Ministry of Health and Social Affairs	Commissioner for Foreigners' Affairs
Local level	Municipal Social Services	Foreigner Advisory Councils		Offices of semi-public welfare agencies	Municipal Commissioners for Foreigners' Affairs

APPENDIX C

International Instruments that Provide Standards Applicable to International Migrants

United Nations

Universal Declaration of Human Rights (1948)
Geneva Convention on the Legal Status of Refugees (1951)
International Convention on the Elimination of All Forms of Racial Discrimination (1965)
International Covenant on Economic, Social, and Cultural Rights (1966)
International Covenant on Civil and Political Rights (1966)
UNESCO Declaration on Race and Racial Prejudice (1978)
Convention on the Elimination of All Forms of Discrimination against Women (1979)
Convention on the Rights of the Child (1990)
International Convention on the Protection of the Rights of All Migrant Workers and Members of Their Families (1990)

International Labor Organization

Convention on Equality of Treatment (1925)
Convention Concerning Migration for Employment (1949)
Recommendation Concerning the Protection of Migrant Workers from Underdeveloped Countries and Territories (1955)
Convention on Equality of Treatment (Social Security) (1962)

Convention on Migrant Workers (Supplementary Provisions) (1975)
Convention on Maintenance of Social Security Rights (1982)
Recommendation Concerning Employment Policy (1984)

Council of Europe

European Convention on the Protection of Human Rights and Fundamental Freedoms (1950)
European Convention on Social and Medical Assistance (1953)
European Convention on Establishment (1955)
European Agreement on Regulations Governing the Movements of Persons between Member States of the Council of Europe (1957)
European Social Charter (1961)
European Convention on the Legal Status of Migrant Workers (1977)

European Community

The European Community has a series of regulations and directives that are binding for the member states regarding freedom of movement of persons pursuing economic activities. There also exist a resolution and an action program for migrant workers and their families (1976), guidelines for a Community policy on migration that define and provide for the rights and status of foreigners (1985), a declaration of human rights (1977), and a declaration against racism and xenophobia (1986).

APPENDIX D

Intergovernmental and Nongovernmental Organizations Concerned with International Migration and Migrant Workers

Intergovernmental

United Nations
  Center for Human Rights
  Center for Social Development and Humanitarian Affairs
  Commission on Human Rights
  Conference on Trade and Development (UNCTAD)
  Educational, Scientific, and Cultural Organization (UNESCO)
  Fund for Population Activities (UNFPA)
  High Commission for Refugees (UNHCR)
Council of Europe
  Committee on Migration, Refugees, and Demography
  Conference of Local and Regional Authorities of Europe
  European Committee on Migration
European Community
Intergovernmental Committee for Migration (ICM)
International Bank for Reconstruction and Development (IBRD)
International Labor Organization (ILO)
Organization for Economic Cooperation and Development (OECD)
World Health Organization (WHO)

Nongovernmental

Catholic Relief Services (CRS)
Diakonisches Werk
International Catholic Migration Commission (ICMC)
International Committee of the Red Cross
International Confederation of Free Trade Unions (ICFTU)
International Council on Social Welfare (ICSW)
International Council of Voluntary Agencies (ICVA)
International Social Service (ISS)
International Union for Child Welfare (IUCW)
League of Red Cross and Red Crescent Societies (LRCS)
Lutheran World Foundation (LWF)
Service Social d'Aide aux Emigrants (SSAE)
World Council of Churches (WCC)
  Churches' Committee for Migrants in Europe
World Relief Refugee Services (WRRS)

NOTES

Chapter One

1. It can be argued that a national model of citizenship has never been realized. Homogeneity has never been a reality for any polity; neither has a uniform status for all citizens. Obviously the national citizenship model is a social construction. It has reality as a model, that states, as well as individuals, have acted upon to approximate it, but as an empirical construct it is always challenged and violated.

2. See, for instance, Walzer 1983 and Brubaker 1992. Both works, by taking the boundaries of already existing "communities" for granted, sustain the presumption of nationally and territorially based distribution of membership and fail to acknowledge the new modalities of citizenship.

3. See Meyer 1980 and Meyer, Boli, and Thomas 1987 for a conceptualization of the world system as a symbolic cultural order. My approach also resonates with what Appadurai and Breckenridge (1988) call "public culture." Following them, I view the global symbolic and discursive order as a "zone of cultural debate," whose modalities and language are "ecumenical, not parochial" and surpass such hierarchies of the elite and the popular. See also Hannerz 1992 for a similar approach to the global system.

4. Sewell (1992:17). My point is inspired by Sewell's perceptive discussion of the "multiplicity of structures and cultural schemas" in a society. Sewell argues that "societies are based on practices that derive from many distinct structures, which exist at different levels, operate in different modalities, and are themselves based on widely varying types and quantities of resources. . . . Social actors are capable of applying a wide range of different and even incompatible [cultural]

schemas and have access to heterogeneous arrays of resources" (1992: 16–17). See also Friedland and Alford 1991 for a conceptualization of society as consisting of "potentially contradictory" institutions that provide "multiple logics" to actors.

5. See Zolberg 1981 on the relation between nation-state sovereignty and international migration.

6. I completed most of my data collection on state policies, legal codes, and organizational structures before the unification of the two Germanies. After the unification, the laws, institutions, and practices of the Federal Republic became the immigration regime of the new Germany.

7. France had a policy of immigration before the Second World War, to compensate for its low birth rate and short labor supply (Verbunt 1985). Also, both France and the United Kingdom have had experience with colonial immigration. For a period after the colonies gained their independence, colonial populations had the right to immigrate to the metropolis. However, even for these two countries, postwar migration trends do not significantly differ in terms of the motivation for recruiting and the perceived temporariness of migrant populations.

Chapter Two

1. In the 1850s there were 500,000 foreigners in France, 250,000 in Belgium, 100,000 in the Netherlands, and more than a million in Germany at the turn of the century (Werner 1986:543). The number of Irish in Britain exceeded 700,000 in 1851 (Power 1979:13). Italians, who emigrated between 1876 and 1920, went to Germany, Switzerland, and France as much as to the United States (Sassen-Koob 1980). After the First World War, faced with demographic decline, France recruited large numbers of workers from Poland, Czechoslovakia, and Italy—a total of 2.5 million by 1926 (Power 1979:11). By the turn of the century, foreigners had already reached 12 percent in Switzerland (Hoffmann-Nowotny 1980:74). See Moch 1992 for a history of European migrations from the seventeenth century on.

2. Tilly (1978:49) argues that migration statistics emerged with the consolidation of national states, reflecting "the concern of [state] bureaucrats to attach people to domiciles where they can be registered, enumerated, taxed, drafted and watched."

3. Tilly 1978 and Zolberg 1978 offer historical analyses of the relationship between international migration and state systems.

4. Although slavery had existed long before, ancient Greece and Rome were the first societies where slavery was "very solidly the base of their socioeconomic structures" (Patterson 1982:vii).

5. Obviously, as Marshall (1964) recounts, the construction of a national citizenry was an uneven and gradual process. Incorporation into the rights and privileges of citizenship took longer for some groups than others. The full political participation of the working classes required the step-by-step abolishment of restrictive property qualifications. In many European countries, women's rights were not fully granted until well into the mid-twentieth century. Colonial populations' ascendance to citizenship was realized through self-rule, after separation from the metropoles. Nevertheless, it was the French Revolution that instituted national citizenship as the modern mode of membership in a polity.

6. The Bracero program, an intergovernmental agreement between Mexico and the United States concluded in 1942, arranged for the importation of Mexican laborers for periods not to exceed six months. Though planned as a temporary wartime measure, the Bracero program lasted until 1964, initiating new patterns of labor migration to the United States (Galarza 1964; Reichert and Massey 1985).

7. The German Democratic Republic had a substantial guestworker population, which came from Vietnam, Angola, Mozambique, and Cuba. After the unification of the two Germanies, most of these workers lost their jobs and some returned voluntarily to their home countries. Those who stayed either receive unemployment benefits like other guestworkers in western Germany or are engaged in petty trade.

8. By the late 1970s, many host governments had announced plans for repatriation. Among these, France and Germany had the most elaborate policies. However, repatriation schemes, including premiums offered to the unemployed on return, did not achieve what was intended, and were virtually dropped by the mid-1980s (Penninx 1986; Seccombe and Lawless 1985).

9. In 1990, the unemployment rate among foreigners was 16 percent in Belgium, 13 percent in the Netherlands, 12.8 percent in France, 11 percent in Austria, 10.8 percent in Germany, and 4.5 percent in Sweden (SOPEMI 1992:26).

10. In the early 1990s, Austria, Britain, France, Germany, and the Netherlands all tightened their asylum provisions to reduce the flow of new refugees (See Darnton 1993).

11. See Brumberg 1986 for a historical account of the crucial role of schooling in the assimilation process.

Chapter Three

1. Selected examples include Abadan-Unat 1985; Brouwer and Priester 1983; Esser 1980; Hoffmann-Nowotny 1973; Hoffmann-

Nowotny and Hondrich 1982; and Mehrländer 1982, 1984, and 1987. For an important exception, see B. Schmitter (1980, 1981), who focuses on organizational structures within host societies as the facilitator of integration.

2. As O'Brien (1988:20) argues, such studies not only justify the modern/traditional dichotomy by providing "multi-faceted image[s]" of the unadjusted or "lost" Turkish migrant, but also legitimize state policies that appropriate the same language and concepts. For another critique of this scholarly practice in guestworker literature, see Çağlar 1990.

3. See Keely 1990 for a synthesis of otherwise distinct concepts of regimes (Krasner 1983) and discourses (Foucault 1973, 1979, 1980).

4. See Castles and Kosack 1972, 1973; and Piore 1979 for the most classical treatment of this point. See also Markovits and Kazarinov 1978, and Schmid 1981b.

5. See especially the chapters on individual countries in Hammar 1985. Switzerland and Britain are the only countries that experienced politicization of immigration before the 1980s (Heisler 1988; Layton-Henry 1992; Saggar 1992).

6. Since the late 1980s, extreme right parties have achieved significant gains in local and national elections in Belgium, France, and Germany. Their electoral success, however, does not follow a consistent trend. In Germany, for example, throughout 1990 and 1991, racist parties lost considerable ground in regional and federal elections; in 1992, they increased their regional parliamentary seats in Schleswig-Holstein and Baden-Württemberg (Husbands 1992).

7. In 1993, amid violent attacks against guestworkers and asylum seekers, the major German political parties agreed upon the drastic restriction of asylum, at the same time engaging in debate over the extension of dual citizenship to second-generation migrants.

8. The thrust of this argument is that institutionalized political structures and organizational principles can and should be studied as a major source of variation among states (Birnbaum 1988; Dobbin 1994; Hall 1986; Jepperson and Meyer 1991; Katzenstein 1978; Skocpol 1985). These factors "give rise to various conceptions of the meaning and methods of 'politics' itself," which, in turn, influence the nature of policies and issues in the political agenda, and the forms of collective action and organizing (Skocpol 1985:22). For example, Skocpol and Finegold (1982), Orloff and Skocpol (1984), and Skowronek (1982) suggest that, by their organization, state structures prevent or facilitate the development of certain types of policy. Katzenstein (1984, 1985) shows that the design of political institutions, in addition to the design of markets, has significantly shaped the postwar industrial policy of western European countries. Tilly's (1986) work stresses that

the nature of social movements and collective organization is significantly affected by state structures and practices. For a synthesizing reprise of "new institutionalist" approaches to political order, see March and Olsen 1984.

9. Swidler (1986) defines culture as a repertoire or "tool kit" of publicly available meanings, symbols, styles, and "modes of regulating conduct" from which individuals construct "strategies of action." Similarly, it can be argued that the institutional logic and repertoire of each polity influence the mode of state action in incorporating migrants. This line of argument parallels Bourdieu's (1977:83) invocation of *habitus* as "transposable dispositions," which render the possibility of extending already existing schemes to new contexts and new problems.

10. This typology draws largely on Meyer 1983; and Jepperson and Meyer 1991; but also benefits significantly from the works of Badie and Birnbaum 1983; Birnbaum 1988; P. Schmitter 1981; Katzenstein 1985; and Esping-Andersen 1990. Meyer 1983, and Jepperson and Meyer 1991 provide a typology that distinguishes modern polities according to the degree of their "collective rationalization" of social actors and functions. Badie and Birnbaum, and later Birnbaum, construct their typology according to the existence (or nonexistence) of a state and/or a center. Schmitter, in contrast, develops his typology on the basis of interest representation in a polity, without particularly referring to the characteristics of the state itself. Katzenstein elaborates his scheme not only on the basis of relationships between interest groups, but also as a distinctive combination of market and state characteristics. Esping-Andersen's classification of welfare-state regimes is based on interactions between the historical legacy of state institutions and the nature of class formation and mobilization. These typological exercises are not necessarily related (and are partly at odds with each other or mine) in their logic or classification; rather, they explicate different organizational characteristics and systems of rules that apply to different issue areas within polities.

Note that my concern is not to account for the origins of particular polity and membership types. The comparative institutional histories of European polities have been studied quite extensively in, for example, Ashford 1982; Badie and Birnbaum 1983; Birnbaum 1988; Flora and Heidenheimer 1981; Grew 1978; Heclo 1974; Heclo and Madsen 1987; Katzenstein 1984, 1987; Lipset and Rokkan 1967; Mann 1986; Nettl 1968; Rokkan 1980; Shefter 1977; Skocpol 1979; Suleiman 1974; and Tilly 1975, 1990.

11. By the term *corporatist,* I do not refer narrowly to a mode of "interest intermediation" or "conflict negotiation," as the term is commonly used in political sociology literature. Rather, I employ the term

to define a relationship between the state, society, and the individual—a particular form of organizing membership in a polity, which takes corporate groups as its basis.

12. Katzenstein (1987) characterizes the German system as a decentralized state and a centralized society, drawing attention to "parapublic" institutions and bureaucracies as the main link between the public and private spheres, for example, the Bundesbank, Federal Employment Office, Labor Courts, the German Conference of University Presidents, and Social Welfare Funds.

13. Regarding the expansion of individual rights, see Boli's (1987b) extensive codification of national constitutions from 1872 to 1970.

14. The definition of the "other," as codified by international instruments, is based on the idea that individuals are alike and equal as human beings, but that they have a right to express their collective differences.

15. The individual person has often been noted as an institutional feature of modernity in contemporary theoretical accounts (among them, Abercrombie, Hill, and Turner 1986; Bourdieu 1984; Giddens 1990, 1991; and Turner 1986b). For two compelling variants, see Foucault 1979 and Meyer 1986a, 1986b. Foucault explains the modern emphasis on the individual person as a product of increased social differentiation and control. Meyer, on the other hand, perceives the development of the idea of the individual as an independent cultural feature of the rationalized Western model of society. They both, however, see the modern individual as subject to much collective regulation and a standardized and rationalized life course. See also Kohli 1985; Buchmann 1989; Rose 1990; and Lamont 1992 for discussions of the core dimensions of modern discourse on the person.

16. The Peace of Westphalia in 1648, for example, included provisions for the treatment of religious minorities in Germany. In the nineteenth century, the issues of slavery and the war-wounded focused efforts to make human rights part of an international agenda (Krasner 1991). The scope of these earlier efforts was limited. Christian and European tolerance was granted to "our kind," not to "strangers" (Zolberg 1990). The religious provisions of Westphalia were developed exclusively for the Christian factions; the Jews and Muslims of Europe were not considered. In the twentieth century, however, "human rights" has become ever more inclusive in scope. A "refugee" is defined as an abstract persecuted person ("all with a fear of persecution"), not necessarily referring to a specific group. For discussions of the development of the international human rights regimes, see Donnelly 1986 and Sikkink 1991.

17. It should be noted that taken-for-grantedness does not necessarily require moral commitment or internalization on the actors' part

(Jepperson 1991). Neither does it mean that institutionalized discourses are unchallenged or uncontested. It does mean that even objections are framed in the language of the dominant discourse. As the 1993 World Conference on Human Rights in Vienna demonstrated, there is wide-ranging debate over the content and definition of human rights. During the conference, speakers for Western countries insisted on defining human rights primarily in civil and political terms, while third-world representatives argued for a definition that emphasized social and economic rights of individuals and national collectives. Despite the different visions articulated, none questioned the value or necessity of human rights.

18. How global discourses and models develop and permeate actors' frames of reference at national and local levels is an important question. Recent studies provide rich accounts of the genesis, reproduction, and adoption of global norms and the role in this process of such collective public actors as international agencies, interest groups, nonprofit organizations, scientists, and experts. For notable examples, see Ferguson 1990; Finnemore 1992; and Sikkink 1991. Ferguson's fascinating ethnographic study of Lesotho shows how the concept of development becomes an intrinsic part of local political discourses and bureaucracies, and describes the crucial role played by global development agencies in this process. Through an account of the institutionalization of human rights ideas in state bureaucratic apparatuses and laws, Sikkink demonstrates how differences in national contexts shape the adoption of global norms and produce different outcomes in the United States and Europe. Finnemore, on the other hand, presents a case study of how, through the activities of the UNESCO, science policy came to be defined as a valuable goal, and was, in turn, adopted by nation-states.

Chapter Four

1. Note that, as early as 1916, France had established institutions that dealt with the recruitment and presence of foreign workers (e.g., the Interministerial Manpower Commission). However, these institutions were dismantled as the foreign workers who were imported for the duration of the war were sent back (Singer-Kérel 1991).

2. See Heclo and Madsen 1987 and Hernes 1988 for the corporatist foundations of Swedish citizenship.

3. Lithman 1987 provides detailed documentation of the instruments of Swedish immigrant policy. Also, the individual country chapters in Hammar's (1985) *European Immigration Policy* present comprehensive reviews of both immigration and immigrant policies, as well as related administrative agencies.

4. In 1992, the Chinese were granted access to certain benefits of minorities policy, even though they still are not defined as a target group (SOPEMI-Netherlands 1992).

5. From the recommendations of an advisory committee to the Ministry of Welfare, Health, and Cultural Affairs, quoted in Rath, Groenendijk, and Penninx 1991:110.

6. After the founding of the Republic of Turkey in 1923, all religious organizing was banned. Mosques, the places of worship, are normally founded and regulated by the state; a government-level office, headed by an appointed high cleric, oversees religious matters, including mosque organizations.

7. See Lijphart 1968 for a classic analysis of Dutch society as a system of pillarization.

8. Freedom of education in accord with one's ideological persuasions has been a basic right guaranteed by the constitution since 1917 (Ministry of Foreign Affairs 1987). The constitutional right is also extended to noncitizen immigrants. This guarantee allows migrant groups to educate their children in their national languages or cultures. A hundred-and-twenty families can get together and found a school based on their own beliefs, and the state has an obligation to fund such initiatives. By 1990, there were nine Islamic elementary schools in Rotterdam, all publicly funded. Similarly, within the Dutch broadcasting system, religious denominations and ethnic organizations are eligible for an allocation of broadcasting time. There is an Islamic Broadcasting Organization (IOS) and Migrant Television (MTV). The latter started by initiative of the Ministry of Welfare, Health, and Cultural Affairs, and in 1988 had a budget of 1 million Fl ($520,000). In general, however, the number of separate institutions set up on ethnic basis by initiative from the migrant groups themselves is slight (SCP 1986).

9. In 1988, there were 63,000 migrant children from preschool to upper secondary school taking classes in more than 60 languages (Swedish Institute 1989). In the Netherlands, 80 percent of minority children received mother-tongue education in primary school (Poulter 1986:180).

10. The conversion rates used throughout this text are as of May 1991; one dollar equals 0.576 British pounds (£), 5.80 French francs (F), 1.712 German marks (DM), 1.93 Dutch florins (Fl), 6.17 Swedish crowns (SKr), and 1.44 Swiss francs (SFr).

11. In the early 1970s, "overforeignization" became an important issue on the public agenda. The present quota system was introduced in response to a series of referenda demands in the Federal Constitution to limit the number of aliens (Hoffmann-Nowotny 1985; Heisler 1988). Though not stated officially, an upper limit exists, the "magic

number" of one million foreigners, not to be exceeded at any point (interview: Federal Office of Industry, Small Business, and Labor [BIGA]). Family members of migrants and refugees are not included in quota allocations.

12. The Federal Law of Abode and Settlement of Foreigners (ANAG), enacted in 1931 and still valid today, refers only to regulations for migration control (Hoffmann-Nowotny 1985). Several decrees and ordinances have been issued since 1931, each with a new set of regulatory measures. Although the last ordinance, issued in 1986, does include "the creation of favorable general conditions for the integration of aliens" as a purpose, no specific provisions are developed in the text. For an English translation of this ordinance, see Swiss-American Chamber of Commerce 1988.

13. The Swiss political administrative system is three-tiered, consisting of federal, cantonal, and communal levels. Individuals are registered as citizens at all three levels. However, the commune, where individuals are registered and have a "hereditary 'right of city,'" is the most crucial unit for the individual (de Rham 1990:168). The commune has to provide for the welfare of its citizens and their families even if they have never resided there.

14. The British education system comprises three types of schools: county schools, grant-aided schools, and independent (private) schools. The first two are public schools in the sense of being financed by local education authorities. Schools owned by religious organizations, as well as other voluntary bodies, can apply for grant-aided status (Poulter 1990b:79). In 1989, the Association of Metropolitan Authorities urged local councils to oppose any attempt to set up Muslim or other religious schools within the state system, on the grounds that they might hamper the process of integration (Runnymede Trust 1989a:7–8). There are currently about 20 Islamic schools, all private. The state has rejected a number of applications from Muslim schools for grant-aided status in the past few years. In a 1992 case, however, the High Court ruled the decision against Muslim schools "manifestly unfair" and asked the education secretary to reconsider its decision (*The Economist*, 19 December 1992).

15. See, for example, the interview in *Atlantic* with Kofi Yamgnane, the French State Secretary for Integration (Kaplan 1992).

Chapter Five

1. Appendix B illustrates the level, extent, and composition of the government, voluntary, and semi-public agencies involved in the organization of incorporation by country.

2. The framework for migrant policy is essentially established on

the basis of the reports of the Netherlands Scientific Council for Government Policy (WRR), a centrally funded committee (Entzinger 1985; Penninx 1984b). Also, the Advisory Committee on Minorities Research (ACOM), a group of academic experts, has served as a consultative council on policy development since 1978.

3. The NCB had six departments and a staff of 60 in 1988. The same year, the Center received 3.5 million florins ($1.8 million) from the Ministry of Welfare, Health, and Cultural Affairs for staffing alone (interview: NCB). In addition, the NCB runs several projects funded by different ministries.

4. The Dutch government funds both the council and subcouncils. The council meets at least four times a year at the Ministry of Home Affairs, where the secretariat for the LAO is located.

5. The business community in Switzerland, which is "well-organized, encompassing, and centralized" (Katzenstein 1980), is consulted regularly by the government regarding foreign worker quotas, both federal and cantonal. A large percentage of these quotas are reserved for seasonal labor.

6. In 1988, the Federal Aliens Office had 120 employees, half of whom, curiously, worked at the Central Register for Aliens.

7. In 1988, the Commission had 26 members, 6 of whom were of foreign origin.

8. In the canton of Zurich alone there are about 3,000 social service organizations, 60 of which specialize in helping foreigners (Informationsstelle des Zürcher Sozialwesens 1988).

9. The CRE is funded by the Home Office. In 1991, the CRE had a staff of 211 and a budget of £14 million ($24.3 million). The Commission has five divisions, two of which specifically deal with discrimination in employment, education, and housing, and one with complaints, and legal representation and services (CRE 1991).

10. Financially, RECs depend on the CRE and local authorities. In 1988, the CRE supplied grants for the employment of full-time staff in 87 of the 101 RECs (CRE 1988). In addition to full-time officers, RECs rely on an advisory body of individuals from various ethnic minority organizations, trade unions, political parties, and local authorities.

11. There is a considerable body of literature that discusses problems and in-fighting within the RECs (formerly, the Community Relations Councils) in regard to representation. In particular, see Gay and Young 1988 and Prashar and Nicholas 1986.

12. Body-Gendrot and Schain (1992) argue that although the unitary structure of the French political system places immigration formally in the domain of central authorities, local authorities also had a considerable say in the definition and implementation of the integration policy until the 1980s.

13. The second component of this ministry's name has evolved over time from National Solidarity, to Employment, and finally to its 1991 version, Integration, reflecting the projected changes in policy orientation.

14. The FAS has ten regional commissions (CRIPI). In 1989, it had a staff of 120, eighty-five of whom worked in its headquarters in Paris.

15. This emphasis on "republican citizenship" was the underlying theme in the address that the French State Secretary for Integration, Kofi Yamgnane, gave at a 1992 conference at Harvard University. See also the interview with the Secretary in Kaplan 1992.

16. Altogether, these three social service organizations had about 600 counseling centers and a staff of 900 in 1990.

17. As I learned in an interview, the Commissioner's office had, in 1988, a budget of around 100,000 DM ($58,000), excluding salaries, 10 percent of which was spent on publications.

18. Berlin was the first state to appoint a Commissioner for Foreigners' Affairs in 1981. The office of the commissioner is attached to the Ministry for Social Affairs of the Berlin Senate. In 1991, the office had 25 employees.

Chapter Six

1. For studies of migrant associations in specific European countries, refer to the volumes edited by Gerholm and Lithman (1988); Jenkins (1988); and Rex, Joly, and Wilpert (1987).

2. For major exceptions, see Schmitter (1980); Heisler (1985, 1986); and Miller (1981), who emphasize the importance of the organizational structures of the host as well as the sending society in providing access to sociopolitical participation. See also de Graaf, Penninx, and Stoové 1988; Werbner 1991; and Layton-Henry 1990b for discussions of the role of the host state on the form and effectiveness of migrant organizations.

3. Migrants from Turkey are the largest group among the foreign migrant populations in Europe. They also constitute the largest foreign group within the European Community: 24.4 percent of all foreigners. In 1990, there were about 1.7 million Turks in Germany; 204,000 in the Netherlands; 201,500 in France; 64,200 in Switzerland; and 25,500 in Sweden (SOPEMI 1992:135–40).

4. As well as self-organizing, migrants do participate in the formal organizational structures of the host society. The most obvious and relevant ones are trade unions and political organizations of various sorts, such as political parties, civil rights groups, and solidarity associations. Turkish migrant membership in the German Social Democratic Party, for instance, was 24,000 in 1990, 2.5 percent of total SPD

membership (Şen 1990). Trade unions, by their field of competence, have a natural interest in labor migrants. However, trade union policies with regard to labor migration vary among host societies, which leads to considerable differences in migrant membership in trade unions. See Freeman 1978; Miller 1981; B. Schmitter 1981; and Vranken 1990 for discussions of trade union politics with respect to migrant labor and migrant participation.

5. Boli reports that 75 percent of all Swedish voluntary associations are affiliated with national-level federations.

6. The idea that "popular movements" can be organized as part of a state administrative structure may sound antithetical, but it simply reflects the excessively organized character of Swedish polity.

7. The Eastern European refugee groups (Polish, Latvian, Estonian, and Hungarian federations) are united as the East European Groups. The Cooperating Immigrant Federation in Europe (SIOS) includes the remaining 10 national federations (Assyrian, Greek, Yugoslav, Finnish, Spanish, Italian, Portuguese, Polish, and Turkish). Both working groups have a permanent secretariat financed by the government. As new national groups organize, they are incorporated into these structures, the latest addition being the Kurdish Federation.

8. At the local level, 30 percent of associations claim to have social service and advising functions (Bäck 1983), which is still fairly low compared to cases like Britain, where 70 percent of the groups claim to perform these services.

9. For instance, in 1987, state funding was distributed according to the following scheme (membership size/amount of funding):

1,000–3,499	250,000 SKr ($ 40,500)
3,500–4,499	400,000 SKr ($ 64,800)
4,500–6,999	650,000 SKr ($105,300)
7,000–10,999	800,000 SKr ($129,600)
11,000–14,999	900,000 SKr ($145,800)
15,000–29,999	1,100,000 SKr ($178,200)
30,000 and up	1,300,000 SKr ($210,600)

(source: SIV).

10. Historically, the free churches began in opposition to the Swedish national church by forming local parishes and committees. Consequently, the funding structure of the free churches is designed according to the church parish model, that is, based on local membership. Although this particular form of organizing is not necessarily consonant with Islamic organizational forms (or with Orthodox, Catholic, or Buddhist practices, for that matter), the very existence of

this organizational and funding structure induces the Islamic groups to organize into parishes and local committees.

11. The Muslim Association works closely with the National Turkish Federation; most migrants are members of both.

12. In 1987, the Swedish Muslim Association, which had 12,000 members, received 344,000 SKr ($55,728), and the United Islamic Congregations (an organization of mostly non-Turkish Muslims), which has 17,000 members, received 437,000 SKr ($70,794).

13. The training courses financed by the NCB are usually administered by outside educational institutions. The courses are designed to teach immigrants how to set up organizations of their own. Topics covered by these courses include how executive committees should function, how to conduct an efficient meeting, what types of associations and organizations exist, how to solicit funding from the state, and how to prepare a budget (Informatie Amsterdam 1987). The National Cooperation of Foreign Workers' Organizations (LSOBA), an umbrella organization of migrants from different nationalities, criticizes this policy on the grounds that "the courses are designed to meet the needs of the government rather than the migrant organizations per se. The government forces the cadres of migrant organizations to take these courses in order to make them cooperate with their existing models and policies" (LSOBA 1986:24).

14. In 1986–87, although the IOT presented separate advisory reports on 14 major governmental legislative proposals, including laws about discrimination and equal opportunity, and the new foreigners' law, only 6 of them were taken into account at the time of final decision making (IOT 1986/87). This circumstance was interpreted as an accomplishment by one of the IOT executives, who said, "Although not all of our proposals are accepted, we still have considerable influence on matters" (interview: IOT).

15. Two considerably active organizations at the national level are the West Indian Standing Conference and the Confederation of Indian Organizations.

16. JCWI, founded in 1967, is a London-based organization whose primary focus is political action against restrictive immigration legislation. It also has a legal service program to help migrants with visa, entry, and naturalization problems.

17. *Maghrebian* refers to Algerian, Moroccan, and Tunisian migrants, who together constitute 40 percent of all foreigners in France.

18. There are, for example, fifteen Portuguese federations, mostly associated at the regional level (CEDEP 1986). The main exceptions are the Spanish and Italian associations, as is the case in Switzerland. Seventy percent of the Spanish associations are united in two large

federations supported by the Spanish state and the Catholic church. Similarly, the Christian Association of Italian Workers (ACLI) and the Catholic Mission gather together a large proportion of Italian migrants (FAS and the Directorate of Migrant Populations 1987).

19. In the 1970s, several migrant associations oriented primarily toward Turkey and its politics came into being. The organizational scene was divided by different political tendencies, replicating the political groupings in Turkey, itself. The four major organizations were the Federation of Turkish Associations in Germany, the Federation of Turkish Workers in Europe, the Federation of Progressive People's Associations, and the Turkish Federation (Özak and Sezer 1987). In 1991, only the Federation of Progressive People's Associations remained active. In the last decade, migrant groups have started to orient themselves toward life in Europe, and the organizations established since then reflect this orientation.

20. In Germany, Muslim organizations can operate legally as registered associations. However, the *Länder* governments are not willing to recognize Muslim associations as equal to other religious bodies, since that would require allocating funding from church tax revenues to these organizations.

21. This conviction was expressed in several interviews I conducted with government officials responsible for migrants and migrant issues.

22. Interestingly enough, despite Islam's appeal for a world religion and its transnational character, Islamic associations in Europe are organized along national lines. See, for example, Bastenier 1988 and Joly 1988a. There are only a few umbrella organizations that gather together Islamic associations from different sending countries. The sending governments also promote a more national base for the organization of Islam in host countries.

23. In a subsequent decision on the case, the Conseil d'Etat, the highest administrative court in France, relegated the decision on veiling to local educational authorities on a case-by-case basis. However, the Conseil at the same time required the local authorities to remain within the bounds of criteria established by the government circular. See Feldblum 1993 for an illuminating analysis of the affair.

Chapter Seven

1. The Common Nordic Labor Market has existed since 1954 among Denmark, Finland, Iceland, Norway, and Sweden.

2. The information in the two paragraphs that follow is mainly drawn from Niessen's (1989) detailed review of the laws and regula-

tions regarding entry and stay in 17 European countries. For a comprehensive source on the legal status of aliens and their rights under national laws, see Frowein and Stein 1987.

3. Restrictions introduced by the new conservative French government in 1993, which denied foreign students the benefits of the family reunion policy and authorized public prosecutors to suspend "marriages of convenience," were rejected by the French Constitutional Council on the grounds that they breach foreigners' human rights (*Le Monde*, 16 August 1993).

4. The most recent legislative changes aim to curb the influx of asylum seekers by tightening application procedures. Germany, for instance, revised its constitutional provisions guaranteeing automatic right to asylum, to bring its policy into line with other European countries.

5. See the by-now classic text by Castles and Kosack (1973) on guestworker programs and the status of guestworkers.

6. The analysis of North, de Wenden, and Taylor is confined to access to social services in Britain, Canada, Germany, France, Sweden, and the United States. See also the volumes edited by Layton-Henry (1990) and Brubaker (1989), which discuss the civil, political, and socioeconomic rights of migrants in selected Western countries. Similar to North, de Wenden, and Taylor 1987, these volumes also conclude that the socioeconomic rights of permanent residents are not different than those of citizens.

7. See Schuck 1987 and Hull 1985 on the rights and status of illegal aliens in the United States.

8. In 1990, the Dutch government adopted a plan to promote the employment of migrants in ministries and government institutions, with the goal of raising the proportion of ethnic minorities in civil services to 5 percent in five years (SOPEMI-Netherlands 1991). Similarly, the municipality of Amsterdam has a regulation requiring that the proportion of people of different ethnic origins (citizen or noncitizen) be reflected in city personnel and in all government-subsidized local organizations (interview: City of Amsterdam, Bureau for Ethnic Minority Affairs).

9. Note also that in the United States, until World War I, aliens voted in local, state, and national elections in 22 states, thus enjoying political rights that many citizens, black and female, did not (Raskin 1993).

10. Trade union activity and participation in work councils can be considered separately as industrial rights (see Vranken 1990, and also Barbalet 1988 for a discussion). Nevertheless, in many European countries, notably Germany and Sweden, where trade unions and

work councils constitute important channels for participation in politics, it is difficult to differentiate the right to participate in them categorically from political rights.

11. Although selectively invoked, national security still plays an important role in defining the boundaries of citizenship. Nevertheless, the issue is more symbolic than real, since security issues are much more internationalized than most of the host society governments appear (or are willing) to accept.

12. See Wölker 1987 for a detailed study of foreigners' civil rights (freedom of speech, assembly, and association for political purposes) in the domestic laws of western European countries.

13. For critiques of Marshall's evolutionary scheme, see in particular Barbalet 1988; Giddens 1985; Mann 1987; and Turner 1986a.

14. The situation is similar for asylum seekers. Switzerland in 1988 had a backlog of 20,000 asylum applicants, three-quarters of whom were expected eventually to be given the legal status of refugee. In 1990, this number reached 58,000 (SOPEMI 1992:29). The understanding, as succinctly put by a high-level bureaucrat at the Federal Aliens Office, was that "these people have been in the country for four or five years and have already settled, brought their children, and established a life. You cannot simply throw them out, on the ground of some legal rules." On the same grounds, in other European countries, at least one-third of asylum seekers whose requests are declined are nonetheless allowed to stay (*The Economist*, 17 August 1991).

15. I have borrowed this term from Stephan Leibfried (personal communication).

Chapter Eight

1. The first international acknowledgment of children's rights was the Declaration of the Rights of the Child, adopted in Geneva in 1923 (Underhill 1979). In 1990, the Convention on the Rights of the Child became international human rights law, affirming the rights of children to survival, protection, development, and education (*International Herald Tribune*, 1 October 1990). See also Boli and Meyer 1987 and Ramirez 1989 for the incorporation of children rights into national constitutions and agendas.

2. Katzenstein (1985) argues that economic openness and vulnerability to fluctuations in the global economy facilitate welfare and corporatist arrangements in the small states of Europe. Similarly, Cameron (1978) shows that trade dependence has a positive effect on social spending in European countries. Freeman (1986) acknowledges the increasing openness of national economies but considers it a source of tension for the "viability" of the welfare state.

3. There had been sporadic laws enacted to control certain population flows, but systematic immigration regulation and control of aliens were established only after World War I in most European countries (Hammar 1986). The "work permit" is also a relatively new innovation; from the early nineteenth century until the 1920s, one did not need such a permit to enter a country as a fully empowered economic actor.

4. In Sweden, there were 100,000 people with dual citizenship in 1985. Each year, about 10,000 new cases are added (Hammar 1985b). France has over one million Franco-Algerian dual nationals (de Rham 1990). In 1985, the total number of people holding dual citizenship in western Europe was estimated to be between 3 and 4 million (Perotti, Costes, and Llaumett 1989).

5. All of the common indicators of state strength show an increase throughout the century (Boli 1987a, 1993). At the same time, nation-states are becoming much more vulnerable to outside influences.

6. The 1981 British Nationality Act even formalizes this "multiple status" through legal categories. According to the act, British citizenship is a three-tier system, composed of British citizens, British overseas citizens, and citizens of dependent territories, each with a differential set of rights (Handsworth Law Centre 1985).

7. Contemporary polities like South Africa and Israel that ventured to institutionalize such unequal statuses have been strongly condemned and have failed to maintain their status quo.

8. The very existence of the category "refugee," referring to persons whose most basic rights are denied in their own countries by their own states, demonstrates the fragility of the ideals of personhood and citizenship. Ironically, refugee status does not apply to people under the sovereignty of their own government, whatever the violation of their basic human rights.

9. See Heisler 1986 for the involvement of sending countries in matters related to the lives of migrants. Most states, for example, recruit and send their own teachers and clergy to perform educational and religious functions for their citizens abroad.

10. Other regional human rights conventions include the American Declaration of the Rights and Duties of Man (1948), the American Convention on Human Rights (1969) accompanied by the Inter-American Court of Human Rights (1979), and the African Charter on Human and People's Rights (1981). Though not in effect, the Arab Charter of Human Rights (1971) and the Draft Arab Covenant on Human Rights (1979) also exist (Donnelly 1986).

11. See Böhning 1988 for a review of ILO activities and labor standards regarding the protection of migrant workers. The Council of Europe, an institution entirely separate from the European Commu-

nity, principally engages in promoting treaties and agreements between member countries concerning a broad range of human rights and social and economic affairs.

12. Certain collective rights are already included in national legislation. For example, Sweden, the Netherlands, and Belgium recognize the right to use the mother tongue and have arrangements to provide for it. Also, all European Community countries have legislation allowing religious rituals that involve slaughtering animals (Poulter 1986).

13. See Böhning 1988; Goodwin-Gill 1989; Goodwin-Gill, Jenny, and Perruchoud 1985; Niessen 1989; Plender 1985, 1988; and the 1991 special issue of the *International Migration Review* for more detailed accounts of these conventions. Niessen (1989) also lists the ratifying countries for various conventions.

14. The provision for local and European voting rights awaits the enactment of the Maastricht treaty, which was ratified by all EC member states in 1993.

15. In 1990, the European Community had agreements with five immigrant-sending countries: Turkey, Algeria, Morocco, Tunisia, and Yugoslavia.

16. These collectivities are referred to as "transnational moral entrepreneurs" (Nadelmann 1990), "epistemic communities" (Ruggie 1975), and "rationalized others" (Meyer 1994). For empirical studies of norm diffusion and policy influence by international organizations, see Finnemore 1992 and McNeely 1990.

17. Justice Minister Pierre Méhaignerie and Social Affairs Minister Simone Veil opposed the proposed legislation on identity checks for foreigners, arguing that it may lead to racial discrimination.

18. The call for dual citizenship has also received support from the liberal Free Democrats (FDP), a partner in the ruling coalition, and such prominent members of the Christian Democrats (CDU), the major partner in the coalition, as the president of parliament, Rita Süssmuth, and the mayor of Berlin, Eberhard Diepgen. In addressing a workshop at the Center for European Studies at Harvard University in January 1992, Barbara John, head of the Office of Foreigners' Affairs in Berlin, likened Germany's existing citizenship codes to "tribal membership," and advocated changes toward "club membership."

19. There are regional protocols and charters that aim at regulating migration for employment, including the Protocol on Free Movement of Persons of the Economic Community of West African States and the Charter of the Organization of African Unity, but they do not contain provisions as comprehensive as the ones I have discussed.

20. The 1993 World Conference on Human Rights was a forum for

expanding and redefining human rights beyond their conventional scope. The Conference recognized for the first time the rights of "poor nations" to economic development and the right of women to protection on the basis of gender as inviolable human rights (*New York Times,* 21 June 1993).

21. An urgency about "control over borders" summarizes official rhetoric. In defending Austria's new restrictive asylum law, the Director of Immigration reasoned that "in international migration, there is a point at which it becomes chaotic and there is no longer a means to control it" (*New York Times,* 10 August 1993).

22. Germany has concluded similar financial aid agreements with other refugee-sending countries such as the former Yugoslavia, Poland, the Czech Republic, and Russia. In 1991, an agreement with the former Yugoslavia for the "reintegration" of Macedonian Gypsies promised a program that included financing of kindergartens and job-training facilities (*Business Week,* 9 September 1991). The practice is not limited to Germany. When Albanian asylum seekers were sent back in 1991, the Italian government allocated "an emergency economic and financial aid package" for Albania (SOPEMI 1992:30).

23. After the political transformations in Eastern Europe, the Baltic states of Latvia and Estonia and the Czech Republic launched exclusive national citizenship schemes creating large noncitizen minorities from populations that had citizenship previously.

24. The right to self-determination is recognized by two major instruments of human rights: the International Covenant on Civil and Political Rights, and the International Covenant on Economic, Social, and Cultural Rights. The first article of both covenants proclaims that "all peoples have the right of self-determination. By virtue of that right, they freely determine their political status and freely pursue their economic, social, and cultural development" (quoted in Dinstein 1976:106).

25. Spain comprises 17 regions with varying degrees of autonomy, some with separate languages. In 1991, Italy recognized 11 minority languages, giving regional authorities substantial discretion to implement bilingualism in schools (*Financial Times,* 22 November 1991). In 1993, the French government asked local authorities to develop bilingual education programs in regions with such indigenous languages as Breton, Flemish, Occitan, Basque, and Catalan (*New York Times,* 3 May 1993).

26. My thanks to John Meyer for reminding me of this point. In 1992 a Viking exhibition, the first of its kind, toured Europe with the usual fare—food tents, on-the-spot craft production, dances and singing, and face-painting. The image presented was a tame, domestic

one, supplanting the "barbaric" swords, shields, and carnage customarily associated with the Vikings. Similarly in 1988, the exhibit, "Süleyman, the Magnificent" toured the world and recast the "warlike" reign of that Ottoman sultan as a history of arts, architecture, and legal and administrative reforms.

BIBLIOGRAPHY

Abadan-Unat, Nermin. 1985. Identity Crisis of Turkish Migrants, First and Second Generation. In *Turkish Workers in Europe: An Interdisciplinary Study,* ed. İ. Başgöz and N. Furniss. Bloomington: Indiana University Turkish Studies.

Abercrombie, Nicholas, Stephen Hill, and Bryan S. Turner. 1986. *Sovereign Individuals of Capitalism.* London: Allen and Unwin.

Abu-Lughod, Janet L. 1989a. *Before European Hegemony: The World System, A.D. 1250–1350.* London: Oxford University Press.

———. 1989b. Restructuring the Premodern World System. Paper presented at the annual meeting of the American Sociological Association, San Francisco.

Amin, Samir, ed. 1974. *Modern Migrations in West Africa.* London: Oxford University Press.

City of Amsterdam. 1986. *Actieprogramma Minderhedenbeleid.* Amsterdam.

———. 1987. *Actieprogramma Minderhedenbeleid.* Amsterdam.

Andersen, Uwe. 1990. Consultative Institutions for Migrant Workers. In *The Political Rights of Migrant Workers in Western Europe,* ed. Z. Layton-Henry. London: Sage.

Anderson, Benedict. 1983. *Imagined Communities: Reflections on the Origin and Spread of Nationalism.* London: Verso.

Anderson, Perry. 1979. *Lineages of the Absolutist State.* London: Verso.

Anwar, Muhammad. 1991. Ethnic Minorities' Representation: Voting and Electoral Politics in Britain, and the Role of Leaders. In *Black and Ethnic Leaderships in Britain: The Cultural Dimensions of Political Action,* ed. P. Werbner and M. Anwar. London: Routledge.

Appadurai, Arjun, and Carol A. Breckenridge. 1988. Why Public Culture? *Public Culture* 1:5–9.

Ashford, Douglas E. 1982. *British Dogmatism and French Pragmatism: Central-Local Policymaking in the Welfare State.* London: George Allen and Unwin.

ATT (Association des Travailleurs de Turquie). 1987. *7. Yılında Perspektifimiz-Aktivitemiz.* Paris: Türkiyeli İşçiler Derneği.

Bäck, Henry. 1983. *Invandrarnas Riksorganisationer.* Report, no. 24. Stockholm: EIFO.

Badie, Bertrand, and Pierre Birnbaum. 1983. *The Sociology of the State.* Chicago: University of Chicago Press.

Baker, David P., Yılmaz Esmer, Gero Lenhardt, and John Meyer. 1985. Effects of Immigrant Workers on Educational Stratification in Germany. *Sociology of Education* 58:213–27.

Barbalet, J. M. 1988. *Citizenship: Rights, Struggle and Class Inequality.* Milton Keynes, England: Open University Press.

Bastenier, Albert. 1988. Islam in Belgium: Contradictions and Perspectives. In *The New Islamic Presence in Western Europe,* ed. T. Gerholm and Y. G. Lithman. London: Mansell.

Bauböck, Rainer, and Hannes Wimmer. 1988. Social Partnership and 'Foreigners Policy': On Special Features of Austria's Guest-worker System. *European Journal of Political Research* 16:659–82.

Bendix, Reinhard. 1977. *Nation-Building and Citizenship: Studies of Our Changing Social Order.* Berkeley and Los Angeles: University of California Press.

BIGA (Bundesamt für Industrie, Gewerbe und Arbeit). 1986. *Weisungen und Erlauterungen zur Verordnung des Bundesrates vom 6. Oktober 1986 über die Begrenzung der Zahl der Ausländer.* Bern.

Birmingham Community Relations Council. 1988. *Annual Report 1987/88.* Birmingham.

Birnbaum, Pierre. 1988. *States and Collective Action: The European Experience.* Cambridge: Cambridge University Press.

Body-Gendrot, Sophie, and Martin A. Schain. 1992. National and Local Politics and the Development of Immigration Policy in the United States and France: A Comparative Analysis. In *Immigrants in Two Democracies: French and American Experience,* ed. D. L. Horowitz and G. Noiriel. New York: New York University Press.

Böhning, W. R. 1978. International Migration and the Western World: Past, Present, Future. *International Migration* 16:11–22.

———. 1979a. International Migration and the International Economic Order. *Journal of International Affairs* 33:187–200.

———. 1979b. International Migration in Western Europe: Reflections on the Past Five Years. *International Labour Review* 118: 401–14.

———. 1988. The Protection of Migrant Workers and International Labour Standards. *International Migration* 26:133–45.

Boli, John. 1987a. World Polity Sources of Expanding State Authority and Organization, 1870–1970. In *Institutional Structure: Constituting State, Society, and the Individual*,ed. Thomas et al. Newbury Park, Calif.: Sage.

———. 1987b. Human Rights or State Expansion? Cross-national Definitions of Constitutional Rights, 1870–1970. In *Institutional Structure: Constituting State, Society, and the Individual*, ed. Thomas et al. Newbury Park, Calif.: Sage.

———. 1989. *New Citizens for a New Society: The Institutional Origins of Mass Schooling in Sweden*. New York: Pergamon Press.

———. 1991. Sweden: Is There a Viable Third Sector? In *Between States and Markets: The Voluntary Sector in Comparative Perspective*, ed. R. Wuthnow. Princeton: Princeton University Press.

———. 1993. Sovereignty from a World Polity Perspective. Paper presented at the annual meeting of the American Sociological Association, Miami.

Boli, John, and John W. Meyer. 1987. The Ideology of Childhood and the State: Rules Distinguishing Children in National Constitutions, 1870–1970. In *Institutional Structure: Constituting State, Society, and the Individual*, ed. Thomas et al. Newbury Park, Calif.: Sage.

Bourdieu, Pierre. 1977. *Outline of a Theory of Practice*. Cambridge: Cambridge University Press.

———. 1984. *Distinction: A Social Critique of the Judgment of Taste*. Cambridge: Harvard University Press.

Boyzon-Fradet, Danielle. 1992. The French Education System: Springboard or Obstacle to Integration? In *Immigrants in Two Democracies: French and American Experience*, ed. D. L. Horowitz and G. Noiriel. New York: New York University Press.

Brouwer, Lenie, and Marijke Priester. 1983. Living in Between, Turkish Women in Their Homeland and in the Netherlands. In *One Way Ticket: Migration and Female Labor*, ed. A. Phizacklea. London: Routledge and Kegan Paul.

Brown, L. Neville, and Jeremy McBride. 1981. Observation on the Proposed Accession by the European Community to the European Convention on Human Rights. *The American Journal of Comparative Law* 29:691–705.

Brubaker, William Rogers. 1989a. Introduction. In *Immigration and Politics of Citizenship in Europe and North America*, ed. W. R. Brubaker. Lanham, Md.: University Press of America.

———. 1989b. Citizenship and Naturalization: Policies and Politics. In *Immigration and Politics of Citizenship in Europe and North America*, ed. W. R. Brubaker. Lanham, Md.: University Press of America.

———. 1989c. Membership without Citizenship: The Economic and Social Rights of Noncitizens. In *Immigration and Politics of Citizenship in Europe and North America,* ed. W. R. Brubaker. Lanham, Md.: University Press of America.

———. 1992. *Citizenship and Nationhood in France and Germany.* Cambridge: Harvard University Press.

Brubaker, William Rogers, ed. 1989. *Immigration and Politics of Citizenship in Europe and North America.* Lanham, Md.: University Press of America.

Brumberg, Stephan F. 1986. *Going to America, Going to School: The Jewish Immigrant Public School Encounter in Turn-of-the-Century New York City.* New York: Praeger.

Buchmann, Marlis. 1989. *The Script of Life in Modern Society: Entry into Adulthood in a Changing World.* Chicago: University of Chicago Press.

Burgdörfer, F. 1931. Migration across the Frontiers of Germany. In *International Migrations,* vol. 2, ed. W. F. Willcox. New York: National Bureau of Economic Research, Inc.

Çağlar, Ayşe Ş. 1990. The Prison House of Culture in the Studies of Turks in Germany. *Sozialanthropologische Arbeitspapiere,* no. 31. Institut für Ethnologie, Freie Universität, Berlin.

CAIF (Conseil des Associations d'Immigrés en France). 1988. *Bulletin d'Information et de Liaison.* May–June. Paris.

Callovi, Giuseppe. 1992. Regulation of Immigration in 1993: Pieces of the European Community Jig-Saw Puzzle. *International Migration Review* 26:353–72.

Cameron, David R. 1978. The Expansion of the Public Economy: A Comparative Analysis. *American Political Science Review* 72:1243–61.

Carens, Joseph H. 1989. Membership and Morality: Admission to Citizenship in Liberal Democratic States. In *Immigration and Politics of Citizenship in Europe and North America,* ed. W. R. Brubaker. Lanham, Md.: University Press of America.

Castles, Stephen. 1984. *Here for Good: Western Europe's New Ethnic Minorities.* London: Pluto Press.

———. 1985. The Guests Who Stayed—The Debate on 'Foreigners Policy' in the German Federal Republic. *International Migration Review* 19:517–34.

Castles, Stephen, and Godula Kosack. 1972. The Function of Labour Immigration in Western European Capitalism. *New Left Review* 73: 3–21.

———. 1973. *Immigrant Workers and Class Structure in Western Europe.* Oxford: Oxford University Press.

CBS (Centraal Bureau voor de Statistiek). 1987. *Minderheden in Nederland, Statistisch Vademecum 1987.* Rotterdam.

CEDEP (Collectif pour l'Etude et la Dynamisation de l'Emigration Portugaises). 1986. *Enfermement et Ouvertures: Les Associations Portugaises en France.* Paris.

Centre for the Study of Islam and Christian–Muslim Relations. 1987. Muslim Demands of the British Political Parties. *News of Muslims in Europe,* no. 40, pp. 6–7. Birmingham.

Cheetham, Juliet. 1988. Ethnic Associations in Britain. In *Ethnic Associations and the Welfare State: Services to Immigrants in Five Countries,* ed. S. Jenkins. New York: Columbia University Press.

Commissioner for Foreigners' Affairs of the Senate of Berlin. 1985. *Foreign Nationals and Policy on Matters Concerning Foreigners.* Berlin.

———. 1986. *Miteinander Leben: Bilanz und Perspektiven.* Berlin.

———. 1991. *Das Aufenthaltsrecht nach dem neuen Ausländergesetz.* Berlin.

———. 1992. *Aufgabenschwerpunkte.* Berlin.

Commission Européenne Immigrés. 1985. What Type of Migrations For Which Europe? Report of the Tenth International Seminar. *Objectif Immigrés.* Brussels.

Commission of the European Communities. 1976. Action Programme in Favour of Migrant Workers and Their Families. *Bulletin of the European Communities,* Supplement 3/76. Luxembourg: Office for Official Publications of the European Communities.

———. 1977. *Freedom of Movement for Workers within the Community.* Official Texts. Luxembourg: Office for Official Publications of the European Communities.

———. 1985a. Migrants in the European Community. *European File,* no. 13/85. Luxembourg: Office for Official Publications of the European Communities.

———. 1985b. Guidelines for a Community Policy on Migration. *Bulletin of the European Communities,* Supplement 9/85. Luxembourg: Office for Official Publications of the European Communities.

———. 1986a. Voting Rights in Local Elections for Community Nationals. *Bulletin of the European Communities,* Supplement 7/86. Luxembourg: Office for Official Publications of the European Communities.

———. 1986b. The Court of Justice of the European Community. *European Documentation,* Periodical 5. Luxembourg: Office for Official Publications of the European Communities.

———. 1987. New Rights for the Citizens of Europe. *European File,* no. 11/87. Luxembourg: Office for Official Publications of the European Communities.

———. 1989a. Proposal for a Council Regulation (EEC) Amending Regulation (EEC) No 1612/68 on Freedom of Movement for Workers within the Community. COM(88) 815 final—SYN 185. Brussels.

———. 1989b. The European Community and Human Rights. *European File,* no. 5/89. Luxembourg: Office for Official Publications of the European Communities.

Council of Europe. 1977. *European Convention on the Legal Status of Migrant Workers.* Strasbourg.

———. 1981. *European Migration in the 1980s: Trends and Policies.* Conference of European Ministers Responsible for Migration Affairs, Strasbourg, 6–8 May 1980, Records. Strasbourg.

———. 1987. *The Culture of Immigrant Populations and Cultural Policies: Socio-Cultural Innovations in the Member States of the CDCC.* DECS/EGT (86) 34. Strasbourg.

CRE (Commission for Racial Equality). 1983a. *Code of Practice: Race Relations.* London.

———. 1983b. *Ethnic Minority Community Languages: A Statement.* London.

———. 1985. *Directory of Ethnic Minority Organisations in the UK.* London.

———. 1988. *Annual Report of the Commission for Racial Equality.* London.

———. 1990. *Annual Report of the Commission for Racial Equality.* London.

———. 1991. *Annual Report of the Commission for Racial Equality.* London.

———. 1992. *Second Review of the Race Relations Act 1976.* London.

Daalder, Hans. 1984. On the Origins of the Consociational Democracy Model. *Acta Politica* 19:97–116.

Danmarks Statistik. 1989. *Statistik om Invandrere.* Copenhagen: Indenrigsministeriet.

Darnton, John. 1993. Western Europe Is Ending Its Welcome to Immigrants. *New York Times,* 10 August.

Davis, Kingsley. 1974. The Migrations of Human Populations. *Scientific American* 231:93–105.

DiMaggio, Paul J., and Walter W. Powell. 1983. The Iron Cage Revisited: Institutionalized Isomorphism and Collective Rationality in Organizational Fields. *American Sociological Review* 48:147–60.

———. 1991. Introduction. In *The New Institutionalism in Organizational Analysis,* ed. W. W. Powell and P. J. DiMaggio. Chicago: University of Chicago Press.

Dinstein, Yoram. 1976. Collective Human Rights of Peoples and Minorities. *The International and Comparative Law Quarterly* 25:102–20.

DGB (Deutscher Gewerkschaftsbund). 1987. *Die deutschen Gewerkschaften und die ausländischen Arbeitnehmer: Beschlüsse, Forderungen, Stellungnahmen und Empfehlungen.* Düsseldorf.

———. 1990. *Informationen zum neuen Ausländergesetz,* no. 4. Düsseldorf.

Dobbin, Frank. 1994. *Forging Industrial Policy: The United States, Britain, and France in the Railway Age.* New York: Cambridge University Press.

Dohse, Knuth. 1981. *Ausländische Arbeiter und bürgerlicher Staat: Genese und Funktion von staatlicher Ausländerpolitik und Ausländerrecht.* Königstein, Germany: Verlag Anton Hain.

Donnelly, Jack. 1986. International Human Rights: A Regime Analysis. *International Organization* 40:559–642.

Doomernik, Jeroen. 1988. Turkish Islamic Institutions and Integration. Department of Social Geography, University of Amsterdam, the Netherlands. Manuscript.

Dumon, W. A. 1977. The Activity of Voluntary Agencies and National Associations in Helping Immigrants to Overcome Initial Problems. *International Migration* 15:113–26.

Ehrenberg, Victor. 1962. *The People of Aristophanes: A Sociology of Old Attic Comedy.* New York: Schocken Books.

EKA (Eidgenössische Konsultativkommission für das Ausländerproblem). 1975. *Konzept zum Ausländerproblem.* Bern.

———. 1977. Die Ausländerfrage in den Aktionsprogrammen der Parteien zur Legislaturperiode 1975–1979. In *Zur Tätigkeit der Eidgenössischen Konsultativkommission für das Ausländerproblem,* pp. 27–34. Bern.

EKA (Eidgenössische Kommission für Ausländerprobleme). 1981. *Information,* no. 13. Bern.

———. 1982. *Information,* no. 14. Bern.

———. 1986. *Auszug aus dem Bericht des Bundesrates über seine Geschäftsführung im Jahre 1986.* Bern.

———. 1987. *Auszug aus der internen Zeitung des Bundesamtes für Zivilschutz.* Bern.

Entzinger, Han B. 1985. The Netherlands. In *European Immigration Policy,* ed. T. Hammar. Cambridge: Cambridge University Press.

———. 1987. Race, Class and the Shaping of a Policy for Immigrants: The Case of the Netherlands. *International Migration* 25: 5–19.

Esman, Milton J. 1992. The Political Fallout of International Migration. *Diaspora* 2:3–41.

Esping-Andersen, Gøsta. 1990. *The Three Worlds of Welfare Capitalism.* Princeton: Princeton University Press.

Esser, Hartmut. 1980. *Aspekte der Wanderungssoziologie: Assimilation und Integration von Wanderern, ethnischen Gruppen und Minderheiten.* Darmstadt: Luchterhand.

FAS (Fonds d'Action Sociale). 1988a. *Le FAS, 1958–1988. 30e Anniversaire.* Paris.

———. 1988b. *Programme et Orientations du FAS pour 1988.* Paris.

———. 1989a. *Annuaire des Organismes Finances par le FAS en 1988.* Paris.

———. 1989b. *Programme 1989 et Orientations 1989–91.* Paris.

FAS and the Directorate of Migrant Populations, Ministry of Social Affairs. 1987. *Le Rôle du Mouvement Associatif dans l'Evolution des Communautés Immigrés.* 3 vols. Paris.

FASTI (Fédération des Associations de Solidarité avec les Travailleurs Immigrés). 1985. *Argumentaire: Pour le Droit de Vote des Immigrés.* Paris.

———. 1989. *Douzième Congrès Documents.* Paris.

FCLIS (Federazione Colonie libere italiane in Svizzera). 1987. *Plattform.* Zurich.

Federal Commissioner for Foreigners' Affairs. 1986a. *Bericht zur Ausländerbeschäftigung.* Mitteilungen, September. Bonn.

———. 1986b. *Das Amt der Ausländerbeauftragten-Tätigkeitsbericht, 1983 bis 1986.* Mitteilungen, November. Bonn.

———. 1987. *Ausländerrecht der Bundesländer.* Mitteilungen, Juli. Bonn.

———. 1988. *Daten und Fakten zur Ausländersituation.* Mitteilungen, Mai. Bonn.

Federal Labor Institute. 1988. *Ratgeber für Türkische Arbeitnehmer.* Nurnberg.

Federal Ministry of Interior. 1987. *Survey of the Policy and Law Regarding Aliens in the Federal Republic of Germany.* Bonn.

Federal Ministry of Labor and Social Affairs. 1981. *Situation der Ausländischen Arbeitnehmer und ihrer Familienangehörigen in der Bundesrepublik Deutschland.* Bonn.

———. 1985. *Ausländerpolitik: Fakten, Rechte, Pflichten, Argumente.* Bonn.

Feldblum, Miriam. 1990. The Politicization of Citizenship in French Immigration Politics. Paper presented at the Seventh International Conference of Europeanists, Washington, D.C.

———. 1993. Paradoxes of Ethnic Politics: The Case of Franco-Maghrebis in France. *Ethnic and Racial Studies* 16:52–74.

Ferguson, Edith. 1974. *Immigrants in Canada.* Guidance Centre, Faculty of Education, University of Toronto.

Ferguson, James. 1990. *The Anti-Politics Machine: 'Development,' Depoliticization, and Bureaucratic Power in Lesotho.* Cambridge: Cambridge University Press.

Finnemore, Martha. 1992. Science, the State, and International Society. Ph.D. diss., Stanford University.

FitzGerald, Marian. 1986. Immigration and Race Relations: Political Aspects—No. 15. *New Community* 13:265–71. London: Commission for Racial Equality.

———. 1988. Different Roads? The Development of Afro-Caribbean and Asian Political Organisation in London. *New Community* 14:385–96. London: Commission for Racial Equality.

Flora, Peter, and Arnold J. Heidenheimer, eds. 1981. *The Development of Welfare States in Europe and America*. New Brunswick, N.J.: Transaction Books.

Foucault, Michel. 1973. *The Order of Things: An Archaeology of the Human Sciences*. New York: Vintage Books.

———. 1979. *Discipline and Punish: The Birth of the Prison*. New York: Vintage Books.

———. 1980. *The History of Sexuality*, vol. 1. New York: Vintage Books.

Freeman, Gary P. 1978. Immigrant Labor and Working-Class Politics: The French and British Experience. *Comparative Politics* 11:24–41.

———. 1979. *Immigrant Labor and Racial Conflict in Industrial Societies: The French and British Experience, 1945–1975*. Princeton: Princeton University Press.

———. 1986. Migration and the Political Economy of the Welfare State. *Annals of the American Academy of Political and Social Science* 485:51–63.

———. 1989. The French State Reconsidered: The Lost World of Social Security Administration. Paper presented at the annual meeting of the American Political Science Association, Atlanta.

Friedland, Roger, and Robert R. Alford. 1991. Bringing Society Back In: Symbols, Practices, and Institutional Contradictions. In *The New Institutionalism in Organizational Analysis*, ed. W. W. Powell and P. J. DiMaggio. Chicago: University of Chicago Press.

Frowein, Jochen Abr., and Torsten Stein, eds. 1987. *Die Rechtsstellung von Ausländern nach staatlichem Recht und Völkerrecht*. 2 vols., with English summaries. Berlin: Springer-Verlag.

Fullinwider, Robert K. 1988. Citizenship and Welfare. In *Democracy and the Welfare State*, ed. A. Gutmann. Princeton: Princeton University Press.

Galarza, Ernesto. 1964. *Merchants of Labor: The Mexican Bracero History*. Charlotte, Calif.: McNally and Loftin.

Gay, Pat, and Ken Young. 1988. *Community Relations Councils: Roles and Objectives*. London: Policy Studies Institute and the Commission for Racial Equality.

Gellner, Ernest. 1983. *Nations and Nationalism*. Ithaca: Cornell University Press.

Gerholm, Tomas, and Yngve Georg Lithman, eds. 1988. *The New Islamic Presence in Western Europe.* London: Mansell.

Giddens, Anthony. 1985. *The Nation-State and Violence.* Berkeley and Los Angeles: University of California Press.

———. 1990. *The Consequences of Modernity.* Stanford: Stanford University Press.

———. 1991. *Modernity and Self-Identity: Self and Society in the Late Modern Age.* Stanford: Stanford University Press.

GISTI (Groupe d'Information et de Soutien des Travailleurs Immigrés). 1988. Dossier: Quels Discours sur l'Immigration? *Plein Droit,* no. 3. Paris.

Gitmez, Ali, and Czarina Wilpert. 1987. A Micro-Society or an Ethnic Community? Social Organization and Ethnicity amongst Turkish Migrants in Berlin. In *Immigrant Associations in Europe,* ed. J. Rex, D. Joly, and C. Wilpert. Aldershot: Gower.

Goodwin-Gill, Guy S. 1989. International Law and Human Rights: Trends Concerning International Migrants and Refugees. *International Migration Review* 23:526–46.

Goodwin-Gill, Guy S., R. K. Jenny, and Richard Perruchoud. 1985. Basic Humanitarian Principles Applicable to Non-Nationals. *International Migration Review* 19:556–69.

de Graaf, Hein. 1985. *Plaatselijke Organisaties van Turken en Marokkanen.* The Hague: Nederlands Instituut voor Maatschappelijk Werk Onderzoek (NIMAWO).

de Graaf, Hein, Rinus Penninx, and Errol F. Stoové. 1988. Minorities Policies, Social Services, and Ethnic Organizations in the Netherlands. In *Ethnic Associations and the Welfare State: Services to Immigrants in Five Countries,* ed. S. Jenkins. New York: Columbia University Press.

Grew, Raymond, ed. 1978. *Crises of Political Development in Europe and the United States.* Princeton: Princeton University Press.

Hall, Peter A. 1986. *Governing the Economy: The Politics of State Intervention in Britain and France.* New York: Oxford University Press.

Hammar, Tomas. 1985a. Dual Citizenship and Political Integration. *International Migration Review* 19:438–50.

———. 1985b. Election Year '85: Immigrant Voting Rights and Electoral Turnout. *Current Sweden,* no. 336. Stockholm: The Swedish Institute.

———. 1985c. On Immigrant Status and Civic Rights in Sweden. Paper presented to the research group, European Consortium for Political Research, Paris.

———. 1985d. Sweden. In *European Immigration Policy,* ed. T. Hammar. Cambridge: Cambridge University Press.

———. 1985e. Comparative Analysis. In *European Immigration Policy,* ed. T. Hammar. Cambridge: Cambridge University Press.

———. 1986. Citizenship: Membership of a Nation and of a State. *International Migration* 24:735–47.

———. 1990a. *International Migration, Citizenship, and Democracy.* Aldershot: Gower.

———. 1990b. The Civil Rights of Aliens. In *The Political Rights of Migrant Workers in Western Europe,* ed. Z. Layton-Henry. London: Sage.

Hammar, Tomas, ed. 1985. *European Immigration Policy: A Comparative Study.* Cambridge: Cambridge University Press.

Handler, Richard. 1988. *Nationalism and the Politics of Culture in Quebec.* Madison: University of Wisconsin Press.

Handsworth Law Centre. 1985. *Immigration Law Handbook: A Comprehensive Guide to Immigration Law and Practice,* 3d ed. Birmingham.

Hannerz, Ulf. 1992. *Cultural Complexity: Studies in the Social Organization of Meaning.* New York: Columbia University Press.

Heclo, Hugh. 1974. *Modern Social Politics in Britain and Sweden: From Relief to Income Maintenance.* New Haven: Yale University Press.

Heclo, Hugh, and Henrik Madsen. 1987. *Policy and Politics in Sweden: Principled Pragmatism.* Philadelphia: Temple University Press.

Heisler, Barbara Schmitter. 1985. Sending Countries and the Politics of Emigration and Destination. *International Migration Review* 19: 469–84.

———. 1986. Immigrant Settlement and the Structure of Emergent Immigrant Communities in Western Europe. *The Annals of the American Academy of Political and Social Science* 485:76–86.

———. 1988. From Conflict to Accommodation: The 'Foreigners Question' in Switzerland. *European Journal of Political Research* 16: 683–700.

Heisler, Barbara Schmitter, and Martin O. Heisler. 1989. Comparative Perspectives on Security and Migration: The Intersection of Two Expanding Universes. Paper presented at the annual meeting of the American Sociological Association, San Francisco.

Heisler, Martin O., and Barbara Schmitter Heisler. 1990. Citizenship—Old, New, and Changing: Inclusion, Exclusion, and Limbo for Ethnic Groups and Migrants in the Modern Democratic State. In *Dominant National Cultures and Ethnic Identities,* ed. J. Fijalkowski, H. Merkens, and F. Schmidt. Berlin: Free University.

Heisler, Martin O., and Barbara Schmitter Heisler, eds. 1986. From Foreign Workers to Settlers? Transnational Migration and the Emergence of New Minorities. *The Annals of the American Academy of Political and Social Science* 485 (May).

Hernes, Helga M. 1988. Scandinavian Citizenship. *Acta Sociologica* 31:199–215.

Hobsbawm, Eric. 1983. Mass-Producing Traditions: Europe, 1870–1914. In *The Invention of Tradition,* ed. E. Hobsbawm and T. Ranger. Cambridge: Cambridge University Press.

———. 1990. *Nations and Nationalism Since 1780: Programme, Myth, Reality.* Cambridge: Cambridge University Press.

Hobsbawm, Eric, and Terence Ranger, eds. 1983. *The Invention of Tradition.* Cambridge: Cambridge University Press.

Hoffmann-Nowotny, Hans-Joachim. 1973. *Soziologie des Fremdarbeiterproblems: Eine theoretische und empirische Analyse am Beispiel der Schweiz.* Stuttgart: Ferdinand Enke.

———. 1980. Sociological, Legal and Political Aspects of the Situation of Immigrants in Switzerland. *Research in Race and Ethnic Relations* 2:73–95.

———. 1985. Switzerland. In *European Immigration Policy,* ed. T. Hammar. Cambridge: Cambridge University Press.

———. 1986. Assimilation and Integration of Minorities and Cultural Pluralism: Sociocultural Mechanisms and Political Dilemmas. In *Education and the Integration of Ethnic Minorities,* ed. D. Rothermund and J. Simon. New York: St. Martin's Press.

Hoffmann-Nowotny, Hans-Joachim, and Karl-Otto Hondrich, eds. 1982. *Ausländer in der Bundesrepublik Deutschland und in der Schweiz.* Frankfurt: Campus Verlag.

Hollifield, James F. 1989. Migrants into Citizens: The Politics of Immigration in France and the United States. Paper presented at the annual meeting of the American Political Science Association, Atlanta.

———. 1992. *Immigrants, Markets, and States: The Political Economy of Postwar Europe.* Cambridge: Harvard University Press.

Holloway, Nigel. 1989. Immigration Anxieties. *Far Eastern Economic Review,* Thursday, 26 January, p. 19.

Home Office. 1977. *Racial Discrimination: A Guide to the Race Relations Act 1976.* London.

———. 1988. *Control of Immigration: Statistics, United Kingdom 1987.* London.

Hoppe, Robert, and Coert Arends. 1986. The Politics and Policy Dynamics of Ethnicity in the Netherlands. Paper presented at the European Consortium for Political Research workshop, Göteborg, Sweden.

Hull, Elizabeth. 1985. *Without Justice for All: The Constitutional Rights of Aliens.* Westport, Conn.: Greenwood Press.

Husbands, Christopher T. 1992. The Other Face of 1992: The Extreme-Right Explosion in Western Europe. *Parliamentary Affairs* 45:267–84.

IGM (Industriegewerkschaft Metall). 1987. *Fakten und Argumente für eine notwendige Forderung: Wahlrecht ist Menschenrecht.* Frankfurt am Main: Union-Druckerei.

ILO (International Labor Office). 1984. *Employment and Manpower Problems and Policy Issues in Arab Countries: Proposals for the Future.* Geneva: ILO Publications.

———. 1986. *The Rights of Migrant Workers: A Guide to ILO Standards for the Use of Migrant Workers and Their Organizations.* Geneva: ILO Publications.

———. N.d. *Provisions of the ILO Conventions and Recommendations Concerning Migrant Workers.* Geneva: ILO Publications.

Informatie Amsterdam. 1985. *Adviesraden-Danışma Kurulları.* City of Amsterdam Information Bureau.

———. 1987. Eğitim İçin Geç Kalınmaz. City of Amsterdam Information Bureau.

Informationsstelle des Zürcher Sozialwesens. 1988. *Soziale Hilfe von A–Z: Verzeichnis der sozialen, pflegerischen und medizinischen Dienste im Kanton Zürich.* Zurich.

International Migration. 1977. Third Seminar on Adaptation and Integration of Permanent Immigrants: Conclusions and Recommendations, vol. 15:17–83.

International Migration Review. 1991. U.N. International Convention on the Protection of the Rights of All Migrant Workers and Members of Their Families. Special Issue 25(4).

IOT (Inspraakorgaan Turken). 1986/87. *Yıllık Çalışma Raporu.* The Hague.

ISA (Informationsstelle für Ausländerfragen). 1988. *Jahresbericht 1987/1988.* Bern.

Jaakkola, Magdalena. 1987. Informal Networks and Formal Associations of Finnish Immigrants in Sweden. In *Immigrant Associations in Europe,* ed. J. Rex, D. Joly, and C. Wilpert. Aldershot: Gower.

JCWI (Joint Council for the Welfare of Immigrants). 1987. *Annual Report 1986/87.* London.

———. 1988. Europe without Frontiers? *Bulletin* 3(8). London.

Jenkins, Shirley, ed. 1988. *Ethnic Associations and the Welfare State: Services to Immigrants in Five Countries.* New York: Columbia University Press.

Jepperson, Ronald L. 1991. Institutions, Institutional Effects, and Institutionalism. In *The New Institutionalism in Organizational Analysis,* ed. W. W. Powell and P. J. DiMaggio. Chicago: University of Chicago Press.

Jepperson, Ronald L., and John W. Meyer. 1991. The Public Order and the Construction of Formal Organizations. In *The New Institutional-*

ism in Organizational Analysis, ed. W. W. Powell and P. J. DiMaggio. Chicago: University of Chicago Press.

Johnson, Mark R. D. 1987. Towards Racial Equality in Health and Welfare: What Progress? *New Community* 14:128–35. London: Commission for Racial Equality.

Joly, Daniele. 1987. Associations amongst the Pakistani Population in Britain. In *Immigrant Associations in Europe*, ed. J. Rex, D. Joly, and C. Wilpert. Aldershot: Gower.

———. 1988a. Making a Place for Islam in British Society: Muslims in Birmingham. In *The New Islamic Presence in Western Europe*, ed. T. Gerholm and Y. G. Lithman. London: Mansell.

———. 1988b. Immigration, Citizenship, and Local Power: Moslems in Birmingham. Centre for Research in Ethnic Relations, University of Warwick, England. Manuscript.

Josephides, Sasha. 1987. Associations amongst the Greek Cypriot Population in Britain. In *Immigrant Associations in Europe*, ed. J. Rex, D. Joly, and C. Wilpert. Aldershot: Gower.

Kantonale Arbeitsgemeinschaft für Ausländerfragen. 1984. *Jahresbericht 1984*. St. Gallen.

Kaplan, Roger. 1992. France: Through Kofi's Eyes. *Atlantic*, April.

Katzenstein, Peter J. 1980. Capitalism in One Country? Switzerland in the International Economy. *International Organization* 34:507–40.

———. 1984. *Corporatism and Change: Austria, Switzerland, and the Politics of Industry*. Ithaca: Cornell University Press.

———. 1985. *Small States in World Markets: Industrial Policy in Europe*. Ithaca: Cornell University Press.

———. 1987. *Policy and Politics in West Germany: The Growth of a Semisovereign State*. Philadelphia: Temple University Press.

Katzenstein, Peter J., ed. 1978. *Between Power and Plenty: Foreign Economic Policies of Advanced Industrial States*. Madison: University of Wisconsin Press.

Keely, James F. 1990. Toward a Foucauldian Analysis of International Regimes. *International Organization* 44:83–105.

Kepel, Gilles. 1987. *Les Banlieues de l'Islam: Naissance d'une Religion en France*. Paris: Seuil.

Kohli, Martin. 1985. Die Institutionalisierung des Lebenslaufes. *Kölner Zeitschrift für Soziologie und Sozialpsychologie* 37:1–29.

Krasner, Stephen D. 1983. Structural Causes and Regime Consequences: Regimes as Intervening Variables. In *International Regimes*, ed. S. D. Krasner. Ithaca: Cornell University Press.

———. 1991. Sovereignty, Regimes, and Human Rights. Department of Political Science, Stanford University. Manuscript.

Lamont, Michèle. 1992. *Money, Morals, and Manners: The Culture of the*

French and American Upper-Middle Class. Chicago: University of Chicago Press.

Layton-Henry, Zig. 1985. Great Britain. In *European Immigration Policy,* ed. T. Hammar. Cambridge: Cambridge University Press.

———. 1990a. The Challenge of Political Rights. In *The Political Rights of Migrant Workers in Western Europe,* ed. Z. Layton-Henry. London: Sage.

———. 1990b. Immigrant Associations. In *The Political Rights of Migrant Workers in Western Europe,* ed. Z. Layton-Henry. London: Sage.

———. 1990c. Citizenship or Denizenship for Migrant Workers? In *The Political Rights of Migrant Workers in Western Europe,* ed. Z. Layton-Henry. London: Sage.

———. 1992. *The Politics of Immigration: Immigration, 'Race' and 'Race' Relations in Post-war Britain.* Oxford: Blackwell.

Layton-Henry, Zig, ed. 1990. *The Political Rights of Migrant Workers in Western Europe.* London: Sage.

Leibfried, Stephan. 1990. Sozialstaat Europa? Integrationsperspektiven europäischer Armutsregimes. *Nachrichtendienst des Deutschen Vereins für öffentliche und private Fürsorge (NDV)* 70:296–305.

Lester, Anthony. 1993. Britain Wrong on Human Rights. *Financial Times,* 26 May.

Leveau, Rémy. 1988. The Islamic Presence in France. In *The New Islamic Presence in Western Europe,* ed. T. Gerholm and Y. G. Lithman. London: Mansell.

Lijphart, Arend. 1968. *The Politics of Accommodation: Pluralism and Democracy in the Netherlands.* Berkeley and Los Angeles: University of California Press.

Lipset, Seymour Martin, and Stein Rokkan. 1967. Cleavage Structures, Party Systems, and Voter Alignments: An Introduction. In *Party Systems and Voter Alignments: Cross-National Perspectives,* ed. S. M. Lipset and S. Rokkan. New York: Free Press.

Lithman, Eva L. 1987. *Immigration and Immigrant Policy in Sweden.* Stockholm: The Swedish Institute.

LO (Landsorganisationen). 1980. *Migrant Workers and the Trade Union Movement.* Stockholm.

Lochak, Danièle. 1989. Les Minorités et le Droit Public Français. Du Refus des Différences à la Gestion des Différences. In *Les Minorités et Leurs Droits Depuis 1789,* ed. A. Fenet and G. Soulier. Paris: Editions L'Harmattan.

LSOBA (Landelijke Samenwerking van Organisaties van Buitenlandse Arbeiders). 1986. *Konsept, Eisenpakket 1986.* Utrecht.

Mann, Michael. 1986. *The Sources of Social Power: A History of Power from the Beginning to A.D. 1760*, vol. 1. Cambridge: Cambridge University Press.

———. 1987. Ruling Class Strategies and Citizenship. *Sociology* 21: 339–54.

March, James G., and Johan P. Olsen. 1984. The New Institutionalism: Organizational Factors in Political Life. *American Political Science Review* 78:734–49.

Markovits, Andrei S., and Samantha Kazarinov. 1978. Class Conflict, Capitalism, and Social Democracy: The Case of Migrant Workers in the Federal Republic of Germany. *Comparative Politics* 10:373–91.

Marshall, T. H. 1964. *Class, Citizenship and Social Development*. Garden City, N.Y.: Doubleday.

McNeely, Connie L. 1990. Cultural Isomorphism among Nation States: The Role of International Organizations. Ph.D. diss., Stanford University.

McNeill, William H. 1979. Historical Patterns of Migration. *Current Anthropology* 20:95–102.

———. 1987. Migration in Premodern Times. In *Population in an Interacting World*, ed. W. Alonso. Cambridge: Harvard University Press.

Mehrländer, Ursula. 1982. Integration Process of Second Generation Migrants: Results of an Empirical Study on Italian Youths in the Federal Republic of Germany. In *Cultural Identity and Structural Marginalization of Migrant Workers*, ed. H. Korte. Strasbourg: European Science Foundation.

———. 1984. Turkish Youth—Occupational Opportunities in the Federal Republic of Germany. *Environment and Planning C: Government and Policy* 2:375–81.

———. 1987. Sociological Aspects of Migration Policy: The Case of the Federal Republic of Germany. *International Migration* 25:87–93.

Memoire Fertile. 1988. *Document Presenté et Adopté par les Associations lors de la Coordination Nationale, Paris le 1 Octobre 1988*. Paris.

Messina, Anthony. 1989. *Race and Party Competition in Britain*. Oxford: Clarendon Press.

Meyer, John W. 1980. The World Polity and the Authority of the Nation-State. In *Studies of the Modern World System*, ed. A. Bergesen. New York: Academic Press.

———. 1983. Conclusion: Institutionalization and the Rationality of Formal Organizational Structure. In *Organizational Environments: Ritual and Rationality*, ed. J. W. Meyer and W. R. Scott. Beverly Hills, Calif.: Sage.

———. 1986a. Myths of Socialization and of Personality. In *Reconstructing Individualism*, ed. T. Heller, M. Sosna, and D. Wellberry. Stanford: Stanford University Press.

———. 1986b. The Self and the Life Course: Institutionalization and Its Effects. In *Human Development and the Life Course: Multidisciplinary Perspectives,* ed. A. B. Sørensen, F. E. Weinert, and L. R. Sherrod. Hillsdale, N.J.: Lawrence Erlbaum Associates.

———. 1994. Rationalized Environments. In *Institutional Environments and Organizations,* ed. W. R. Scott and J. W. Meyer. Newbury Park, Calif.: Sage.

Meyer, John W., John Boli, and George M. Thomas. 1987. Ontology and Rationalization in the Western Cultural Account. In *Institutional Structure: Constituting State, Society, and the Individual,* ed. Thomas et al. Newbury Park, Calif.: Sage.

Meyer, John W., and Brian Rowan. 1977. Institutionalized Organizations: Formal Structure as Myth and Ceremony. *American Journal of Sociology* 83:340–63.

Miller, Mark J. 1981. *Foreign Workers in Western Europe: An Emerging Political Force.* New York: Praeger.

———. 1989. Political Participation and Representation of Noncitizens. In *Immigration and Politics of Citizenship in Europe and North America,* ed. W. R. Brubaker. Lanham, Md.: University Press of America.

Ministry of Foreign Affairs. 1987. *The Netherlands in Brief.* The Hague.

Ministry of Home Affairs. 1983. *Summary of the Policy Document on Minorities.* The Hague.

———. 1987/88. *Actieprogramma Minderhedenbeleid 1988.* The Hague.

Ministry of Labor. 1984. *Swedish Immigration Policy.* Stockholm.

Ministry of Social Affairs and Employment. 1988. *1986–1987, Le Point sur l'Immigration et la Présence Etrangère en France.* Documents Affaires Sociales. Paris: La Documentation Française.

Ministry of Social Affairs and National Solidarity. 1986. *1981–1986, Une Nouvelle Politique de l'Immigration.* Documents Affaires Sociales. Paris: La Documentation Française.

Ministry of Welfare, Health, and Cultural Affairs. 1984. Organisaties van Minderheden, by J. Goutier. *Handboek Minderheden.* Rijswijk.

———. 1986a. *Policy Toward Minorities.* Rijswijk.

———. 1986b. Welfare Work for Minorities (I). *Fact Sheet* 1-E. Rijswijk.

———. 1986c. Welfare Work for Minorities (II). *Fact Sheet* 2-E. Rijswijk.

———. 1988. *Rijksprogramma, Welzijn Minderheden 1988.* Rijswijk.

Moch, Leslie P. 1992. *Moving Europeans: Migration in Western Europe since 1650.* Bloomington: Indiana University Press.

Nadelmann, Ethan A. 1990. Global Prohibition Regimes: The Evolution of Norms in International Society. *International Organization* 44:479–526.

Nakhleh, Emile A. 1977. Labor Markets and Citizenship in Bahrayn and Qatar. *The Middle East Journal* 31:143–56.

Nettl, J. P. 1968. The State as a Conceptual Variable. *World Politics* 20:559–92.

Nielsen, Jørgen S. 1986. Islamic Law and Its Significance for the Situation of Muslim Minorities in Europe: Report of a Study Project. *Research Papers: Muslims in Europe,* no. 35, pp. 1–49.

Niessen, Jan. 1989. Migration and (Self-) Employment, Residence, and Work Permit Arrangements in Seventeen European Countries. Maastricht: European Center for Work and Labor. Manuscript.

North, David S., Catherine Wihtol de Wenden, and Chris Taylor. 1987. Non-Citizens' Access to Social Services in Six Nations: Canada, F.R.G., France, Sweden, U.K., and U.S. Paper presented at the conference on Reaching for Citizenship: The Process of Political and Economic Integration, German Marshall Fund of the United States, Berkeley Springs, W.Va.

O'Brien, Peter. 1988. Turks against Themselves: Political Activity among Turkish Migrants in West Germany. Ph.D. diss., University of Wisconsin, Madison.

———. 1990. The Civil Rights of West Germany's Migrants. *German Politics and Society* (19):27–40.

OECD (Organization of Economic Cooperation and Development). 1987. *The Future of Migration.* Paris: OECD.

d'Oliveira, H. U. Jessurun. 1984. Electoral Rights for Non-nationals. *Netherlands International Law Review* 31:59–72.

OMI (Office des Migrations Internationales). 1988. Le Journal des Activités de l'OMI. *Actualités Migrations,* Special Issue, no. 231/32. Paris.

———. 1989a. Le FAS en 1989. *Actualités Migrations,* no. 264/65, pp. 13–15. Paris.

———. 1989b. La Naturalisation: L'Aboutissement d'une Intégration Réussie. *Actualités Migrations,* Special Issue, no. 267/68. Paris.

———. 1989c. Discours de M. Evin. *Actualités Migrations,* no. 271, pp. 1–4. Paris.

ONI (Office National d'Immigration). 1986. *Office National d'Immigration, 1946–1986. 40e Anniversaire.* Paris.

Orloff, Ann Shola, and Theda Skocpol. 1984. Why Not Equal Protection? Explaining the Politics of Public Social Spending in Britain, 1900–1911, and the United States, 1880s–1920. *American Sociological Review* 49:726–50.

Özak, İbrahim H., and Ahmed Sezer. 1987. Türkische Organisationen in der Bundesrepublik Deutschland. *Informationsdienst zur Ausländerarbeit,* nos. 3–4, pp. 54–62. Frankfurt am Main: Institut für Sozialarbeit und Sozialpädagogik.

Patterson, Orlando. 1982. *Slavery and Social Death: A Comparative Study.* Cambridge: Harvard University Press.

———. 1991. *Freedom: Freedom in the Making of Western Culture.* New York: Basic Books.

Penninx, Rinus. 1984a. Immigrant Populations and Demographic Development in the Member States of the Council of Europe. Population Studies 12–13, Council of Europe CDDE (84)12, Strasbourg.

———. 1984b. Research and Policy with Regard to Ethnic Minorities in the Netherlands: A Historical Outline and the State of Affairs. *International Migration* 22:345–65.

———. 1986. International Migration in Europe: Developments, Mechanisms, and Controls. Report prepared for the conference on Demographic Impact of Political Action, Institut für Bevölkerungsforschung und Sozialpolitik, Bielefeld, Germany.

Perotti, Antonio, André Costes, and Maria Llaumett. 1989. L'Europe et l'Immigration. Part 1: Les Constats. *Migrations Société* 1:23–46. Paris: CIEMI.

Perruchoud, R. 1986. The Law of Migrants. *International Migration* 24:699–716.

Pillard, J. P. 1986. Patterns and Forms of Immigrant Participation and Representation at the Local and National Levels in Western (Continental) Europe. *International Migration* 24:501–13.

Piore, Michael J. 1979. *Birds of Passage: Migrant Labor and Industrial Societies.* Cambridge: Cambridge University Press.

Plender, Richard. 1985. Migrant Workers in Western Europe. *Contemporary Affairs Briefing,* vol. 2, no. 14.

———. 1986. Rights of Passage. In *Towards a Just Immigration Policy,* ed. A. Dummett. London: Cobden Trust.

———. 1987. The Economic Rights of Non-Citizens. Paper presented at the conference on Reaching for Citizenship: The Process of Political and Economic Integration, German Marshall Fund of the United States, Berkeley Springs, W. Va.

———. 1988. *International Migration Law.* 2d ed., rev. Dordrecht: Martinus Nijhoff.

Poulter, Sebastian M. 1986. *English Law and Ethnic Minority Customs.* London: Butterworths.

———. 1990a. Cultural Pluralism and Its Limits: A Legal Perspective. In *Britain a Plural Society: Report of a Seminar.* London: Commission for Racial Equality.

———. 1990b. *Asian Traditions and English Law: A Handbook.* London: The Runnymede Trust with Trentham Books.

Power, Jonathan. 1979. *Migrant Workers in Western Europe and the United States.* New York: Pergamon Press.

Prashar, Usha, and Shān Nicholas. 1986. *Routes and Roadblocks? Consulting Minority Communities in London Boroughs.* London: The Runnymede Trust and the Greater London Council.

Ramirez, Francisco O. 1989. Reconstituting Children: Extension of Personhood and Citizenship. In *Age Structuring in Comparative Perspective,* ed. D. Kertzer and K. W. Schaie. Hillsdale, N.J.: Lawrence Erlbaum Associates.

Ramirez, Francisco O., and Yasemin Nuhoğlu Soysal. 1989. Women's Acquisition of the Franchise: An Event History Analysis. Paper presented at the annual meeting of the American Sociological Association, San Francisco.

Raskin, Jamin B. 1993. Time to Give Aliens the Vote (Again). *The Nation,* 5 April.

Rath, Jan. 1988. Political Action of Immigrants in the Netherlands: Class or Ethnicity? *European Journal of Political Research* 16:623–44.

———. 1990. Voting Rights. In *The Political Rights of Migrant Workers in Western Europe,* ed. Z. Layton-Henry. London: Sage.

Rath, Jan, Kees Groenendijk, and Rinus Penninx. 1991. The Recognition and Institutionalisation of Islam in Belgium, Great Britain and the Netherlands. *New Community* 18:101–14.

Rath, Jan, and Shamit Saggar. 1987. Ethnicity as a Political Tool: The British and Dutch Cases. Paper presented at the conference on Ethnic and Racial Minorities in Advanced Industrial Societies, University of Notre Dame, South Bend, Indiana.

Reichert, Josh, and Douglas Massey. 1985. Guestworker Programs: Evidence from Europe and the United States and Some Implications for U.S. Policy. Working Paper, no. 1. Program in Population Research, University of California, Berkeley.

Reuter, Lutz R. 1990. Political Participation of Immigrants in the European Community and the Current Suffrage Debate. Paper presented at the Seventh International Conference of Europeanists, Washington, D.C.

Rex, John, Daniele Joly, and Czarina Wilpert, eds. 1987. *Immigrant Associations in Europe.* Aldershot: Gower.

de Rham, Gérard. 1990. Naturalisation: The Politics of Citizenship Acquisition. In *The Political Rights of Migrant Workers in Western Europe,* ed. Z. Layton-Henry. London: Sage.

Rhoades, Robert E. 1978. Foreign Labor and German Industrial Capitalism, 1871–1978: The Evolution of a Migratory System. *American Ethnologist* 5:553–73.

Rist, Ray C. 1978. *Guestworkers in Germany: The Prospects for Pluralism.* New York: Praeger.

Robertson, Roland. 1992. *Globalization: Social Theory and Global Culture.* London: Sage.

Rocha-Trindade, Maria B. 1988. Migration and the European Community after 1992. Paper presented at the colloquium on Current Trends in Migration and Social Mobility of Migrants, Utrecht, the Netherlands.

Rogers, Rosemarie. 1992. The Future of Refugee Flows and Policies. *International Migration Review* 26:1112–43.

Rokkan, Stein. 1980. Territories, Centres, and Peripheries: Toward a Western Europe. In *Spatial Variation in Politics*, ed. J. Gothmann. Newbury Park, Calif.: Sage.

Rosaldo, Renato. 1989. *Culture and Truth: The Remaking of Social Analysis*. Boston: Beacon Press.

Rose, Nikolas. 1990. *Governing the Soul: The Shaping of the Private Self*. London: Routledge.

Ruggie, John Gerard. 1975. International Responses to Technology: Concepts and Trends. *International Organization* 29:557–83.

Runnymede Trust. 1984a. Migrant Workers in Britain. *Race and Immigration*, no. 164, pp 9–15. London.

———. 1984b. Racism and Immigration in France. *Race and Immigration*, no. 170, pp. 8–15. London.

———. 1989a. Education Round-Up. *Race and Immigration*, no. 224, pp. 6–8. London.

———. 1989b. Race Units under Threat. *Race and Immigration*, no. 224, pp. 10–11. London.

Saggar, Shamit. 1992. *Race and Politics in Britain*. London: Harvester-Wheatsheaf.

Salt, John. 1992. The Future of International Labor Migration. *International Migration Review* 26:1077–111.

Sassen, Saskia. 1988. *The Mobility of Labor and Capital: A Study in International Investment and Labor Flow*. Cambridge: Cambridge University Press.

Sassen-Koob, Saskia. 1980. The Internationalization of the Labor Force. *Studies in Comparative International Development* 15:3–25.

Schain, Martin A. 1988. Immigration and Changes in the French Party System. *European Journal of Political Research* 16:597–621.

Schmid, Carol L. 1981a. *Conflict and Consensus in Switzerland*. Berkeley and Los Angeles: University of California Press.

———. 1981b. Economic Necessity and Social Marginality: Gastarbeiter in Germany and Switzerland. *Ethnic Groups* 3:355–71.

Schmitter, Barbara E. 1980. Immigrants and Associations: Their Role in the Socio-Political Process of Immigrant Worker Integration in West Germany and Switzerland. *International Migration Review* 14:179–92.

———. 1981. Trade Unions and Immigration Politics in West Germany and Switzerland. *Politics and Society* 10:317–34.

Schmitter, Philippe C. 1981. Interest Intermediation and Regime Governability in Contemporary Western Europe and North America. In *Organizing Interests in Western Europe: Pluralism, Corporatism, and the Transformation of Politics*, ed. S. Berger. Cambridge: Cambridge University Press.

———. 1992. Interests, Powers, and Functions: Emergent Properties and Unintended Consequences in the European Polity. Department of Political Science, Stanford University. Manuscript.

Schuck, Peter H. 1987. The Status and Rights of Undocumented Aliens in the United States. *International Migration* 25:125–39.

Schuck, Peter H., and Rogers M. Smith. 1985. *Citizenship Without Consent: Illegal Aliens in the American Polity*. New Haven: Yale University Press.

SCP (Social and Cultural Planning Office). 1986. *Social and Cultural Report*. Rijswijk.

Seccombe, I. J., and R. J. Lawless. 1985. Some New Trends in Mediterranean Labour Migration: The Middle East Connection. *International Migration* 23:123–48.

Semyonov, Moshe, and Noah Lewin-Epstein. 1987. *Hewers of Wood and Drawers of Water: Noncitizen Arabs in the Israeli Labor Market*. Ithaca: ILR Press, Cornell University.

Şen, Faruk. 1987. *Turks in the Federal Republic of Germany: Achievements, Problems, Expectations*. Bonn, Germany: Zentrum für Türkeistudien.

———. 1990. Yeni Bir Model. *Milliyet*, 3 May.

Sewell, William H., Jr. 1992. A Theory of Structure: Duality, Agency, and Transformation. *American Journal of Sociology* 98:1–29.

Shefter, Martin. 1977. Party and Patronage: Germany, England, and Italy. *Politics and Society* 7:403–51.

Sica, Mario. 1977. Involvement of the Migrant Worker in Local Political Life in the Host Country. *International Migration* 15:143–52.

Sikkink, Kathryn. 1991. The Political Power of Foreign Policy Ideas: The Origins of Human Rights Policy in the U.S. and Western Europe. Paper presented at the annual meeting of the American Political Science Association, Washington, D.C.

Silverman, Maxim. 1991. Citizenship and the Nation-State. *Ethnic and Racial Studies* 14:333–49.

Singer-Kérel, Jeanne. 1991. Foreign Workers in France, 1891–1936. *Ethnic and Racial Studies* 14:279–93.

SIV (Statens Invandrarverk). 1983. *Sweden: A General Introduction for Immigrants*. Norrköping.

———. 1987a. *Facts About the Immigration Board: Its Activities and Organisation*. Norrköping.

———. 1987b. *Swedish Citizenship*. Norrköping.

———. 1987c. *Kultur Tidskriften 1988*. Göteborg.

———. 1988/89. *Annual Report 1987/88*. Norrköping.

Skocpol, Theda. 1979. *States and Social Revolutions: A Comparative Analysis of France, Russia, and China*. Cambridge: Cambridge University Press.

———. 1985. Bringing the State Back In: Strategies of Analysis in Current Research. In *Bringing the State Back In*, ed. P. B. Evans, D. Rueschemeyer, and T. Skocpol. Cambridge: Cambridge University Press.

Skocpol, Theda, and Kenneth Finegold. 1982. State Capacity and Economic Intervention in the Early New Deal. *Political Science Quarterly* 97:255–78.

Skowronek, Stephen. 1982. *Building a New American State: The Expansion of National Administrative Capacities, 1877–1920*. Cambridge: Cambridge University Press.

Smith, Anthony D. 1986. *The Ethnic Origins of Nations*. Oxford: Basil Blackwell.

SOPEMI. 1989. *Continuous Reporting System on Migration*. Paris: OECD.

———. 1992. *Trends in International Migration: Continuous Reporting System on Migration*. Paris: OECD.

SOPEMI–Netherlands. 1991. *Migration, Minorities and Policy in the Netherlands: Recent Trends and Developments*. Report for the Continuous Reporting System on Migration of the OECD, by Philip J. Muus. Centre for Migration Research, University of Amsterdam.

———. 1992. *Migration, Minorities and Policy in the Netherlands*. Report for the Continuous Reporting System on Migration of the OECD.

Soysal, Yasemin Nuhoğlu, and David Strang. 1989. Construction of the First Mass Education Systems in Nineteenth-Century Europe. *Sociology of Education* 62:277–88.

Spectre of Organized Racism, The. 1986. *Inside Sweden*, no. 3/4. Stockholm.

Statistics Sweden. 1989. *Befolkningsförändringar 1988*. Stockholm.

City of Stockholm. 1987. *Invandrare och Flyktingar i Stockholm*. Stockholm.

Suleiman, Ezra N. 1974. *Politics, Power, and Bureaucracy in France: The Administrative Elite*. Princeton: Princeton University Press.

Swann Committee Report. 1985. Education for All: The Report of the Committee of Inquiry into the Education of Children from Ethnic Minority Groups. London: Her Majesty's Stationery Office.

Swart, A. H. J. 1987. The Legal Position of Aliens in Dutch Law. In *Die Rechtsstellung von Ausländern nach staatlichem Recht und Völkerrecht*, vol. 1, ed. J. A. Frowein and T. Stein. Berlin: Springer-Verlag.

Swedish Institute. 1987. *Fact Sheets on Sweden: Immigrants in Sweden*. Stockholm.

———. 1989. *Fact Sheets on Sweden: Immigrants in Sweden*. Stockholm.

Swidler, Ann. 1986. Culture in Action: Symbols and Strategies. *American Sociological Review* 51:273–86.

Swiss-American Chamber of Commerce. 1988. *Swiss Work Permit Regulations*. Zurich.

Taft, Donald R., and Richard Robbins. 1955. *International Migrations: The Immigrant in the Modern World*. New York: The Ronald Press Company.

Teitelbaum, Michael S. 1984. Immigration, Refugees, and Foreign Policy. *International Organization* 38:429–50.

Thomas, Eric-Jean, ed. 1982. *Immigrant Workers in Europe: Their Legal Status*. Paris: UNESCO.

Thomas, George M., and John W. Meyer. 1984. The Expansion of the State. *Annual Review of Sociology* 10:461–82.

Thomas, George M., John W. Meyer, Francisco O. Ramirez, and John Boli, eds. 1987. *Institutional Structure: Constituting State, Society, and the Individual*. Newbury Park, Calif.: Sage.

Thomson, Janice. 1990. State Practices, International Norms, and the Decline of Mercenarism. *International Studies Quarterly* 34:23–47.

Thomson, Janice E., and Stephen D. Krasner. 1989. Global Transactions and the Consolidation of Sovereignty. In *Global Changes and Theoretical Challenges: Approaches to World Politics for the 1990s*, ed. E. O. Czempiel and J. N. Rosenau. Lexington, Mass.: Lexington Books.

Tilly, Charles. 1975. *The Formation of National States in Western Europe*. Princeton: Princeton University Press.

———. 1978. Migration in Modern European History. In *Human Migration: Patterns and Policies*, ed. W. H. McNeill and R. S. Adams. Bloomington: Indiana University Press.

———. 1986. *The Contentious French: Four Centuries of Popular Struggle*. Cambridge: Harvard University Press.

———. 1990. *Coercion, Capital, and European States, A.D. 990–1990*. Oxford: Basil Blackwell.

TRAG (Tamil Refugee Action Group). 1987. *Annual Report 1987*. London.

Turkiska Riksförbundet. 1987. *Tenth Anniversary Pamphlet*. Stockholm.

Turner, Bryan S. 1986a. *Citizenship and Capitalism: The Debate over Reformism*. London: Allen and Unwin.

———. 1986b. Personhood and Citizenship. *Theory, Culture, and Society* 3:1–16.

UKIAS (United Kingdom Immigrants Advisory Service). 1989. *Annual Report 1987/88*. London.

Underhill, E. 1979. The Situation of Migrant and Refugee Children in Relation to the United Nations Declaration of the Rights of the Child. *International Migration* 17:122–38.

Verbunt, Gilles. 1985. France. In *European Immigration Policy: A Comparative Study,* ed. T. Hammar. Cambridge: Cambridge University Press.

Vranken, Jan. 1990. Industrial Rights. In *The Political Rights of Migrant Workers in Western Europe,* ed. Z. Layton-Henry. London: Sage.

Waardenburg, Jacques. 1988. The Institutionalization of Islam in the Netherlands, 1961–86. In *The New Islamic Presence in Western Europe,* ed. T. Gerholm and Y. G. Lithman. London: Mansell.

Wallerstein, Immanuel. 1974. *The Modern World System I.* New York: Academic Press.

Walzer, Michael. 1983. *Spheres of Justice: A Defense of Pluralism and Equality.* New York: Basic Books.

Weber, Eugen. 1976. *Peasants into Frenchmen: The Modernization of Rural France, 1870–1914.* Stanford: Stanford University Press.

Weber, Max. 1978. *Economy and Society: An Outline of Interpretive Sociology,* vol. 1, ed. G. Roth and C. Wittich. Berkeley and Los Angeles: University of California Press.

de Wenden, Catherine Wihtol. 1984. The Evolution of French Immigration Policy after May 1981. *International Migration* 22:199–213.

———. 1987. France's Policy on Migration from May 1981 till March 1986: Its Symbolic Dimension, Its Restrictive Aspects and Its Unintended Effects. *International Migration* 25:211–20.

———. 1988a. Trade Unions, Islam, and Immigration. *Economic and Industrial Democracy* 9:65–82.

———. 1988b. Les Pays Européens Face à l'Immigration. *Pouvoirs, Revue Française d'Etudes Constitutionnelles et Politiques,* no. 47, pp. 133–44.

———. 1990. The Absence of Rights: The Position of Illegal Immigrants. In *The Political Rights of Migrant Workers in Western Europe,* ed. Z. Layton-Henry. London: Sage.

Wendt, Alexander. 1992. Anarchy Is What States Make of It: The Social Construction of Power Politics. *International Organization* 46: 391–425.

Werbner, Pnina. 1991. The Fiction of Unity in Ethnic Politics: Aspects of Representation and the State among British Pakistanis. In *Black and Ethnic Leaderships in Britain,* ed. P. Werbner and M. Anwar. London: Routledge.

Werbner, Pnina, and Muhammad Anwar, eds. 1991. *Black and Ethnic Leaderships in Britain: The Cultural Dimensions of Political Action.* London: Routledge.

Werner, H. 1986. Post-War Labour Migration in Western Europe: An Overview. *International Migration* 24:543–57.

Widgren, Jonas. 1982. The Status of Immigrant Workers in Sweden. In *Immigrant Workers in Europe: Their Legal Status,* ed. E. Thomas. Paris: UNESCO.

de Wit, Willem. 1988. Mosque-communities in Amsterdam. *Research Papers: Muslims in Europe,* no. 37, pp. 24–36.

Wölker, Ulrich. 1987. *Zu Freiheit und Grenzen der politischen Betätigung von Ausländern.* Berlin: Springer-Verlag.

Wong, Ernest P. 1978. Chinese Exclusion and Public Policy. M.A. thesis, San Francisco State University.

WRR (Wetenschappelijke Raad voor het Regeringsbeleid). 1979. *Ethnic Minorities.* Reports to the Government, no. 17. The Hague.

Yeni Birlik. 1988. Kongre Çekişmeli Geçti. No. 3, pp. 4–12, Stockholm.

Zentrales Ausländerregister. 1987. *Ausländische Bevölkerung in der Schweiz.* Bern: Bundesamt für Ausländerfragen.

Zolberg, Aristide R. 1978. International Migration Policies in a Changing World System. In *Human Migration: Patterns and Policies,* ed. W. H. McNeill and R. S. Adams. Bloomington: Indiana University Press.

———. 1981. International Migrations in Political Perspective. In *Global Trends in Migration: Theory and Research on International Population Movements,* ed. M. M. Kritz, C. B. Keely, and S. M. Tomasi. Staten Island: Center for Migration Studies.

———. 1990. Stranger Encounters. In *Les Etrangers dans la Ville: Le Regard des Sciences Sociales,* ed. I. Simon-Barouh and P. Simon. Paris: Editions l'Harmattan.

Citations for newspaper and magazine articles and wire service reports (Reuter and the United Press International) are given in the text. The following is a list of non-English-language newspapers and magazines by place of publication.

Cumhuriyet Hafta, Frankfurt, Germany.
İkibine Doğru, Istanbul, Turkey.
Kirpi, Essen, Germany.
Milliyet, Frankfurt, Germany.
Le Monde, Paris, France.
Süddeutsche Zeitung, Munich, Germany.
Der Tagesspiegel, Berlin, Germany.

INDEX

Page numbers in italics refer to tables or figures.